EXPRESS

ITALIAN

A self-st
business and pleasure

by
MARINA FARDEGHINI • PAOLI NIGGI

English text by
Marcel Danesi, PhD
Julia Messenger, BA, L-ès-L, DipTELFA

Illustrations by
Giuseppe Quattrocchi and Xavier de Sierra

EUROPEAN
SCHOOLBOOKS
PUBLISHING

*All enquiries should be addressed to:
European Schoolbooks Publishing Limited
The Runnings,
Cheltenham, GL51 9PQ
England*

ISBN 0 85048 158 9

English edition first published in the United States 1990 by Barron's Educational Series, Inc.

This revised edition published in the United Kingdom and Eire by European Schoolbooks Publishing Ltd in May 1994 by arrangement with Barron's Educational Series Inc., Hauppauge, N.Y.

Welcome to Express Track Italian

Maybe you have never learned Italian, and feel that now is the time; or you learned Italian years ago, and want to take it up again. Perhaps you are interested in learning more about Italy and its people, their customs, culture and language. Or maybe you are going to work with Italians, and need a basic business vocabulary. Whoever you are, the authors of Express Track Italian wish you a warm welcome - in Italian: Benvenuti! - and offer you this carefully designed, step-by-step guide to the Italian language.

What you will find in Express Track Italian

- *This full-colour textbook contains dialogues, vocabulary lists, exercises, games, articles about Italy and the Italian people, a short story, a tourist guide and an alphabetic glossary;*
- *Four cassettes, total playing time nearly 6 hours, with dialogues, games and numerous exercises;*
- *A separate booklet with translations of the dialogues, further grammar, and a complete transcript of the cassettes.*

How to use Express Track Italian

Each lesson begins with a dialogue in simple but natural everyday Italian. Read it through once in the textbook, and check the translation in the booklet. Then listen as often as necessary, until you can distinguish all the words. Key phrases are highlighted at the end of each dialogue. Listen for the signal, and repeat each phrase and sentence aloud until you achieve an easy rhythm and intonation.

Important words and phrases from the dialogues are translated and explained in the sections VOCABULARY and HOW TO SAY IT, together with further useful vocabulary on the same topic. The meanings given are only those relevant to the context. To explore deeper, you should also have a good bilingual dictionary.

ORAL PRACTICE gives you a series of structured exercises on tape (with sound signals and pauses for you to respond). Grammar buffs will find explanations of all the structures in the grammar sections of the accompanying booklet.

After every five units you will find WRITTEN PRACTICE - a series of exercises covering everything you have learned in those five units. This is followed by a section of MORE VOCABULARY.

Finally, for lighter moments, in each unit you will find short, humorous accounts of some of the good and not so good things about Italy and the Italians; a selection of famous Italian songs with translations; listening games, word puzzles, quizzes and crosswords to fill in on the page; and a selection of the sort of Italian colloquial sayings and expressions that you may hear any day in the streets.

So plan your route, and let's get on the Express Track to Italian. Buona fortuna!

TABLE OF CONTENTS

TABLE OF CONTENTS

UNIT 1

1.1 DIALOGUE

LISTEN

ALL' AEROPORTO DI MILANO

At Milan airport the head of a business school welcomes people on a new course.

Il responsabile: *Mi presento: sono Mario Rossi, il responsabile del Centro di formazione.*

Un corsista: *Buongiorno, mi chiamo John Miller. Sono il capo del personale della Austin Rover.*

Il responsabile: *Lei è inglese, vero?*

J. Miller: *No, non sono inglese, sono americano, ma lavoro a Londra.*

Un corsista: *E io sono Dàmaso Carrasco. Sono il direttore amministrativo della casa editrice Anagrama di Barcellona.*

Il responsabile: *Spagnolo?*

D. Carrasco: *Catalano, per la precisione!*

Una corsista: *Piacere. Il mio nome è Chantal Dulac. Sono il direttore delle vendite alla Danone.*

Il responsabile : *Molto lieto. Lei...?*

C. Dulac : *Sì, sì, sono francese!*

Un corsista: *E io sono Hans Bauer. Sono tedesco.*

Il responsabile: *Lei è della ditta...?*

H. Bauer: *Siemens. Sono il responsabile della divisione sviluppo.*

Il responsabile: *Benissimo. Ci siamo tutti? Ah, no! Manca ancora una persona. Mentre aspettiamo, andiamo a prendere un caffè.*

LISTEN AND REPEAT

You will find the translation of this dialogue on page 1 of the accompanying booklet.

The "Duomo"

1.1 VOCABULARY

NOUNS

l'aeroporto — airport
il/la corsista — participant on a course
il/la responsabile — director, manager, head
il centro — centre
la formazione — training
il capo del personale — personnel manager
il direttore amministrativo — administrative/executive director
la casa editrice — publishing house
il nome — name
il direttore delle vendite — sales manager
la ditta — company
il/la responsabile della divisione sviluppo — head of development
la persona — person

---

lo stage — training course
la gestione — management
l'azienda — business/company
l'informatica — computing
la professione — profession
il/la segretario/a — secretary
l'assistente (m/f) — assistant
l'impiegato/a — employee
l'ingegnere (m/f) — engineer

Il paese — country
l'Italia — Italy
la Spagna — Spain
la Francia — France
la Germania — Germany
l'Inghilterra — England

---

il Portogallo — Portugal
la Svizzera — Switzerland
gli Stati Uniti — the United States
la nazionalità — nationality

ADJECTIVES

inglese — English
americano — American
spagnolo — Spanish
francese — French
tedesco — German
italiano — Italian
portoghese — Portuguese
svizzero — Swiss

VERBS

presentarsi — to introduce oneself
essere — to be
chiamarsi — to be called
lavorare — to work
mancare — to lack
aspettare — to wait for
andare — to go
prendere — to take

MISCELLANEOUS

Lei — you (formal) ***(1)***
vero? — right?
ma — but
benissimo — very well
ancora — again/yet
mentre — while

HOW TO SAY IT

1. INTRODUCING YOURSELF

Mi presento, sono Mario Rossi — Let me introduce myself. I'm Mario Rossi.
Mi chiamo Mario Rossi — I'm called Mario Rossi.
Il mio nome è Mario Rossi — My name is Mario Rossi. ***(2)***

2. BEING POLITE

Piacere — It's a pleasure!
Molto lieto(a) — Delighted! How nice to meet you!

3. NATIONALITIES

Sono francese — I'm French ***(3)***
Non sono inglese, sono americano — I'm not English, I'm American.

3. NATIONALITIES

Sono francese — I'm French ***(3)***
Non sono inglese, sono americano — I'm not English, I'm American.

4. ASKING A NAME AND NATIONALITY

Come si chiama? — What's your name? *(formal)* ***(1)***
Qual è il Suo nome? — What's your name? *(formal)*
Di che nazionalità è? — What's your nationality? *(formal)*
Qual è la Sua nazionalità? — What is your nationality? *(formal)*

5. GIVING YOUR PROFESSION

Sono il direttore delle vendite — I'm the sales manager. ***(4)***
Sono il responsabile della divisione sviluppo — I'm head of the development section

REMARKS REMARKS REMARKS REMARKS

(1) *When being formal, use the third person singular of verbs. The formal subject pronoun is "Lei" (see* **Grammar**, *L.5.) —* ***(2)*** *The word "nome" means both "name" and "first name". The word for "family name" or "surname" is "cognome". —* ***(3)*** *No subject pronoun is necessary: the verb ending changes to show the subject (see Grammar, L.) —* ***(4)*** *The definite article is always used with professions: "Sono il direttore della vendite" = I'm (the) sales manager.*

1.1 ORAL PRACTICE

1. ANSWERING IN THE AFFIRMATIVE

LISTEN

Lei è italiano?
- *Sì, sono italiano.*

Lei è tedesco?
- *Sì, sono tedesco.*

Answer affirmatively, as in the model.
Lei è italiano? - Lei è tedesco? — Lei è spagnolo? — Lei è francese? — Lei è inglese? — Lei è americano? — Lei è portoghese? — Lei è svizzero?

(See Grammar, L.4.)

2. MASCULINE AND FEMININE ADJECTIVES

LISTEN

Mario è italiano/Maria
- *Maria è italiana*

Jean è francese/Chantal
- *Chantal è francese*

Give the nationality of each person as in the model.
Mario è italiano/Maria — Jean è francese/Chantal — John è inglese/Mary — Carlos è spagnolo/Carmen — Hans è tedesco/Karin — Robert è americano/Jenny.

(See Grammar, C.1.)

3. NATIONALITIES

LISTEN

Di che nazionalità è Carlos?
- *Carlos è spagnolo.*

Di che nazionalità è Jenny?
- *Jenny è americana.*

Give the nationalities of people in the previous exercise.
Di che nazionalità è Carlos? — Di che nazionalità è Jenny? — Di che nazionalità è Chantal? — Di che nazionalità è Mario? — Di che nazionalità è Karin? — Di che nazionalità è Jean? — Di che nazionalità è Mary? — Di che nazionalità è Carmen?

(See Grammar, C. 1.)

4. GIVING YOUR NAME

LISTEN

Come si chiama?/Mario Rossi
- *Mi chiamo Mario Rossi.*

Answer as if you were the following people.
Mario Rossi — Chantal Dulac — John Miller — Carlo Bianchi — Hans Bauer — Maria Verdi — Gianni Belli.
Now give your name. (See Grammar, L. 3.)

5. THE VERB "TO BE"

sono, sei, è, siamo, siete sono,

LISTEN

io
- *Sono impiegato*

lui
- *è impiegato*

Give the appropriate form of the verb "to be", as in the model.
io — lui — noi — Roberto — Beatrice e Anna — lei — tu — voi — Mario e Giani. (See Grammar, L.1.)

6. INTRODUCING YOURSELF

LISTEN

Mi presento : sono Mario Rossi/John Miller
- *Piacere. Il mio nome è John Miller.*

Imagine you are the following people. Introduce yourself to Mario Rossi.
John Miller — Chantal Dulac — Hans Bauer — Gianni Belli — Maria Verdi — Carlo Bianchi — Jean Rollin.
Now introduce yourself.

7. PRONUNCIATION

LISTEN AND REPEAT

Centro — direttore — casa editrice — responsabile — caffè — tutti — ditta — per la precisione

IS MILAN THE CENTRE OF THE UNIVERSE?

To choose Milan as your starting point for seeing Italy is to go straight for the bullseye. For Milan is the real financial and cultural capital of Italy. Throbbing with life, buzzing with activity, the principal city of Lombardy sees itself as a serious rival to Rome. Major economic and banking centre, vital link in the communications network with the main centres of northern Europe, fashion and design capital, Mecca of modern art: Milan is truly a metropolis on a world scale.

In climate damp and foggy, Milan is closer to Munich than to Rome or Naples. More than anywhere else in Italy, the raincoat and umbrella are valued accessories. It is perhaps because of the climate that the Milanese, who have to keep moving just to keep warm, and have less need of a siesta than most of their compatriots, have always been so astonishingly successful in business. The financial importance of Milan can be most easily summarised by one statistic: the Milanese constitute just 3% of Italy's population, but pay 25% of the country's taxes.

It is easy to understand the differences, sometimes even antagonisms, which exist between Milan and the rest of Italy. The Milanese can be patronising and distrustful, while other Italians sometimes show the sort of jealous resentment that school children feel for the super-bright "top of the class". The rest of Italy says, envyingly, that the Milanese spend their entire lives rushing around; and freely accuses them of being "prepotenti".

But enough of this back-biting. The hard-working, industrious and indeed industrial side of Milan should not be allowed to obscure its many charms. Firstly, the Duomo, a wonderful cathedral, one of the most emphatically Gothic in Italy, which bristles with statues, and inspired not only Stendhal but also Napoleon, who was indeed responsible for finishing it. The Piazza del Duomo is the heart of Milan, a patchwork like the city itself. There is, for example, the Italian Touring Club building, a monument of pure Fascist style; and there too is the entrance to one of the liveliest centres of Milan social life, the famous Galleria Vittorio Emanuele II.

Milan also boasts the Castello Sforzesco (the palace of the Sforzas), the Basilica of St. Ambrogio, the most illustrious local saint, La Scala, the legendary opera house, the Brera Palace fine art collection, the luxury shops in the via Monte Napoleone, and the bustling Navigli, a vivid reminder of the days when Milan was criss-crossed by canals. Then there are the Roman columns in front of San Lorenzo, Leonardo da Vinci's famous fresco "The Last Supper" at Santa Maria delle Grazie, and an unusual, mysterious fountain by Giorgio de Chirico.

But it is for its intellectual life rather than its monuments that Milan is most exciting. The city is bursting with galleries unashamedly devoted to the most daring modern art; and its theatres, notably the Piccolo Teatro, are equally avant garde.

Milan is also the home of most of Italy's great publishing houses, and its local newspaper, the Corriere della Sera, is also the leading national daily. Which explains why Milan sees itself sometimes as a kind of spiritual guide for Italy ...

1.1 TAKE-A-BREAK

No. 1 LISTEN

You will hear these four people giving their name and nationality. Write their number in the appropriate box.
1. *Claudio Valli* ***2.*** *Peter Weber* ***3.*** *Christiane Duval* ***4.*** *Carmen Vasco*

IMPIEGATA	☐	SEGRETARIA	☐	FRANCESE	☐
INGEGNERE	☐	SPAGNOLA	☐	ITALIANO	☐
DIRETTORE	☐	TEDESCO	☐		

No. 4

Can you place these cities on the map of Europe?

Lisbona - Parigi - Londra - Roma - Bruxelles - Madrid - Atene - Bonn - Berna - Amsterdam.

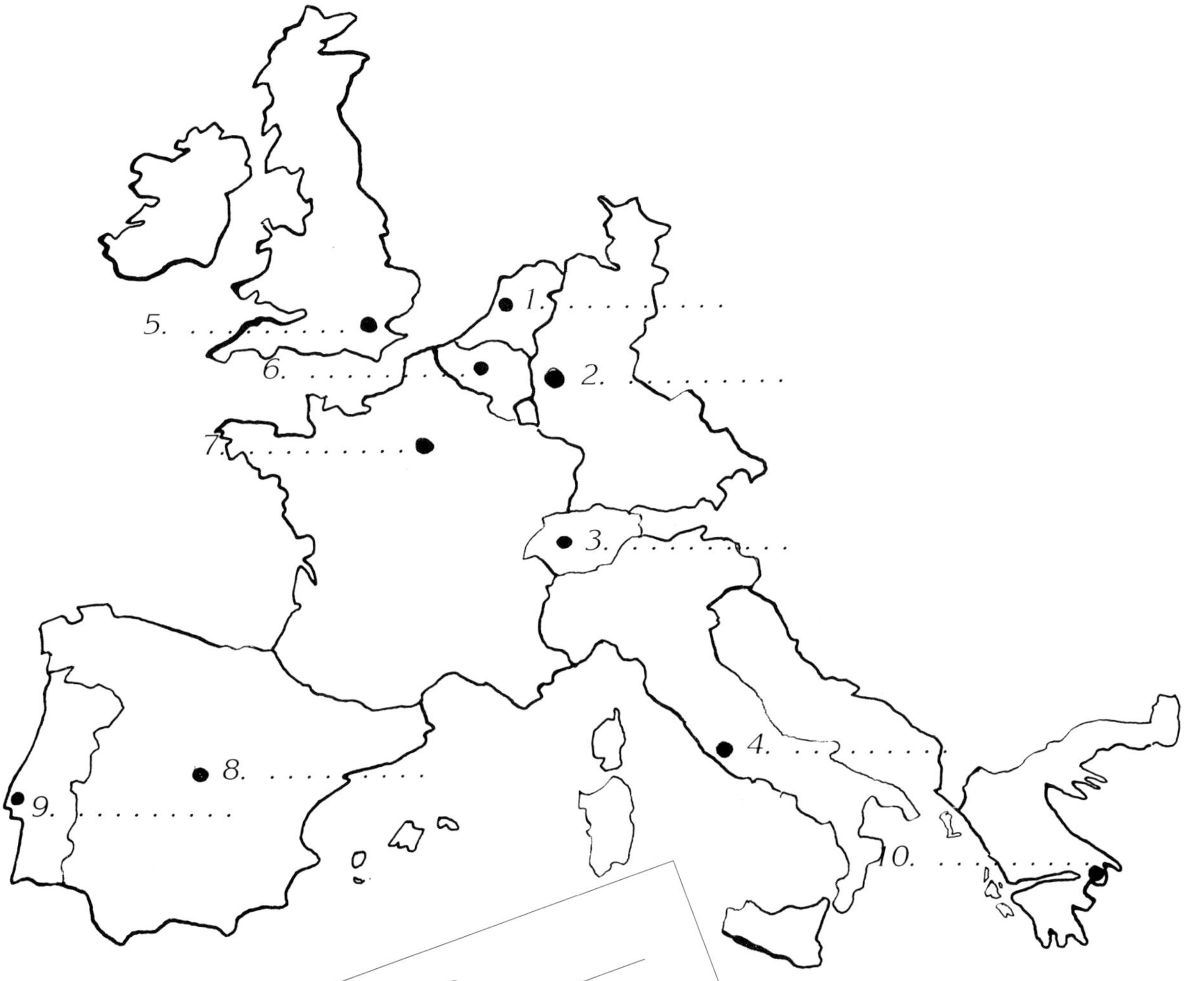

PROVERBIO

LISTEN

Il buon giorno si vede dal mattino (lit. A good day can be seen by its morning)

Start as you mean to go on.

(Answers on page 2 of the booklet)

1.2 DIALOGUE

LISTEN

UN CONTRATEMPO

Mr. Marchi arrives at the airport, but is unable to find his suitcase.

Alla consegna dei bagagli.

Sig. Marchi : *Signorina, per cortesia... Manca la mia valigia.*

L'impiegata : *Lei da dove viene?*

Sig. Marchi : *Vengo da Genova.*

L'impiegata : *Ah. Ha lo scontrino?*

Sig. Marchi : *Sì, un attimo. Ce l'ho sul biglietto. Eccolo!*

L'impiegata : *Un momento. Ora controllo. È strano! Tutti gli altri bagagli sono arrivati...*

Sig. Marchi : *Eh sì, ma mia valigia non c'è!*

L'impiegata : *Ha fretta?*

Sig. Marchi: *Abbastanza : sono già molto in ritardo.*

L'impiegata : *Aspetti! Per caso è una valigia blu molto grande?*

Sig. Marchi : *Sì*

L'impiegata : *Allora è in dogana. L'hanno appena trovata.*

Sig. Marchi : *Ah, per fortuna! Grazie mille.*

L'impiegata : *Di niente.*

All'appuntamento con i corsisti

Sig. Marchi : *Eccomi, scusate! Sono in ritardo! Mi chiamo Giulio Marchi. Sono il responsabile della formazione dell'Elsag di Genova.*

Il responsabile : *Noi ci conosciamo già, Dottor Marchi!*

Sig. Marchi : *Certo! Buongiorno Ingegner Rossi! Ho avuto dei problemi con i bagagli.*

Il responsabile : *Tutto a posto, adesso?*

Sig. Marchi : *Sì, sì, grazie.*

LISTEN AND REPEAT

You will find the translation on page 2 of the booklet.

1. Piazza del Duomo
2. and 4. Galleria Vittorio Emanuele
3. The old district of Naviglio grande
5. A publishing house
6. A Milanese tram

coiffeur
BAR TABACCHI
coiffeur pour dames Milva
Numismatica
NUMISMATICA
PEDICURE
prm
MI Y60389

2

MOBILI
3

4

RIZZOLI
5

STITVTO
1588
Niagara
6

1.2 VOCABULARY

NOUNS

il contrattempo — hitch/mishap
i bagagli — luggage
la consegna dei bagagli — luggage counter
l'impiegato/a — clerk/employee
la valigia — suitcase
lo scontrino — ticket-stub
l'attimo — instant
il biglietto — ticket
il momento — moment
in ritardo — late
il dogana — customs
l'appuntamento — appointment
il problema — problem ***(1)***

---

la signorina — young lady
la signora — lady
il signore — gentleman ***(2)***

ADJECTIVES

strano — strange
altro — other
blu— (dark) blue
grande — big/large
piccolo — small/little

VERBS

venire — to come
avere — to have
controllare — to check
arrivare — to arrive
avere fretta — to be in a hurry
trovare — to find
scusare/scusarsi — to excuse /apologise
conoscere/conoscersi — to know (someone)/to know each other

MISCELLANEOUS

per cortesia — please
da dove — from where
eccolo — here it is
eccomi — here I am
ora — now
adesso — now
c'è (non c'è) — it's there (it's not there)
abbastanza — quite/enough
già — already
molto — very/much/a lot
per caso — by chance
allora — then
per fortuna — fortunately (Thank goodness!)
certo — certainly (indeed)
tutto a posto — everything is fine.

HOW TO SAY IT

1. GREETING SOMEONE

Buongiorno, Signor Verdi! — Hello/Good day/ Good morning, Mr. Verdi! ***(3)***
Buongiorno, Signora Verdi! — Hello/Good day/Good morning, Mrs. Verdi!
Buongiorno, Signorina Verdi! — Hello/etc. Miss/Ms. Verdi!
Buonasera, Dottor Marchi! — Hello/Good evening, Dr. Marchi, (from mid-afternoon)
Buonasera, Ingegner Rossi! — Hello/etc. Engineer Rossi!

2. THANKING SOMEONE

Grazie — Thank you!
Grazie mille! — Many thanks (lit. thanks a thousand)
La ringrazio — Thank you very much (formal) ***(4)***

3. RESPONDING TO THANKS

Prego! — You're welcome! ***(5)***
Di niente — It's nothing/Think nothing of it!
Non c'è di che! — Don't mention it!

4. SAYING WHERE YOU COME FROM

Vengo da Genova — I come from Genoa.
Vengo dalla Francia — I'm from France.

5. TELLING SOMEONE TO WAIT

Un momento! — One moment (please)!
Un attimo! — One minute/second (please)!
Aspetti! — Wait (please)!

REMARKS REMARKS REMARKS REMARKS

(1) *This is an irregular masculine nouns ending in -a. Its plural is formed regularly with -i. —* ***(2)*** *Used with a name, these terms correspond to Miss, Mrs, and Mr. They can also be used on their own, as a polite form of address, the way the French use Mademoiselle, Madame and Monsieur. —* ***(3)*** *In front of a name, masculine titles ending in -e drop this vowel - "Signor Marchi". —* ***(4)*** *Using "Lei" . —* ***(5)*** *It is usual to respond to thanks.*

1.2 ORAL PRACTICE

1. THE VERB "TO HAVE"

ho, hai, ha, abbiamo, avete, hanno

LISTEN

Il signor Marchi - lo scontrino.
- *Il signor Marchi ha lo scontrino.*

lo
- *Ho lo scontrino.*

Give the correct form of the verb.
Il signor Marchi — io — noi —tu — voi — lei — loro — Marco — Francesca e Roberto — io — tu.

(See Grammar, L.1.)

2. POSSESSIVE ADJECTIVES

LISTEN

Io ho la valigia
- *Ecco la mia valigia!*

Giulio ha il biglietto
- *Ecco il suo biglietto!*

Change the sentences as in the model
Io ho la valigia — Giulio ha il biglietto — Lei ha lo scontrino — Noi abbiamo il biglietto — Voi avete la valigia — Tu hai lo scontrino — Loro hanno il biglietto — Maria ha la valigia — Loro hanno la valigia.

(See Grammar, D.1.)

3. PLURALS

LISTEN

Jean e Luc (francese)
- *Jean e Luc sono francesi*

Marta e Laura (italiano)
- *Marta e Laura sono Italiane*

Give the nationalities of the following people.
Jean e Luc (francese) — Marta e Laura (italiano) — John e Mary (inglese) — Peter e Hans (tedesco) — Pablo e José (spagnolo) — Burt e Ron (americano) — Amelia e Carmen (portoghese) — Franka e Karin (tedesco).

4. THE NEGATIVE

LISTEN

John Miller è inglese? (americano)
- *Non, non è inglese , è americano*

Il signor Verdi è avvocato (ingegnere)
- *No, non è avvocato, è ingegnere.*

Answer the questions as in the model.
John Miller è inglese? (americano) — Il signor Verdi è avvocato? (ingegnere) — Chantal Dulac è spagnola? (francese) — Hans Bauer è svizzero? (tedesco) — La signora Belli è segretaria? (ingegnere) — Il signor Marchi è il capo del personale? (il responsabile della formazione)

(See Grammar, L.4.)

5. ASKING QUESTIONS

LISTEN

Il signor Marchi ha lo scontrino
- *Il signor Marchi ha lo scontrino?*

È una valigia blu
- *È una valigia blu?*

Change the statements into questions by changing the intonation.
Il signor Marchi ha lo scontrino — È una valigia blu — Giulio è italiano — I bagagli sono arrivati — È il responsabile — Ha fretta — Marco è in ritardo — Hai il biglietto. (See Grammar, L.4.)

6. SAYING WHERE YOU COME FROM

LISTEN

Genova
- *Vengo da Genova*

La Francia
- *Vengo dalla Francia*

Continue, following the model
Genova — La Francia — Parigi — Londra — Il Portogallo — La Svizzera — Madrid — L'Italia _ Nantes — L'Inghilterra — Roma — Gli Stati Uniti.

(See Grammar, F.)

7. PRONUNCIATION

LISTEN AND REPEAT

Il biglietto — i bagagli — la valigia — gli altri biglietti — un attimo — aspetti! — la consegna.

DO YOU HAVE A RECEIPT?

All too often, Italy is pictured abroad as a country which is not just ungovernable, but is dominated by chaos and improvisation. Not so: for a relatively new country - the unification of Italy dates only from 1860 - Italy has an impressive, even pernickety bureaucracy.

If you ever stay long in the country, you will come up against that mainstay of the average Italian existence: the rubber stamp. Nearly everything official you might do will require the sacred "carta bollata", a document with imposing rubber stamps, the cornerstone of the Italian state.

This state, widely perceived as weak, (except while Mussolini was in power), is forever making its presence felt, if only through the state-owned monopolies. Italy's favourite cigarette, and the mostly widely sold abroad, is, after all, M.S., which simply stands for "Monopolio di Stato" (state monopoly) ... and not forgetting that up to a few years ago, salt was only sold in the eponymous "Sali e Tabbacchi", since salt was also a state monopoly.

It could be that the state itself is the cause of tax dodging ... the tax-returns are grotesquely dfficult to fill in. Salary earners don't have too hard a time, since there is the P.A.Y.E. scheme, but anyone who is self-employed , or who has freelance earnings is snowed under with "moduli" (forms) of such hideous complexity that it takes an accountant to sort them out.

The state's constant battle against `l'evasione fiscale' affects the customer as well. It is worth knowing that when eating in a restaurant you should not only check the bill - as you would anywhere else - but you should also insist on having a receipt, in case the police are carrying out spot-checks as you leave. If you have not got a receipt, you might just end up accused of being accessory to defraud the inland revenue! Not the best way to digest a hearty meal of pasta.

Admittedly, such checks are not common, but forewarned is forearmed ...

The same applies if you go to the hairdresser, have your car serviced etc., etc. - always take your receipt. It goes without saying that the Italians are better used to this system of receipts than we are, for in most of their bars, "tavole calde", and "latterie" (all forms of snack or sandwich bars) you have to pay for what you want before going to the counter, where you claim them by presenting your famous "scontrino". It is the same in the station buffet, and anyone arriving in Italy by train quickly masters the system!

Nothing is perfect, and in this organisational paradise when it comes to actually paying, you quickly come up against the Italians' major defect: their blithe refusal to queue. In post-offices, banks, bread-shops, anywhere, in short, that there may be a bit of a crowd, this national characteristic may be freely observed. The spectacle of a rush of people all claiming to be first is enough to try even the celebrated British phlegm.

1.2 TAKE-A-BREAK

No. 1

LISTEN

Mark down the destination or point of origin of each flight, and whether it has been cancelled (annullato), is late (in ritardo), or is about to depart (in partenza).

ALITALIA	*DESTINAZIONE :*	. . . .
BRITISH AIRWAYS	*DESTINAZIONE :*	. . . .
LUFTHANSA	*PROVENIENZA :*	. . . .
AIR FRANCE	*PROVENIENZA :*	. . . .

No. 2

Put each of the following groups of sentences into the right order to make a short dialogue.

1. Allora, l'hanno appena trovata.
2. Manca la mia valigia...
3. Signorina, per cortesia!
4. È per caso una valigia blu?
5. Sì.
6. È in dogana.

....
....

1. Sono in ritardo
2. Scusate.
3. Mi chiamo Giulio Marchi.
4. Eccomi.

....
....

No. 3

Dingbat.

3 Ni

Ni

PROVERBIO LISTEN

Chi cerca trova (lit. He who searches, will find).

Seek and you shall find.

(Answers on page 3 of the booklet)

1.3 DIALOGUE

LISTEN

AL BAR DELL'AEROPORTO

The course members have a drink at the bar.

Il responsabile : *Caffè per tutti?*

J. Miller : *Per me va bene, io però lo vorrei lungo.*

C. Dulac : *Anch'io. Il caffè italiano è buono ma è troppo forte per me!*

G. Marchi : *Per me invece un caffè ristretto, per contesia.*

H. Bauer : *Ah, se bevo un caffè adesso, poi questa notte non dormo. Per me è meglio una birra.*

D. Carrasco : *E io vorrei un cappuccino!*

Il responsabile : *Allora una birra, un cappuccino e quattro caffè : uno normale, due lunghi e uno ristretto.*

Il cameriere : *Ha la scontrino?*
Il responsabile : *Ah sì! è vero : devo pagare prima?*

Il cameriere : *Sì, signore : deve pagare alla cassa.*

Alla cassa

Il responsabile : *Una birra, un cappuccino e quattro caffè.*

La cassiera : *Ecco lo scontrino.*

....

Il cameriere : *Per chi sono i caffè?*

C. Dulac : *Per noi, grazie.*

G. Marchi : *Quanto zucchero, signora?*

C. Dulac : *Niente zucchero, grazie ... Piuttosto vorrei una goccia di latte freddo.*

Il cameriere : *Eccolo.*

G. Marchi : *Lei è francese?*

C. Dulac : *Sì, sono francese.*

G. Marchi : *E di dov'è?*

C. Dulac : *Sono di Nantes, ma abito e lavoro a Parigi da anni.*

G. Marchi : *Ah, Parigi! Che bella città! La conosco bene perché vengo spesso in Francia per lavoro.*

C. Dulac : *E Lei, di dov'è?*

G. Marchi : *Io sono di Genova.*

C. Dulac : *Non conosco Genova. So solamente che è un porto importante e che si trova nel nord dell'Italia.*

G. Marchi : *È anche la città di Cristoforo Colombo!*

Il responsabile : *Bene, adesso ci siamo tutti, possiamo andare. Le macchine sono qui fuori.*

LISTEN AND REPEAT

You will find the translation on page 3 of the booklet

1. 3. 4. Typical bars
2. A bar in the bohemian quarter of Brera

DONINI
GINROSA
1

BAR BRERA
BAR B
2

Bar
BAR MARINO
NARDY
Bar
BAR MARINO
CAFFÈ
3

CAFFE' MoKamag
l'oasi
BAR GELATERIA
Gelateria
4

1.3 VOCABULARY

NOUNS

il bar — espresso bar ***(1)***
il caffè — coffee ***(1)***
il cameriere — waiter
la notte — night
la birra — beer
la cassa — cashier/cash desk
lo zucchero — sugar
la goccia — drop
il latte — milk
l'anno — year
la città — city, town ***(1)***
il lavoro — job/work
il porto — port
la macchina — car

ADJECTIVES

lungo/corto — long/short
lungo/ristretto — weak/strong (coffee)
buono/cattivo — good/bad
forte/leggero — strong/light
freddo/caldo — cold/hot
bello/brutto — beautiful/ugly
importante — important

VERBS

volere — to want to
bere — to drink
dormire — to sleep
dovere — to have to
pagare — to pay
abitare — to live (somewhere)
sapere — to know
potere — to be able to

ADVERBS

anche — also, too
troppo — too, too much
invece — instead, rather
meglio — better
poi — then, after
prima — before, first
piuttosto — rather
bene/male — well/badly
spesso — often
solamente — only
qui/lì — here/there
fuori/dentro — inside/outside

MISCELLANEOUS

per tutti — for everyone
per me — for me
per noi — for us
però — but, however
niente (zucchero) — no (sugar)
perché — why
quanto? — how much?

HOW TO SAY IT

1. ORDERING DRINKS

Un caffè, per cortesia — A coffee, please.
Per me un cappuccino — A cappuccino for me.
Vorrei una birra — I would like a beer.

2. BEING FROM

Di dov'è Lei? — Where are you from? ***(2)***
Sono di Bristol — I'm from Bristol.

3. SAYING WHERE YOU LIVE

Dove abita? — Where do you live?
Abito a Roma — I live in Rome.

4. FOR HOW MANY YEARS....

Lavoro a Parigi da anni — I've worked in Paris for years. ***(3)***
Sono capo del personale da cinque anni — I've been personnel manager for five years.
Abito in Francia da venti anni — I have lived in France for twenty years.

5. INDICATING PREFERENCES

Piuttosto vorrei una birra — I would rather have a beer.
Preferirei un cappuccino — I would prefer a cappuccino.
Per me invece un caffè ristretto — For me, a strong coffee instead.

6. EXCLAMATIONS

Che bella città!— What a beautiful city!
Che bella donna! — What a beautiful woman!
Bene! — OK/Fine!

REMARKS REMARKS REMARKS REMARKS

(1) *See Grammar, C. 3. -* ***(2)*** *Formal pronouns need a capital letter even within a word or sentence. -* ***(3)*** *The ordinary present tense is used here.*

1.3 ORAL PRACTICE

1. ORDERING DRINKS

LISTEN

un caffè

- *Un caffè per cortesia*

Order the following things.

un caffè — un cappuccino — un tè — una birra — un caffè ristretto — un caffè lungo — un'aranciata — un aperitivo — una Coca-Cola.

2. POSSESSIVES

LISTEN

Ho i biglietti

- *Ecco i miei biglietti!*

Abbiamo i biglietti

- *Ecco i nostri biglietti!*

Change the sentences as in the model.

Ho i biglietti —Abbiamo i biglietti — Ho le valigie — Abbiamo le valigie — Avete i biglietti — Hanno le valigie — Hai i biglietti — Avete le valigie — Hanno i biglietti — Hai le valigie — Ha i biglietti — Ha le valigie.

(See Grammar, D.1.)

3. VERBS ENDING IN *-ARE*

LISTEN

Lei lavora alla FIAT (io)

- *Io lavoro alla FIAT*

(il signor Bianchi)

- *Il signor Bianchi lavora alla FIAT*

Change each sentence using the correct form of the verb.

io — il signor Bianchi — noi — tu — voi — io — Gianni e Paolo — Maria — Marta e Laura — noi — tu.

4. HOW MUCH

LISTEN

zucchero

- *Quanto zucchero vuole, signora?*

biglietti

- *Quanti biglietti vuole, signora?*

Ask questions as in the model.

zucchero— biglietti — birra — latte — tè — aranciata — caffè — caffè (pl.) — birre — aranciate.

(See Grammar, G 2.0)

5. I LIVE IN ....

LISTEN

Francia, Parigi

- *Abito in Francia, a Parigi.*

Italia, Milano

- *Abito in Italia, a Milano*

Say where you live (as in the model).

Francia, Parigi — Italia, Milano — Spagna, Madrid — Inghilterra, Londra — Germania, Monaco — Portogallo, Lisbona — Svizzera, Zurigo.

(See Grammar, F.)

6. "ANCHE:

LISTEN

Per me un caffè

- *Anch'io vorrei un caffè.*

Per me un caffè — Per me una birra — Per me un cappuccino — Per me un tè — Per me un caffè ristretto — Per me un caffè lungo — Per me una Coca-Cola.

(See Grammar, J 2.)

7. PRONUNCIATION

LISTEN AND REPEAT

Birra - cappuccino - spesso - troppo - vorrei - caffè - latte - notte - adesso.

LETS GO FOR A COFFEE!

As soon as you go to Italy, the one thing that strikes you - apart from the language - is the coffee: that special aroma, that unique flavour, as the adverts say: only this time it is true: the coffee you drink in Italy really is that good.

In Naples, they would of course narrow the field still further and claim that it is only in Naples that the coffee is as good as all that ... a slight exaggeration perhaps, even though the famous percolator is called the "Neapolitan". It would seem that the method of infusion is indeed one of the Italians' secrets for concocting this heavenly brew: the roasting being the other.

Remember that coffee goes back a long way in Italy. When they were not at war with them, the Venetians traded with the Turks, and introduced coffee into the peninsula, where it at once became popular. It spread from there to other parts of Europe. It was even - though few Frenchmen like to acknowledge it - a Sicilian, Francesco Procopio dei Coltelli, who opened the first Parisian café, later to become the famous "Procope".

Coffee punctuates the day. From the moment they get up, Italians, who suffer from that Mediterranean failing of eating nothing first thing, must have their coffee. Better still, is to have it brought to them in bed, by their devoted "mamma", loving spouse, or besotted "fidanzato" or "fidanzata": what better way to start the day? This coffee is drunk black or "macchiato", "spotted" with milk, and usually well sugared.

The ritual of coffee-drinking would be incomplete without the sugar. Strong, black coffee being very bitter, sugar is its natural complement, giving rise to a sort of mystical aura to the whole process: the bitter/sweet reflecting the ying/yang. Thus, the fact of drinking very sweet coffee does not satisfy a mere physical need - since it neither nourishes nor quenches the thirst - but gives a sense of well-being, of luxury.

At first, it is quite astonishing to see the amount of sugar that some Italians manage to cram into one tiny cup of coffee. But you get used to it, and if you stay any length of time in Italy, you will probably find that your own ration of sugar has got much larger. Sugar must be an essential ingredient of the famous Italian "dolce vita".

Apart from the first reviving cup of the morning, the day offers further opportunities for further cups: with friends, colleagues, or alone. During the morning, the bars serve coffee with Italian "brioches", rather like French croissants, filled with jam. Very welcome by ten o'clock to an empty stomach! The coffee will vary according to the customers' preferences: "normale" (classic expresso), "ristretto" (even stronger), "lungo" (watered down a bit), "macchiato"... Then there is that wonder of the world, the "cappucino", coffee with just the right amount of milk to give it the warm, brown colour of the wool worn by the Capucines. Hence the name. Just a spot of milk, not enough to drown the flavour.

There are many other possibilities: "corretto" (corrected), with a dash of brandy, or poured over ice-cream, usually vanilla, known by the word for drowned: "affogato".

Apart from the countless small bars, where you drink standing at the counter, major institutions have grown up, thanks to the cult of coffee: great coffee-houses which have been the hub of the country's cultural life - as in the London of Dr. Jonson and Samuel Pepys, and the Paris of Sartre and Camus. Some have a real place in Italian history - the Florian in Venice, the Pedrocchi in Padua, the Rivoire in Florence, or the Greco in Rome - and really should be seen.

1.3 TAKE-A-BREAK

No. 1 LISTEN

Write down the drinks chosen by the people in the drawings.

☐ ______________________

☐ ______________________

☐ ______________________

☐ ______________________

☐ ______________________

PROVERBIO LISTEN

Chi troppo vuole nulla stringe.
(lit. He who wants too much gets nothing)

Count your blessings

No. 2

Complete each of the following as you wish, choosing among the cities shown on the map.

- *Lei è di Genova?*
  No, non sono di Genova, sono di.........
- *Lei è di Milano?*
  No, ...
- *Lei è di Palermo?*
  No, ...
- *Lei è di Reggio Calabria?*
  No, ...
- *Lei è di Firenze?*
  No, ...
- *Lei è di Roma?*
  No, ...

(Answers on page 5 of the booklet)

1.4 DIALOGUE

LISTEN

ALL'ALBERGO

The course director accompanies the participants to a Milan hotel.

Il responsabile : *Buongiorno, ci devono essere sei camere singole prenotate per oggi.*

L'impiegata : *Il suo nome, per cortesia?*

Il responsabile : *La prenotazione è a nome del Centro di formazione Michelangelo.*

L'impiegata : *Attenda un attimo. Sì, ecco. Sono sei camere singole con bagno?*

Il responsabile : *Sì.*

L'impiegata : *Ha i documenti di queste persone?*

Il responsabile : *Sì, ecco i passaporti.*

L'impiegata : *Bene. Questi li restituisco domani. Le camere sono tutte al quarto piano. Ecco le chiavi.*

G. Marchi : *È possible avere la sveglia domani mattina?*

L"impiegata : *Certamente. A che ora?*

C. Marchi : *Alle sette e mezzo.*

L'impiegata : *Benissino : alle sette e mezzo, stanza 407.*

C. Dulac : *A che ora è la prima colazione?*

L'impiegata : *La colazione è servita dalle 7.30 alle 9.30 nella sala a destra in fondo al corridoio.*

C. Dulac : *Grazie.*

H. Bauer : *Scusi, vorrei telefonare in Germania. È possibile avere la linea in camera?*

L'impiegata : *Naturalmente. La linea è diretta.*

H. Bauer : *Per cortesia, qual è il prefisso per l'estero?*

L'impiegata : *Guardi, deve fare 00, poi aggiungere il prefisso per la Germania e il prefisso della città, poi il numero che vuole chiamare.*

H. Bauer : *Benissimo. Grazie mille.*
Il responsabile : Bene. Se volete, potete cenare qui in albergo: c'è un tavolo prenotato per voi.

J. Miller : *A che ora ci vediamo domani?*

Il responsabile : *L'appuntamento per l'inizio dello stage è per domani mattina alle dieci al Centro di formazione. Arrivederci, a domani.*

I corsisti : *ArrivederLa.*

LISTEN AND REPEAT

You will find the translation on page 5 of the booklet.

Milanese design:
1. Hotel façade
2. and 3. Department store windows
4. An avant-garde furniture shop
5. On the Corso Vittorio Emanuele

HOTEL EXECUTIVE
HOTEL EXECUTIVE
HOTEL EXECUTIVE
HOTEL EXECUTIVE

3

arflex

4

BVLGARI

2

5

1.4 VOCABULARY

NOUNS

l'albergo — hotel
la camera (la stanza) — room
singola — single
doppia — double
matrimoniale — double (bed)
la prenotazione — reservation
il bagno — bath
il documento — document
il passaporto — passport
il piano — floor
la chiave — key
la sveglia — early morning call
la mattina — morning
l'ora — time/hour
la prima colazione — breakfast
la sala — room/hall
il corridoio — corridor
la linea — line
il prefisso — code
l'estero — abroad
il tavolo — table
l'inizio — start/beginning

---

il letto — bed
la carta d'identità — identity card
la patente — driving licence
l'orologio — watch/clock
il minuto — minute

---

il pranzo — lunch
la cena — dinner
oggi — today
domani — tomorrow
ieri — yesterday
il pomeriggio — afternoon
la sera — evening
il giorno — day

ADJECTIVES

primo — first
secondo — second
terzo — third
quarto — fourth
quinto — fifth
sesto — sixth
settimo — seventh
ottavo — eighth
nono — ninth
decimo — tenth
undicesimo — eleventh
ventesimo— twentieth

VERBS

prenotare — to reserve
attendere — to wait
restituire — to give back/return
servire — to serve
telefonare — to phone
fare — to do/make
aggiungere — to add (on)
chiamare— to call
cenare — to dine/have dinner
vedere — to see
vedersi — to see each other/meet

---

fare colazione — to have breakfast
pranzare — to have lunch

MISCELLANEOUS

certamente (certo) — certainly, of course
a nome di ... — in the name of ...
questo — this
a destra — to the right
a sinistra — to the left
in fondo a ... — at the end of

HOW TO SAY IT

1. CHECKING INTO A HOTEL

Buongiorno, ci deve essere una camera singola prenotata per oggi — Hello. There should be a single room reserved for today.
La prenotazione è a nome della ditta X — The reservation is in the name of Company X.

2. ASKING SOMEONE'S NAME

Il Suo nome, per cortesia? — Your name please?
Qual è il Suo nome? — What is your name?
Come si chiama? — What is your name?

3. ASKING FOR AN ALARM CALL

Scusi, è possibile avere la sveglia domani mattina alle 7.00? — Excuse me, is it possible to have an early morning call tomorrow at 7.00?

4. ASKING AND SAYING WHEN

A che ora? — At what time
A mezzogiorno — At noon/midday
A mezzanotte — At midnight
All'una — at 1.00. ***(1)***
Alle due — At two o'clock
Alle 2 e cinque — At 2.05.
Alle 2 e un quarto — At 2.15.
Alle 2 e mezzo — At half past two/2.30.
Alle 3 meno un quarto — At a quarter to three/2.45.

5. FROM WHEN TO WHEN

La colazione è servita dalle 7.30 alle 9.30 — Breakfast is served from 7.30 to 9.30.

6. TAKING LEAVE

ArrivederLa! — Goodbye (formal)
Arrivederci! — Goodbye (informal) ***(2)***
A domani! — See you tomorrow!
A presto! — See you soon!
A stasera! — See you this evening!

REMARKS REMARKS REMARKS REMARKS

(1) *Official time (trains, planes, etc.) uses the 24 hour clock. But in everyday conversation the tendency is to say, for instance, 4.00 in the afternoon.* — ***(2)*** *This is the most general form used in all kinds of speech, formal and informal.*

1.4 ORAL PRACTICE

1. ASKING NAMES AND NATIONALITIES

LISTEN

Mi chiamo Giulio Marchi
- *Qual è il Suo nome?*

Sono italiano
- *Qual è la Sua nazionalità?*

Form questions as in the example.
Mi chiamo Giulio Marchi — Sono italiano — Mi chiamo Hans Bauer — Sono tedesco — Mi chiamo John Miller — Sono inglese — Mi chiamo Chantal Dulac — Sono francese — Mi chiamo Damaso Carrasco — Sono spagnolo.

(See Grammar, G.2.)

2. ASKING THE TIME

LISTEN

La colazione è alle 7
- *A che ora è la colazione?*

Va all'albergo alle 3
- *A che ora va all'albergo?*

Continue asking questions in the same way.
La colazione è alle 7 — Va all'albergo alle 3 — La sveglia è alle 8 — Va all'aeroporto alle 2 — Va al bar alle 11 — Ha l'appuntamento alle 10 — Va a letto a mezzanotte — Arriva a Torino alle 6.

(See Grammar, G.2.)

3. IS IT POSSIBLE TO....?

LISTEN

Una camera singola
- *È possibile avere una camera singola?*

La sveglia domani mattina
- *È possibile avere la sveglia domani mattina?*

Ask questions as in the model.
Una camera singola — La sveglia domani mattina — Una camera doppia — La chiave della camera (12) — Una camera matrimoniale — La colazione in camera — Una camera con bagno.

(See Grammar, L 1.)

4. SPECIFYING A LAPSE OF TIME

LISTEN

A che ora è la colazione? (7.30/9.30)
- *La colazione è dalle 7.30 alle 9.30*

Answer the following questions.
A che ora è la colazione? (7.30/9.30) — A che ora è la cena? (19.30/21) — A che ora è il pranzo? (12.30/14) — A che ora è la colazione?(8/10) — A che ora è la cena? (20/22.30) — A che ora è il pranzo? 12/13.30) (See Grammar, F.)

5. ORDINAL NUMBERS

LISTEN

A che piano è la camera 17 ? (1°)
- *La camera 17 è al primo piano.*

Answer the following questions in the same way.
A che piano è la camera 17? (1°) — A che piano è la camera 16? (3°) — A che piano è la camera 21? (2°) — A che piano è la camera 19? (4°) — A che piano è la camera 28? (8°) — A che piano è la camera 51? (5°) — A che piano è la camera 60? (6°) — A che piano è la camera 70? (7°) (See Grammar, K. 2.)

6. VERBS ENDING IN -*ERE*

LISTEN

Mario prende un caffè (io)
- *Anch'io prendo un caffè*

noi
- *Anche noi prendiamo un caffè*

Answer as in the model
io — noi — tu — voi — loro — Chantal — Giulio e Mario — Luisa — tu — il signor Rossi — io.

(See Grammar, L.2.)

7. PRONUNCIATION

LISTEN AND REPEAT

Prenotazione — colazione — mezzanotte — mezzogiorno — inizio — stanza — mezzo — terzo.

SOCIAL NICETIES

Italians are thought of as being warm-hearted and straightforward. No doubt that is why they are usually presented as happy-go-lucky, much less pernickity than their fellow Europeans in matters of etiquette. This is a misapprehension: there is a rigid social code, and its formal expressions, to an English or French person, would be more in keeping with Imperial China than a modern, industrial society!

If your Lordship would care to follow me ...?

In Italian, the way to address a person you do not know well, is to use the third person singular, feminine, giving it a capital letter just to show you really mean it: "Lei". For the last word in formal elegance, it is possible to make this plural, by using "Loro", all that remains of the original "Loro Signorie" (their lordships). Happily, this is increasingly rare, and the simple "voi" tends to be used for all plurals. The Fascisti tried to ban this use of "Lei", as "not virile", and replace it with "Voi" (as in French). With the Liberation, this was speedily abandoned, and the "Lei" reinstated.

That said, this use of "voi" is frequently found in the south, and in business correspondence, since it avoids misunderstandings. In such cases, it normally has a capital letter: Voi, Vi, Vostro etc. Curiously, it is also often used in comics and cartoons.

It is all a bit bewildering for an outsider.

It is as well to realise that the "Lei" is a way of marking a hierarchical order, whether in rank,

or, more often, between generations: parents will often call their children's friends "tu", while expecting to be called "Lei" back. For the post 1968 brigade, the "tu" is almost universal, symbolising the democratic, egalitarian spirit of that time. Their children, ironically, sometimes show a preference for more formal manners.

Most excellent Doctor ...

Most Italians do not like using simple forms of address, unless it really cannot be avoided. As in French, the ordinary titles are used on their own: "Signore", "Signora", "Signorina". But wherever possible, they like to embellish it with a title, to distinguish the person from everyone else. Such titles are used in conversation, in letters, on visiting cards (much more widely used than in the U.K.), and even appear - abbridged - in the telephone directory.

So it is polite to call an architect "Architetto"(Arch.), a barrister "Avvocato"(Avv.), a doctor (of medicine, philosophy, divinity, law etc etc) "Dottore" (Dott.), a surveyor "Geometra" (Geom.), an engineer "Ingegnere" (Ing.), a teacher, or a research worker, "Professore" (Prof.), an accountant "Ragionere" (Rag.). Should you encounter any MPs, they are all addressed as "~~Onervole~~"(On.) and an onorevole *ambassador is "Eccellenza".*

With the exception of "Dottoressa" (Dott.ssa.) and Professoressa" (Prof.ssa.) there are no female equivalents of these honorifics. In fact, some women practising these professions take it very much amiss if you attempt to feminise their title, and it is wise to address them as "Avvocato", or whatever is appropriate, as the feminine form means " the wife of"...

Once the complexities of the "Lei", the "voi" (or should it be "Voi"?), and the "tu" have been absorbed, and the essential titles mastered, in letters there is still required, in front of the Signore, or the Professoressa, a suitably respectful adjective, designed to ease professional relations.

Even a company should never just be addressed as "A.B.C. Industries", as in English. In Italian it is always "Spettabile" (respectable) or "P~~regiatta~~" Pregiata *(highly-esteemed): rather charming and propitious. As for people, they are "Egregio (excellent) Signore", (or "Signor Direttore", or Avvocato, etc.) for men, and "Gentile" or even "Gentilissima Signora" for women. Which is all very polite.*

Meanwhile, gentle reader, (gent. mi. lett.) as Charlotte Brontë would say, I remain your very humble servant (equivalent: Vogliate gradire i nostri distinti saluti).

1.4 TAKE-A-BREAK

No. 1

LISTEN

Fill in the hotel register on the basis of the information you hear.

PRENOTAZIONE	TIPO CAMERA	N° CAMERA	PIANO	CON BAGNO	SENZA BAGNO
Sarti	....	....	....	....	....
Verdi	....	....	....	....	....
Chiari	....	....	....	....	....
Bianchi	....	....	....	....	....

No. 2

LISTEN

Put in the missing times (writing it out in full) on the basis of what you hear. Don't forget to use "alle" (alle due e mezzo = at 2.30).

*Il dottor Marchi domanda la sveglia .... Poi, ...
fa colazione al bar dell'albergo e, ..., va all'appuntamento con l'ingegner Rossi. La signora Dulac domanda la sveglia ....
Fa colazione .... e, ...è nella hall dell'abergo.*

No. 3

Complete each sentence with "dalle...alle..." to specify the times during which the various meals are served.

La colazione è servita ....

Il pranzo è servito ....

La cena è servita ....

1° giorno :

il corso della mattina è ....

il corso del pomeriggio è ....

2° giorno

il corso della mattina è ....

il corso del pomeriggio è ....

PROVERBIO

LISTEN

Chi tardi arriva male alloggia
(lit. He who arrives late, gets bad lodgings.)

Don't put off till tomorrow what you should do today

(Answers on page 6 of the booklet)

1.5 DIALOGUE

LISTEN

UNA CONVERSAZIONE DOPO CENA

Mr. Marchi and Ms. Dulac strike up a conversation in the hotel foyer.

Sig. Marchi : *Permette? Non La disturbo?*

Sig.ra Dulac : *Prego! Si figuri!*

Sig. Marchi : *Gradisce une sigaretta?*

Sig.ra Dulac : *No, grazie. Non fumo.*

Sig. Marchi : *Anche Lei resta in albergo questa sera, eh?*

Sig.ra Dulac : *Sì, è già molto tardi e domani dobbiamo essere all'appuntamento alle 10.*

Sig. Marchi : *Conosce già Milano?*

Sig.ra Dulac : *Veramente, no.*

Sig. Marchi : *Ma, è la prima volta che viene in Italia?*

Sig.ra Dulac : *No, ci vengo spesso per ragioni di lavoro, ma vado soprattutto a Roma.*

Sig. Marchi : *Lei parla molto bene l'italiano.*

Sig.ra Dulac : *Grazie del complimento. In effetti è la lingua che preferisco.*

Sig. Marchi : *Parla anche altre lingua?*

Sig.ra Dulac : *Sì, parlo anche il tedesco e un po' di russo.*

Sig. Marchi : *Perbacco! Lei mi stupisce!*

Sig.ra Dulac : *Perché?*

Sig. Marchi : *Beh! A vederLa sembra una ragazzina! E invece....*

Sig.ra Dulac : *Eh! Mai fidarsi delle apparenze!*

Sig. Marchi : *Senta, perché invece di dire sempre Lei, Lei... non ci diamo del tu?*

Sig.ra Dulac : *Perché no? È vero che è più simpatico...*

Sig. Marchi : *Perfetto! lo mi chiamo Giulio.*

Sig.ra Dulac : *E io mi chiamo Chantal. Tu, Giulio, parli francese?*

Sig. Marchi : *Oh! Lo parlo abbastanza bene, anche perché mia moglie è francese. Tu sei sposata?*

Sig.ra Dulac : *Sì, sono sposata, e ho anche un bambino.*

Sig. Marchi : *Davvero? E quanti anni ha?*

Sig.ra Dulac : *Oh! È ancora piccolo, ha due anni e mezzo.*

Sig. Marchi : *Incredible! Ma dove trovi il tempo di fare tutte queste cose?*

Sig.ra Dulac : *Oh, in fondo è solo una questione di organizzazione....*

LISTEN AND REPEAT

You will find the translation on page 7 of the booklet.

1. Foyer of La Scala
2. Auditorium of La Scala
3. Michelangelo's "Pietà"
4. Brera Art Gallery
5. The Castello Art Gallery

1

3

4

2

5

1.5 VOCABULARY

NOUNS

la conversazione — conversation
la prima volta — the first time
la ragione — reason
il complimento — compliment
la lingua — language
la ragazzina — little girl ***(1)***
l'apparenza — appearance
la moglie — wife
il/la bambino/a (m/f) — child
il tempo — time
la cosa — thing
la questione — question/matter
l'organizzazione (f) — organisation

---

la ragazza — girl
il ragazzo — boy
il ragazzino — little boy
il marito — husband

---

i giorni della settimana— days of the week
lunedì (m) — Monday
martedì (m) — Tuesday
mercoledì (m) — Wednesday
giovedì (m) — Thursday
venerdì (m) — Friday
sabato (m) — Saturday
domenica (f) — Sunday
i mesi dell' anno — months of the year
gennaio — January
febbraio — February
marzo — March
aprile — April
maggio — May
giugno — June
luglio — July
agosto — August
settembre — September
ottobre — Octrober
novembre — November
dicembre — December

ADJECTIVES

vero — true
simpatico — nice/friendly
piccolo — little, small
falso — false
antipatico — unpleasant (esp. of people)
grande — big/large

VERBS

disturbare — to disturb
fumare — to smoke
restare — to remain
parlare — to speak/talk
preferire — to prefer
stupire — to surprise *(stupirsi* — to be surprised)
sembrare — to seem
fidarsi (di) — to trust
sentire — to hear ***(2)***
dire — to say/tell
dare (darsi) del tu — to call (eachother) tu
dare (darsi) del Lei — to call (eachother) Lei
sposarsi — to get married
fare — to do/make

MISCELLANEOUS

permette? — May I?
prego — please, of course
si figuri! — not at all
già — already
domani — tomorrow
in effetti — actually, in effect
un po' (un poco) — a bit, a little
perbacco! — Wow!
sempre — always
mai — ever (never)
perfetto! — perfect!
davvero? — really?
incredibile! — incredible!
solo — only

HOW TO SAY IT

1. FINDING OUT ABOUT SOMEONE (formal)

È la prima volta che viene in Italia? — Is this the first time that you have been to Italy?
È sposato/a? — Are you married?
Ha bambini? — Do you have children?
Quanti anni ha? — How old are you/is he/is she?

2. EXPRESSING SURPRISE

Perbacco! — Wow!
Davvero? — Really?
Incredibile! — Incredible!
Lei mi stupisce! — You surprise/astonish me!

3. BREAKING THE ICE

Senta, perché non ci diamo del tu? — Listen, why don't we use "tu"?
Gradisce una sigaretta? — Would you like a cigarette?
Diamoci del tu! — Let's use "tu"!

4. AGREEING

Perché no? — Why not? *Perfetto!* — Perfect! *D'accordo!* — OK/Fine/Agreed

5. BASIC SOCIAL CONVENTIONS

Ciao! Come stai? — Hello, how are you?
Buongiorno, Signor Rossi! Come sta? — Hello Mr. Rossi, how are you?
Come va? — How are things going?
Bene, grazie, e tu? — Well, thanks, and you?
Non c'è male, grazie, e Lei? — Not bad, thank you, and you?
Abbastanza bene — Quite/rather well.

6. GIVING THE DATE

Oggi è martedì — Today is Tuesday.
Oggi è il 12 settembre — Today is September 12.
Siamo nel 1994 — This is 1994 (lit. We are in 1994.)

REMARKS REMARKS REMARKS REMARKS

(1) -ino is a diminutive suffix. — (2) The most common usage of this verb is in the expression "Senta!" = "Listen!"

1.5 ORAL PRACTICE

1. FORMAL QUESTIONS

LISTEN

Mi chiamo Giulio Marchi

• *Come si chiama?*

Ho 32 anni

• *Quanti anni ha?*

Can you form the appropriate questions? Don't forget to use "Come?", "Quanto?", "Dove?", "Perché?" and "A che ora?" when needed.

Mi chiamo Giulio Marchi — Ho 32 anni — Sono a Torino per lavoro — Abito a Parigi — Ho due bambini — Ho l'appuntamento all'aeroporto — Arrivo alle 4 — Mi chiamo Chantal Dulac — Lavoro alla FIAT — Ho 35 anni.

(See Grammar, L.5.)

2. GIVING THE DATE

LISTEN

giovedì

• *Oggi è giovedì*

12 settembre

• *Oggi è il 12 settembre*

Give the date as in the example

giovedì — 12 settembre — sabato — 20 luglio — domenica — 1° maggio — martedì — 7 marzo — mercoledì — 28 agosto — venerdì — 15 febbraio — lunedì — 15 giugno — 7 gennaio.

3. HOW ARE THINGS WITH YOU?

LISTEN

Mario

• *Ciao, Mario! Come stai?*

il signor Rossi

• *Buongiorno, signor Rossi! Come sta?*

Ask the following people how they are.

Mario — Il signor Rossi — Marta — Luigi — L'ingegner Bianchi — La signora Verdi — Il professore — Il dottor Marchi — Paola.

4. "ALWAYS" AND "NEVER"

LISTEN

Lavoro sempre il venerdì

• *Io invece non lavoro mai il venerdì*

Change each sentence as in the model.

Lavoro sempre il venerdì — Ceno sempre alle 8 — Prendo sempre l'aereo — Parlo sempre inglese — Parto sempre in agosto — Prendo sempre il caffè ristretto — Vado sempre in Francia per lavoro.

(See Grammar, J.3.)

5. VERBS ENDING IN *-IRE*

LISTEN

Mario dorme in albergo (io)

• *Dormo in albergo*

(lui)

• *Dorme in albergo*

Change each sentence, making sure that subject and verb agree!

Mario dorme in albergo — io — lui — il signor Rossi — voi — noi — tu — Mario e Franco — la signora Verdi — tu — noi — io.

(See Grammar, L.2.)

6. VERBS ENDING IN *-IRE (-ISC)*

LISTEN

Il signor Rossi vuole una birra

• *Il signor Rossi preferisce una birra*

Replace "volere" with "preferire".

Il signor Rossi vuole una birra — Io voglio un caffè — Noi vogliamo un caffè ristretto — Tu vuoi un'aranciata — Maria vuole un aperitivo — L'ingegnere vuole un cappuccino — Loro vogliono una Coca—Cola — Io voglio un caffè lungo — Tu vuoi una birra.

(See Grammar, L.2.)

7. PRONUNCIATION

LISTEN AND REPEAT

Tedesco - mi stupisce! - preferisco - preferisce - conoscere - conosco - finisci - capisce.

WHAT EXACTLY DO ITALIANS SPEAK?

It quickly becomes clear that, even for Italians who live abroad and therefore tend to idealise, Italy does not have a single, clear identity, but is multi-faceted, and varies considerably from region to region. This is why, according to where they come from, Italians can give such varied accounts of their country that they could be describing somewhere completely different.

The Milanese have one Italy, the Venetians have another. The Florentines have a third, totally unlike the Sicilians'. And so forth. Each of these several "Italies" has, of course, its own particular "Italian".

That's one of the first surprises encountered by foreigners in Italy - everyone seems to speak a language different from the one taught abroad, and different from each other.

Sometimes these differences mean no more than a slight variation in pronunciation, intonation, or individual sounds - for instance, the Florentines have a characteristic "c", like the Spanish "jota". But sometimes, whole words change. Do not be alarmed, or think you have not understood anything, or that your phrase-book is useless, or that your teacher has been having you on ... No, it is simply that you have just discovered something you would never have thought: most Italians are bi-lingual; the length and breadth of the peninsula, for everyday things, most people use their dialect, especially in the country.

So that is the reason! In most other parts of Europe, dialects are dying out fast, and are now only spoken by the very elderly, or as a conscious effort to recapture "the good old days". In Italy, on the other hand, they are alive and kicking. It is felt that their dialects are more intimate, warmer, closer to the heart than "standard" Italian. Some people even claim that it is a richer language....

Dialects can use different words and grammatical constructions; some of these words are easy to recognise and understand, but others are not. A foreigner will have different problems with each dialect. The Piedmontese speak a dialect that is half way between French and Italian, so for a French speaker, it is relatively easy. On the other hand, the Genovese dialect has some similarities to Portuguese. And the Sicilian dialect is more or less incomprehensible to anyone not born Sicilian!

It is reassuring to see that often your Italian friends have as much difficulty as you in understanding the other dialects of their fellow countrymen. Some of the dialects are better known than others outside their region: Venetian has its place as the language par excellence of the theatre (think of the Commedia dell'Arte, of Goldoni...) and Roman was generally the language of Cinecittà (which does not, however, mean that everyone understands Roman).

All this is less true of the major northern cities, where the language tends to be the "standard" Italian of the media. By imposing this synthesised Romano-Milanese mixture, first radio and now television have contributed enormously to the linguistic unification of Italy since the end of the war. While written Italian was fixed long before English (in the 13th century, when Chaucer was writing), spoken Italian has always been two-fold: the cold, official "posh" language, the "lingua romana in bocca toscana", and the warm, familiar dialect, the language of the emotions.

That dialects still flourish can be explained historically, (it is little more than a century since Italy was unifed), but also by an essential quality that the Italians have: their "campanalismo", the village pump syndrome. More important than being Italian, is their sense of being Genovese, Neapolitan, Calabrese. Italy sometimes seems like an all-enveloping mantle, covering lots of smaller Italies, each with its own traditions, folklore, dialect and even climate, and keeping them alive.

1.5 TAKE-A-BREAK

LISTEN

INNAMORATI A MILANO

(M. Remigi - A. Testa)
Sung by Memo Remigi

Sapessi com'è strano
sentirsi innamorati
a Milano

Coro : a Milano

Senza fiori
senza verde
senza cielo
senza niente
fra la gente

Coro : a Milano

Sapessi com'è strano
darsi appuntamento
a Milano

Coro : a Milano

In un grande magazzino
in piazza
o in galleria
che pazzia

Coro : che pazzia

Eppure
in questo posto
impossibile
tu mi hai detto "ti amo"
io ti ho detto "ti amo"

Lovers in Milan

You can't imagine how strange it is
to fall in love
in Milan

Chorus : in Milan

With no flowers
With no grass (*lit.* green)
With no sky
With nothing
among the people

Chorus : in Milan

You can't imagine how strange it is
arranging to meet
in Milan

Chorus : in Milan

In a department store
in a square
in an arcade
what madness

Chorus : what madness

Still
in this place
(an) impossible (place)
you said "I love you"
and I said "I love you."

Figures of Speech

NON SBOTTONARSI
(sbottonarsi: lit. *to unbutton)*
To keep it all buttoned up

FARSI LE OSSA
(lit. to develop one's bones)
To cut one's teeth

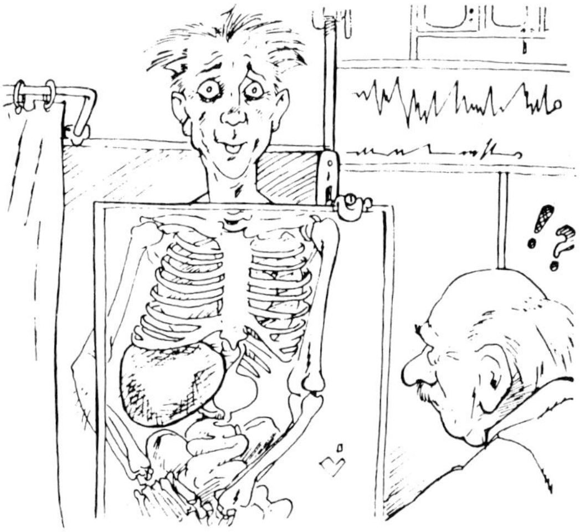

AVERE FEGATO
(lit. to have liver)
To have guts

SAPERNE UNA PIÙ DEL DIAVOLO
(lit. to know one more thing than the Devil)
To have something up one's sleeve

1. WRITTEN PRACTICE

1.1

PUT THE DEFINITE ARTICLE TO COMPLETE THE FOLLOWING: *... direttore — ... segretaria — ... impiegato — ... professione — ... ingegnere — ... stage — ... formazione — ... ditta — ... aeroporto — ... nazionalità — ... paese — ... centro.*
TRANSLATE: *Jenny è americana — Chantal è francese — Carmen è spagnola.*
Mr. Bauer is German — Maria is Italian — José is Portuguese — John is English

1.2

PUT THE POSSESSIVE ARTICLE TO COMPLETE THE FOLLOWING: *Mario ha la valigia : questa è .... valigia. — Noi abbiamo il biglietto : questo è .... biglietto. — Voi avete lo scontrino : questo è.................scontrino. — Tu hai una segretaria : questa è ....segretaria. — Loro hanno il biglietto : questo è ....biglietto. — Io ho la valigia : questa è .... valigia.*
TRANSLATE: *I corsisti sono al bar — Tu sei francese — Il signor Bauer e la signora Dulac hanno il biglietto. — Io sono il direttore delle vendite.*
I have the ticket. — We're at the airport. — You (formal) have a secretary. — Mr. Marchi is at the luggage counter. — We have an appointment.

1.3

PUT EACH INFINITIVE INTO ITS APPROPRITATE FORM: *Il sig. Marchi (lavorare)....... a Genova — I corsisti (aspettare) .... al bar dell' aeroporto — Io (abitare) .... a Parigi — Tu (arrivare) .... in ritardo . — Voi non (trovare) .... la valigia — Noi (parlare) .... italiano.*
TRANSLATE: *Sono in ritardo — Lei è di Londra? No, sono di Leeds. — La valigia è in dogana — Sono qui per lavoro.*
Italian coffee is too strong for me. — I'd like a drop of milk. — I've been working in Paris for years. — I often come to England. — Where do you come from, Sir? From Paris.

1.4

PUT EACH INFINITIVE INTO ITS APPROPRIATE FORM: *L'ingegner Rossi (ricevere) .... i corsisti. — Noi (prendere) .... un caffè. — Il sig. Marchi (conoscere) .... Parigi. — Io non (conoscere) .... Milano. — Tu (vivere) .... in Francia. — I corsisti (attendere) .... al bar. — Voi (vedere)................... il direttore.*
TRANSLATE: *A che ora è la cena? - Le camere prenotate sono al quarto piano. — Ci vediamo domani mattina alle 10.*
The director accompanies the course members to the hotel. — Breakfast is served from 7.30 to 9.30. — The rooms are on the fourth floor. — Mr. Marchi arrives at the airport.

1.5

PUT EACH INFINITIVE INTO ITS APPROPRIATE FORM: *Chantal (preferire) .... un caffè lungo. — Noi (preferire) .... un caffè ristretto. — Loro (preferire)................... una birra. — I corsisti (dormire) .... all'albergo Ambasciatori. — Io (partire) .... domani. — Voi (partire) .... alla cinque. — Lui (dormire) .... ancora! — Tu, a che ora (partire) ....? — L'impiegato (restituire) .... i documenti.*
TRANSLATE: *È la prima volta che vengo in Italia. — Perché non ci diamo del tu? — Quanti anni hai?*
Do you (formal) speak Italian? — My name is John. — Are you married? — Yes, I'm married and I have two children.

(Answers on page 36 of the booklet)

MORE VOCABULARY

CONTINENTS

Europa (f) — Europe
Asia (f) — Asia
Africa (f) — Africa
America (f) — America
Australia (f) — Australia
Antartide (f)— Antartica

COUNTRIES OF THE EU

Italia (f) — Italy
Francia (f)— France
Regno Unito (m) — United Kingdom
Spagna (f) — Spain
Repubblica Tedesca (f) — German Republic
Portogallo (m) — Portugal
Belgio (m) — Belgium
Lussemburgo (m) — Luxembourg
Paesi Bassi (m/pl) — Netherlands
Grecia (f) — Greece
Danimarca (f) — Denmark
Irlanda (f) — Ireland

OTHER COUNTRIES

Bosnia-Erzegovina (f) — Bosnia
Croazia (f) — Croatia
Serbia (f) — Serbia
Svizzera (f) — Switzerland
Austria (f) — Austria
Polonia (f) — Poland
Ungheria (f) — Hungary
Romania (f) — Roumania
Bulgaria (f) — Bulgaria
La Repubblica Ceca (f) — The Czech Republic
Slovacchia (f) — Slovakia
Russia (f) — Russia
Ucraine (f) — Ukraine
Svezia (f) — Sweden
Norvegia (f) — Norway
Finlandia (f) — Finland
Marocco (m) — Morocco
Senegal (m) — Senegal
Costa d'Avorio (f) — Ivory Coast
Nigeria (f) — Nigeria
Angola (m) — Angola
Zaire (m) — Zaire
Repubblica Sudafricana (f) — South Africa
Mozambico (m) — Mozambique
Kenia (m) — Kenya
Somalia (f) — Somalia
Etiopia (f) — Ethiopia
Madagascar (m) — Madagascar
Sudan (m) — Sudan
Ciad (m) — Chad
Algeria (f) — Algeria
Tunisia (f) — Tunisia
Libia (f) — Libya
Egitto (m) — *Egypt*
Libano (m) — Lebanon
Siria (f) — Syria
Giordania (f) — Jordan
Arabia Saudita (f) — Saudi Arabia
Israele (m) — Israel
Turchia (f) — Turkey
Iran (m) — Iran
Irak (m) — Iraq
Pakistan (m) — Pakistan
Afghanistan (m) — Afghanistan
India (f) — India
Cina (f) — China
Tailandia (f) — Thailand
Nepal (m) — Nepal
Indonesia (f) — Indonesia
Giappone (m) — Japan
Corea (f) — Korea
Canada (m) — Canada
Stati Uniti (m/pl) — United States
Messico (m) — Mexico
Guatemala (m) — Guatemala
Nicaragua (m) — Nicaragua
Antille (f/pl) — Antilles
Venezuela (f) — Venezuela
Colombia (f) — Colombia
Perù (m) — Peru
Brasile (m) — Brazil
Argentina (m) — Argentina
Cile (m)— Chile
Nuova Zelanda (f) — New Zealand

PROFESSIONS

operaio (m) — worker
impiegato (m) — employee
commerciante (m) — dealer, trader
rappresentante (m) — representative
industriale (m) — industrialist
libero professionista (m) — freelance professional
ragioniere (m) — accountant
commercialista (m) — businessperson
fisico (m) — physicist
biologo (m) — biologist
chimico (m) — chemist
geologo (m) — geologist
chirurgo (m) — surgeon
architetto (m) — architect
ingegnere (m) — engineer
avvocato (m) — lawyer
disegnatore industriale (m) — industrial designer
maestro (m) — school teacher
professore/professoressa (m/f) — college/university teacher/professor
insegnante (m/f) — teacher
assistente (m/f) — assistant
assistente sociale (m/f) — social worker
psicologo/a (m/f) — psychologist
psichiatra (m/f) — psychiatrist
medico (m/f) — doctor
ginecologo (m) — gynaecologist
giornalista (m/f) — journalist
traduttore/trice (m/f) — translator
interprete (m/f) — interpretor
autista (m/f) — driver
fattorino (m) — errand-boy, deliveryman

THE WORK PLACE

salario (m) — salary
stipendio (m) — wage
foglio-paga (m) — payslip
ferie (f/pl) — paid holidays
tredicesima (f) — holiday pay
anzianità (f) — seniority
licenziamento (m) — sacking
indennità (f) — indemnity
dipendente (m/f) — salaried worker
sindacato (m) — trade-union
sciopero (m) — strike
datore di lavoro (m) — employer
capufficio (m) — office manager
pensione (f) — pension
pensionato/a (m/f) — pensioner
dirigente (m) — manager
casalinga (f) — housewife
socio (m) — member/partner
disoccupato (m) — unemployed
disoccupazione (f) — unemployment

1. TEST YOURSELF

1. PUT THE FOLLOWING SENTENCES INTO THE PLURAL

La signora è francese ....
L'ingegnere ha il biglietto ....
La mia valigia non arriva ....
Ecco il mio biglietto ....
Il viaggio è lungo ....
La camera singola è prenotata ....
Lo scontrino della valigia ....
Questo caffè è buono ....

2. COMPLETE WITH : "Quanto, Che, A che, Como, Perché, Qual, Dove"

.... *si chiama?*
.... *zucchero, Signora?*
.... *ore è la colazione?*
.... *giorno è oggi?*
.... *anni ha?*
.... *è la sua professione?*
.... *abita?*
.... *è a Milano, per affari o per turismo?*
....*piano è la camera?*

3. WHAT WOULD YOU SAY IF YOU HAD TO....

thank someone ....
respond to someone who has just thanked you ....

greet a lady ....
introduce yourself ....
ask someone how he/she is ....
say goodbye ....

ask for an alarm call ....
order a coffee ....
ask someone his/her name ....

4. COMPLETE WITH "devono, fanno, andiamo, volete, possiamo, potete," AS THE CASE MAY BE

Se .... cenare qui in albergo.
Il signor Marchi e la signora Dulac ....conoscenza.
Mentre aspettiamo, ...a prendere un caffè.
Adesso ci siamo tutti, ...andare!
Ci ....essere 6 camere singole prenotate.

5. ONLY ONE SENTENCE IN EACH SET IS CORRECT. CAN YOU FIND IT?

A. *Questi sono i sui biglietti* ☐
B. *Questi sono i suoi biglietti* ☐
C. *Questi è suoi biglietti* ☐

A. *Il sign. Marchi viene di Genova* ☐
B. *Il sign. Marchi viene per Genova* ☐
C. *Il sign. Marchi viene da Genova* ☐

A. *No sono francese* ☐
B. *Non sono francese* ☐
C. *Sono non francese* ☐

A. *Ciao Mario, come stai?* ☐
B. *Ciao Mario, come sta?* ☐
C. *Ciao Mario, come state?* ☐

A. *Hans e Karl Bauer sono tedesco* ☐
B. *Hans è Karl Bauer sono tedeschi* ☐
C. *Hans e Karl Bauer sono tedeschi* ☐

6. MATCH EACH QUESTION TO ITS ANSWER

A. *Sono spagnola.*
B. *No, ci vengo spesso per ragioni di lavoro.*
C. *Sì, parlo anche il tedesco e un po'di russo.*
D. *Abbastanza, sono già molto in ritardo!*

1. *Ha fretta?*
2. *È la prima volta che viene in Italia?*
3. *Di che nazionalità è, signora?*
4. *Parla anche altre lingue?*

(Check your answers on page 38 of the booklet)

IN BOCCA AL LUPO

He had not even had time to open the door before the telephone rang. Milan. It had to be. Ambrogio was in no doubt about it.

Ever since he had taken this job in London, he had not had a single uninterrupted evening. No sooner did he get home than the telephone would start ringing again. And there would be no soft voice whispering sweet nothings - it was always, but always, per motivi di lavoro. Even when he stayed on for hours slaving over his files, his keyboards, his contracts, there was never any escape.

"Why can't I have a normal boss, one who switches off after five-thirty?" he muttered to himself.

This was certainly not the case with his. Ambrogio di qua, Ambrogio di là, mi puoi verificare quell'elenco, chiamare il tal dei tali, dare il recapito di tal altro: it was never ending. Unless it was some journalist or other, trying to sell him some rubbish under pretext of inviting him out..

So, regularly every evening, Ambrogio was beset by the same nagging doubt: had he been wise to accept the Managing-Director's offer of the London job? Of course, there was enormous prestige attached to the job of representing Magagnati, one of Italy's premier publishing houses, but there were certain snags.

Ambrogio heaved a deep sigh: One of his nightly dilemmas was whether to answer with a confident "pronto"? or try a timid "hello?" That evening, however, the caller gave him no time to wonder.

"Pronto, Ambrogio?" said a voice. Obviously not standing on ceremony.

"Sì, sono io."

"Ce la pagherai cara."

And the line went dead. Judging by the interference, it was a call from Italy. He had no idea what he was going to have to pay for, but at least if he had enemies they were not apparently living in the next-door flat. Finding this thought comforting, he ran a bath. Ten minutes later, damning and blasting. he was leaping out of it to take the inevitable call from head-office in Milan.

Crossing the Thames on his way to work next morning, he noticed icicles hanging on the edge of the Embankment. It was going to be a hard winter. He was not over pleased by this. He loathed staying wrapped up indoors. He should have been used to it: after years of living in Milan, he had tolerated fog and frost, and even grown to quite like them.

In fact, sometimes of a January morning, the Po valley swathed in fog from Pavia to Vigevano, he would decide to leave the car at home, and take the tram to work. He would quickly swallow a cappuccino at his *local bar, and go and wait patiently by the tram-lines.. He liked times like this, in the still black night, as yet unbroken by dawn.*

When the tram came, he would mount as if it were the steps to some great house. He would move into the long tube, whose orange paintwork was its one claim to modernity, punch his ticket, and slip through the crush of people, huddled in his overcoat against the cold of the unheated tram. Once there, however, he could enjoy the warmth of the others, pressed up against him.

Ambrogio would watch the orange street-lamps through the icy windows: via Torino, piazza Cordusio, and, finally, piazza Duomo, where he got off. He would cross in front of the cathedral, just a misty shadow on such mornings, cut through the galleria Vittorio Emanuele, past La Scala, completely shrouded, and walk up the via Verdi. He was entranced by this feeling of isolation, in the mist, in the heart of Milan.

All that was in the past. London did not arouse the same emotions. Its temperate climate, which he approved of in theory, left him unmoved. The least drop in temperature could be desolating; one or two icicles on the Trafalgar Square fountains were enough to make it feel as cheerless as camping with Scott in the Antarctic.

Ambrogio was in a black mood. Such meteorological ponderings were making him nostalgic - and his appointments diary made him positively home-sick. And when his assistant, Lucia, announced with a knowing smile: "E arrivata la Piper-Sharp", *his melancholy knew no bounds. In the whole of London, there was no one more relentlessly tedious. And he knew quite a few -* per motivi di lavoro, *needless to say.*

"Più falsa di questa, si muore", *he hissed to Lucia, who instantly vanished.*

Reluctantly, he rose to welcome his visitor.

"Ambrogio, darling, how simply lovely to see you...."

With each meeting, Ambrogio felt increasingly that she was not above intrigue, and was utterly addicted to affectation.

"So, you're not missing the glorious sunshine of that beautiful country of yours? are you getting used to our rough climate? But of course, at your age, one survives the winter."

Mrs. Piper-Sharp jabbered on and on with the ruthless persistence some women give to their crochet.

"You're not looking terribly bright today. You look like someone who has just fallen into the jaws of the wolf, and speaking of wolves, that reminds me of what I'm doing here today. If I haven't completely forgotten my Italian. Mind you with a bit of Latin..."

Ambrogio nodded.

"Yes, a bit of Latin makes all the difference. Well, anyway, Magagnati have published a book entitled, I understand, "Into the Jaws of the Wolf", *or something of the sort. You know about it?"*

"In bocca al lupo....*Yes, I do. Milan has just sent us some copies. I haven't had time to look at it yet."*

"That must be the one. It's the one about an underworld killer, telling all about the gory details of his links with the world of international finance?

"I think it is, but I'd better make sure."

"Don't bother, Ambrogio, darling. That's good enough for me. I won't beat about the bush: we are seriously interested in the book. We would like to take an option out on it. I hope that we might be ready to sign a contract within a week."

To be continued . . .

UNIT 2

2.1 DIALOGUE

LISTEN

IN BANCA

Mr. Moreau is a tourist visiting Rome. He is in a bank to change some of his money.

Allo sportello del cambio.

L'impiegata : *Buongiorno, dica!*

Sig. Moreau : *Buongiorno, vorrei sapere qual è la quotazione del franco francese.*

L'impiegata : *Dunque, oggi il franco francese è a 220 lire.*

Sig. Moreau : *Va bene. Vorrei cambiare 1.000 franchi.*

L'impiegata : *1.000 franchi a 220 lire fanno 220.000 lire. Ha un documento, per favore?*

Sig. Moreau : *Sì, eccolo.*

L'impiegata : *Attenda un attimo, per cortesia. Ecco, firmi qui.*

Sig. Moreau : *Ecco fatto.*

L'impiegata : *Benissimo, si accomodi alla cassa no.2, in fondo al corridoio a destra.*

Sig. Moreau : *Grazie mille. Ancora una cosa. È possibile cambiare dei soldi con una carta di credito internazionale?*

L'impiegata : *Che carta di credito ha?*

Sig. Moreau : *Ho la carta VISA*

L'impiegata : *Certamente, noi accettiamo la carta VISA però ci vuole il libretto degli assegni e bisogna compilare un assegno.*

Sig. Moreau : *Va bene. La ringrazio..... Un'ultima informazione, mi scusi.*

L'impiegata : *Sì, dica...*

Sig. Moreau : *Quali sono le condizioni per aprire un conto corrente in Italia?*

L'impiegata: *Per aprire un conto corrente, bisogna avere la residenza in Italia.*

Sig. Moreau: *Ah...Perché ho intenzione di trasferirmi in Italia l'anno prossimo...*

L'impiegate : *Allora quando Lei arriva deve fare il cambio di residenza e solo dopo può aprire un conto.*

Sig. Moreau : *Bene, grazie mille.*

L'impiegata : *Di niente, ArrivederLa.*

Sig. Moreau : *ArrivederLa.*

LISTEN AND REPEAT

You will find the translation on page 9 of the booklet.

1.Rome

2. The Roman Forum (in the heart of the modern city)

1

2

2.1 VOCABULARY

NOUNS

la banca — bank
lo sportello — bank counter
il cambio — exchange
la quotazione — exchange rate
il franco — franc
la cassa — cash desk
i soldi (pl) — money
la carta di credito — credit card
il libretto degli assegni — cheque book
l'assegno (m) — cheque
la condizione — condition
il conto corrente — current account
la residenza — residence
l'intenzione (f) — intention

----

il denaro — money ***(1)***
il franco francese — French franc
il franco svizzero — Swiss franc
il franco belga — Belgian franc
la lira italiana — Italian lira
il marco tedesco — German mark
la sterlina inglese — British pound
il dollaro USA — American dollar
lo scellino austriano — Austrian schilling
la peseta spagnola — Spanish peseta
lo scudo portoghese — Portuguese escudo

ADVERBS

dunque — therefore/thus/so
quando — when
dopo — after

----

quindi — therefore/thus
prima — before

VERBS

cambiare — to change/exchange
accomodarsi (alla cassa) — to go to (the cash desk) ***(2)***
accettare — to accept
ci vuole — it's necessary
bisogna — it's necessary ***(3)***
compilare — to fill out
ringraziare — to thank
aprire — to open
chiudere — to close

MISCELLANEOUS

aver intenzione di... — to intend to..
l'anno prossimo — next year
l'anno scorso — last year

REMARKS REMARKS REMARKS REMARKS

(1) *"Denaro" is the general term for "money". But in common speech the plural form "i soldi" is often used. —* ***(2)*** *This expression literally means "to make yourself comfortable". It is a polite way of saying "Come in", "Sit down", " Move over there", etc. —* ***(3)*** *See Grammar, L.15.*

HOW TO SAY IT

1. CHANGING MONEY

Vorrei sapere qual è la quotazione (della sterlina inglese) — I'd like to know the exchange rate (of the pound).
Vorrei sapere a quanto è la sterlina? — What's the rate for the pound?
Vorrei cambiare 100 sterline — I'd like to change £100.
Posso cambiare 100 sterline con la carta di credito? — Can I change £100 with a credit card?

2. HOW MUCH .... IS WORTH

100 sterline a 2,200 lire fanno 220.000 lire — £100 at 2,200 liras comes to 220,000 liras.

3. ASKING FOR MORE INFORMATION

Senta, ancora una domanda, per cortesia — If you don't mind, one more question.
Senta, ancora una cosa — One more thing.
Un'ultima informazione, mi scusi — One last bit of information, sorry.

4. EXPRESSING NEED

Ci vuole il libretto degli assegni? — Is a cheque book required?
Bisogna compilare un assegno — You have to make out a cheque.
Lei deve fare il cambio de residenza — You need to register your new address.
Bisogna avere la residenza in Italia — You must have a permanent address in Italy.

5. GIVING WHAT HAS BEEN ASKED FOR

Ha il passaporto? Sì, eccolo! — Have you got a passport? Yes, here it is!
Ha la carta d'identità? Sì, eccola! — Have you got an identity card? Yes, here it is!
Ha i franchi? Sì, eccoli! — Have you got any francs? Yes, here they are!
Ha le lire? Sì, eccole! — Have you got any liras? Yes, here they are!

2.1 ORAL PRACTICE

1. ASKING WHAT THE RATE IS

LISTEN

Il marco

- *Vorrei sapere a quanto è il marco.*

Continue asking what the rate is.
il marco — la sterlina — il franco — la lira — il dollaro — lo scudo — lo scellino — la peseta.

(See Grammer, G.2.)

2. NUMBER PRACTICE

LISTEN

1.000 franchi

- *Vorrei cambiare 1.000 franchi*

Continue saying how much money you want to change.
1.000 franchi — 2.000 franchi — 300 marchi — 50 dollari — 80 sterline — 500 franchi svizzeri — 750 pesetas — 900 scellini — 600.000 lire.

(See Grammar, K.1.)

3. GIVING WHAT HAS BEEN ASKED FOR

LISTEN

Ha il passaporto?

- *Sì, eccolo!*

Ha la carta d'identità?

- *Sì, eccola!*

Answer the following as in the model.
Ha il passaporto? — Ha la carta d'identità? — Ha la patente? — Ha un documento? — Ha il libretto di assegni? — Ha il franchi? — Ha le lire? — Ha la chiave? — Ha i documenti? — Ha la carta di credito? — Ha i biglietti?

(See Grammar, E.6.)

4. EXPRESSING NEED

LISTEN

Avere un libretto di assegni

- *Bisogna avere un libretto di assegni.*

Il libretto di assegni

- *Ci vuole il libretto di assegni.*

Continue expressing need by using "ci vuole" or "bisogna".
Avere un libretto di assegni — Il libretto di assegni — Avere la residenza in Italia — La residenza in Italia — Avere il passaporto — Il passaporto — Avere un conto corrente — Un conto corrente — Avere la carta di credito — La carta di credito.

(See Grammar, L.15)

5. THE VERB "DOVERE"

LISTEN

Il sig. Moreau (compilare un assegno)

- *Il sig. Moreau deve compilare un assegno*

io

- *Devo compilare un assegno*

Continue using the correct form of "dovere".
Il sig. Moreau — io — lui — noi — Marco e Luisa — Lei — lei — voi — loro — tu — io — noi — Roberto.

(See Grammar, L.6.)

6. THE VERB "POTERE"

LISTEN

Il sig. Moreau (cambiare con la carta di credito)

- *Il sig. Moreau può cambiare con la carta di credito.*

io

- *Posso cambiare con la carta di credito.*

Continue using the correct form of "potere".
Il sig. Moreau — io — tu — Franco e Mario — la signora Rossi — noi — voi — io — loro — Lei — tu.

(See Grammer, L.6.)

7. PRONUNCIATION

LISTEN AND REPEAT

Quotazione - franco - franchi - accettare - dunque - certamente - quale - ci vuole

A POCKETFUL OF LIRAS

Italy is one of the ten richest countries in the world. This proves, as does Japan's recent history, that wealth and economic growth are not necessarily linked to a strong currency. In fact, both the yen and the lira have often been weak currencies.

Understandably, there has been talk for ten years or more of revaluing the lira, and creating a "lira pesante" (heavy lira), worth 1,000 liras at the current value, or approximately 40 pence Sterling. Some politicians go on about how such a revaluation would enhance Italy's prestige abroad.

But quite apart from the fact that the "heavy lira" would seem ill-suited to a people widely admired for their ingenuity and liveliness, the expense the changeover would involve, (issuing new coins and notes and withdrawing the old ones), would seem to put the whole thing out of the question, at least for the time being. It seems far more likely that the present system is set to run and run, so we had better get used to it.

It is a good while since the "centesimi" (1/100 of a lira) disappeared from circulation. Like the French franc, the lira was rapidly eroded in the aftermath of the second world war. Nowadays, however, the 5, 10 and 15 lire coins, which replaced the old "centesimi", are also dying out. Anyone working or travelling in Italy - especially southern Italy - ten or so years ago, will recall the rich harvest of "franco-bolli" (stamps), or "caramelle" (sweets), gathered in lieu of small change. The smallest coins had literally disappeared. Rumours abounded at the time that the Japanese had bought vast amounts of these coins as scrap metal! The fact remains that these small coins are now virtually unobtainable, and the normal practice, in a super-market, is to give away plastic bags instead of the long-lamented coins. Since prices never seem to be rounded up or down, you quickly amass an impressive collection ...

The use of cash is very much more in evidence south of the Alps than to the north, largely because of different banking methods. Current accounts have interest paid on them, and therefore, as a logical consequence, cheque-trans-actions cost money. Whereas in most of the developed world, even minor purchases are paid for by cheque or credit card, in Italy for even major purchases, hard cash in the norm. And when you take into account how little a lira is worth, this entails fistfuls of notes.

This must be why, at home or abroad, Italians insist on walking around with enormous sums of money stuffed in their pockets, the sort of sums that would give the rest of us a nervous breakdown. When travelling, this might mean several million liras (at currently just over 2,400 to the £1), well before reaching even the strictest official foreign exchange limits ...

2.1 TAKE-A-BREAK

No. 1 LISTEN

Write down the numbers as you hear them.

....

....

....

No. 2 LISTEN

Circle V *if the statement is "vero" (true), or* F *if it is "falso"(false).*

1. *Il signore vuole cambiare dei dollari*	V	F
2. *Il cambio della sterlina oggi è 2.338 lire*	V	F
3. *Il signore vuole cambiare 50 sterline*	V	F
4. *Il signore riceve 233.800 lire*	V	F

No. 3

Make out the following cheque, writing the amount in letters, then dating and signing it.

li
19
lir 475.000
BANCO DI SANTO SPIRITO
FONDATO NEL 1605
A vista pagate per questo assegno bancario
lire
a
Firma

No. 4

Dingbat.

SCIOGLILINGUA*

LISTEN

Trentatrè trentini entrarono in Trento tutti e trentatrè trotterellando.

Thirty-three riders of Trento entered Trento, all thirty-three trotting.

* tongue-twister

(Answers on page 10 of the booklet)

2.2 DIALOGUE

LISTEN

PRENDERE L'AUTOBUS

Mr. Moreau wants to know how to get to the Trevi Fountain.

Sig. Moreau : *Senta, scusi. Per cortesia, è lontana da qui la fontana di Trevi?*

Il passante : *Guardi, a piedi ci vuole circa mezz'ora. Però può prendere l'autobus. Con l'autobus ci vogliono solo dieci minuti.*

Sig Moreau : *Con questo caldo preferisco prendere l'autobus. C'è una fermata qui vicino?*

Il passante : *Sì, guardi, proprio davanti al tabaccaio.*

Sig. Moreau : *Grazie mille. Per cortesia, mi sa dire anche che autobus devo prendere?*

Il passante : *Il 35.*

Sig. Moreau : *È a che fermata devo scendere?*

Il passante : *Al capolinea, cioè all'ultima fermata.*

Sig. Moreau : *Ancora une domanda, scusi : dove posso comprare il biglietto?*

Il passante : *Dal tabaccaio.*

Sig. Moreau : *Grazie mille.*

Il passante : *Di niente, si figuri!*

Il signor Moreau sale sull'autobus 35 e scende al capolinea. Qui domanda altre informazioni.

Sig. Moreau : *Senta, scusi.*

La passante : *Sì!*

Sig. Moreau : *Per cortesia, mi sa dire dov'è la fontana di Trevi?*

La passante : *Guardi, è molto facile! Vada dritto, alla prima traversa giri a destra e subito a sinistra c'è la fontana di Trevi.*

Sig. Moreau : *È lontano?*

La passante : *È molto vicino, non può sbagliare, ci vogliono due minuti.*

Sig. Moreau : *La ringrazio.*

La passante : *Non c'è di che!*

LISTEN AND REPEAT

You will find the translation on page 10 of the booklet.

1. Piazza Navona 2. A Swiss Guard at the Vatican 3. The Trevi Fountain 4. Piazza di Spagna 5. Four-Rivers Fountain 6. Statue in the Piazza del Popolo

2

4

6

2.2 VOCABULARY

NOUNS

l'autobus (m) — bus ***(1)***
la fontana — fountain
il passante — passerby
il caldo — heat
la fermata — stop
il tabaccaio — tobacconist
il capolinea — terminus
il biglietto — ticket ***(2)***
la domanda — question
la traversa — road junction

---

il freddo — cold
la risposta — answer
il treno — train
il tram — tram ***(1)***
l'aereo — aeroplane
la nave — boat, ship
la macchina — car ***(3)***
la bicicletta — bicycle

ADJECTIVES

ultimo — last
facile — easy
lontano — far

---

difficile — difficult
vicino — near

VERBS

sentire — to listen/hear
scendere — to go down/to get off (a bus, etc)
comprare — to buy
salire — to go up/to get on (a bus, etc)
domandare — to ask
girare — to turn
sbagliare — to make a mistake

MISCELLANEOUS

a piedi — on foot
cioè — that is
di niente, si figuri! — don't mention it!
dritto — straight ahead
dietro — behind
vicino a — near to
lontano da — far from

REMARKS REMARKS REMARKS REMARKS

(1) *Nouns ending in a consonant do not change in the plural. —* ***(2)*** *This can also mean bank note.—* ***(3)*** *The word "automobile" (f) is a synonym for "macchina". —* ***(4)*** *"Senta!", ("Listen!"), is often used to attract attention when you need to ask a question. The reply often starts "Guardi.." ("Look.."). These are simply polite expressions like "Excuse me", or "Let's see..." —* ***(5)*** *See booklet L.15.*

HOW TO SAY IT

1. ASKING FOR DIRECTIONS

Senta, scusi. Mi sa dire dov'è la fontana di Trevi? — Excuse me, can you tell me where the Trevi Fountain is? ***(4)***
Per cortesia, è lontana da qui la fontana di Trevi? — Please, is the Trevi Fountain far from here?
Scusi, come si fa per andare al Colosseo? — Excuse me, how do you get to the Colosseum?

2. GIVING DIRECTIONS

Vada dritto — Go straight ahead.
Giri a destra — Turn right
Giri a sinistra — Turn left
È molto vicino — It's very near
È qui — It's here
È abbastanza lontano — It's quite far
È a 10 minuti a piedi — It's ten minutes away on foot.
È proprio davanti al tabaccaio — It's right in front of the tobacconist's.

3. ASKING ABOUT BUSES

Che autobus devo prendere? — Which bus should I take?
A che fermata devo scendere? — Which stop should I get off at?
C'è una fermata qui vicino? — Is there a stop nearby?
Dove posso comprare il biglietto? — Where can I buy a ticket?

4. THE LENGTH OF TIME NEEDED

A piedi ci vuole circa mezz'ora — It's about half an hour on foot. ***(5)***
Con l'autobus ci vogliono solo 10 minuti — With the bus it'll only take 10 minutes.
E molto vicino, ci vogliono due minuti — It's very close. It only takes two minutes.

5. RESPONDING TO THANKS

(Grazie mille)
Prego! — You're welcome!
Di niente! — Don't mention it.
Si figuri! — Not at all!

2.2 ORAL PRACTICE

1. ASKING FOR DIRECTIONS

LISTEN

La fontana di Trevi
• Senta, scusi. Mi sa dire dov'è la fontana di Trevi?

Ask for directions as in the model.
La fontana di Trevi — Il Colosseo — La fermata dell'autobus — Il tabaccaio — La stazione — L'albergo Aurora — Via Veneto — Piazza Navona — Corso Garibaldi.

2. GIVING DIRECTIONS

LISTEN

Vado dritto?
• Sì, vada dritto.

Continue, using the formal imperative.
Vado dritto? — Giro a destra? — Prendo l'autobus? — Scendo al capolinea? — Giro a sinistra? — Prendo via Marconi? — Vado dal tabaccaio? — Prendo il 35? — Vado dritto?

(See Grammar, L.10)

3. ASKING QUESTIONS

INTERROGATIVE PRONOUNS

LISTEN

Prenda l'autobus 35!
• Che autobus devo prendere?
Scenda alla prima fermata!
• A che fermata devo scendere?

Ask questions as in the model.
Prenda l'autobus 35 — Scenda alla prima fermata — Prenda il treno per Firenze — Scenda alla seconda fermata — Prenda l'autobus 21 — Scenda all'ultima fermata.

(See Grammar, G.2.)

4. HOW LONG DOES IT TAKE?

LISTEN

A piedi, mezz'ora
• A piedi ci vuole mezz'ora
A piedi, 10 minuti
• A piedi ci vogliono 10 minuti

Say how long it takes, as in the model.
A piedi, mezz'ora — A piedi, 10 minuti — A piedi 1 ora — In macchina, 20 minuti — In treno, 2 ore — In aereo, 1 ora — In autobus, un quarto d'ora — A piedi, 2 minuti.

(See Grammar, L.15.)

5. "TO GO" + PREP + INFINITIVE

LISTEN

Prendo l'autobus
• Vado a prendere l'autobus
Comprano il biglietto
• Vanno a comprare il biglietto.

Use the verb "to go" as in the model.
Prendo l'autobus — Comprano il biglietto — Vede la fontana di Trevi — Prendete un caffè — Compriamo le sigarette — Prendi il treno — Compro i fiammiferi — Mangiano al ristorante — Dormiamo in albergo.

(See Grammar, F.)

6. DIRECT PRONOUNS

LISTEN

Conosci Mario? • Sì, lo conosco
Conosci Maria? • Sì, la conosco
Conosci Mario e Franco? • Sì, li conosco
Conosci Maria e Laura? • Sì, le conosco.

Answer the questions as in the model.
Conosci Mario? — Conosci Maria? — Conosci Mario e Franco? — Conosci Maria e Laura? — Conosci la città? — Conosci la fontana di Trevi? — Conosci il sig. Moreau? — Conosci la signora Dupond? — Conosci l'albergo Ligure? — Conosci queste persone? — Conosci gli amici di Mario? — Conosci le vie di Roma? — Conosci Giovanni e Filippo?

(See Grammar, E.1)

7. PRONUNCIATION

LISTEN AND REPEAT

Autobus - aereo - capolinea - miei - suoi - puoi - vuoi - fuori - mai - tabaccaio.

THE NORTH, THE SOUTH AND ROME: ALL PULL TOGETHER

As far as Italians are concerned, there is no such thing as one, single Italy. We have already explained why. Rome is in a sense the capital of two different countries:- "Alta Italia" - High Italy, to the North, "Bassa Italia" - Low Italy, to the South.

Is it by chance, or is it symbolic, that one of the stock characters in "barzellette" (jokes) is that mainstay of the United Italy, a "carabiniere", or state policeman? Either way, it is soon apparent that in the North there is an extra dimension to stories about carabinieri, since most of them are recruited in the South. The North/South antagonism rears its head again.

When you hear people talking about "Italia Saudita", it does not take much imagination to sense their lack of tenderness towards the famous "Mezzogiorno", a name invariably coupled to the word "problema". It has always been a fact that, ever since a certain well-known hot-head, Garibaldi, put on a red shirt and came out with the wierd idea that Northern and Southern Italians should live together in a single state, successive regimes have failed to solve the problem. The divide is still there, in some ways getting even deeper.

Many Northern Italians see the South with its large population and poor economy as a burden which has hampered the country's

economic growth. They are often ashamed of the South, which they see as underdeveloped, not only economically, but socially and culturally, at the same time obstructive, traditional and dominated by the Mafia and racketeers of all kinds.

Southern Italians, for their part, often feel that the North has taken them over, draining the South of its abundant work-force and its economic potential to fuel the industries of Milan and Turin, which then keep the benefits for themselves.

Whatever the factors, historical, geographical or cultural, behind this antagonism, the fact remains that it exists; and it has to be acknowledged that relations between the two are not always smooth. The North's attitude varies from patronising to sarcastic ("Southerner" stories are just as popular in Turin bars as "carabiniere" stories) to the frankly contemptuous: in Northern cities, the Southern migrants are sometimes known as "terroni" (country bumkins).

What about Rome, you might well ask; what part does Rome play in all this? And who could define its precise position "geographically"? Rome falls between two stools - between the notion that proverbially the "Mezzogiorno" starts south of Rome, and the unflattering view of the citizens of the North in Milan, Turin and Genoa that Romans are above all, parasites.

Sometimes, indeed, the foreigner may well wonder what induced a modern state to choose as its capital a city that is really only a living museum, and one of the country's least active to boot. There are ideological reasons: Rome was the capital of the Roman Empire and still is the centre of a world-wide religious faith, Catholicism. Perhaps it is their overwhelming past, and fifteen centuries of "malgoverno" which explain the Romans' characteristic "menefreghismo" (their "don't-give-a-damn" attitude) and one other inconvenient fact: Rome is the part of Italy where the least work is done and where, for instance, the shops stay open least long. But would it be fair to cast the first stone at the inhabitants of a city with only three real employers: the State, the Church and the Cinecittà? Especially nowadays, with the cinema falling on hard times.

This is why Rome, scene of so many "combinazioni" (junketings) is badly placed to act as umpire in the North/South match. But what does it matter: as you approach Rome by the motorway from the North, with the sun setting behind it, the view is simply breath-taking.

2.2 TAKE-A-BREAK

No. 1 LISTEN

Following the directions given on the tape, show where to find the museum, the bus stop, the bank, and the post office. Put the corresponding number in the box.

MUSEO	☐	BANCA	☐
FERMATA DELL'AUTOBUS	☐	POSTA	☐

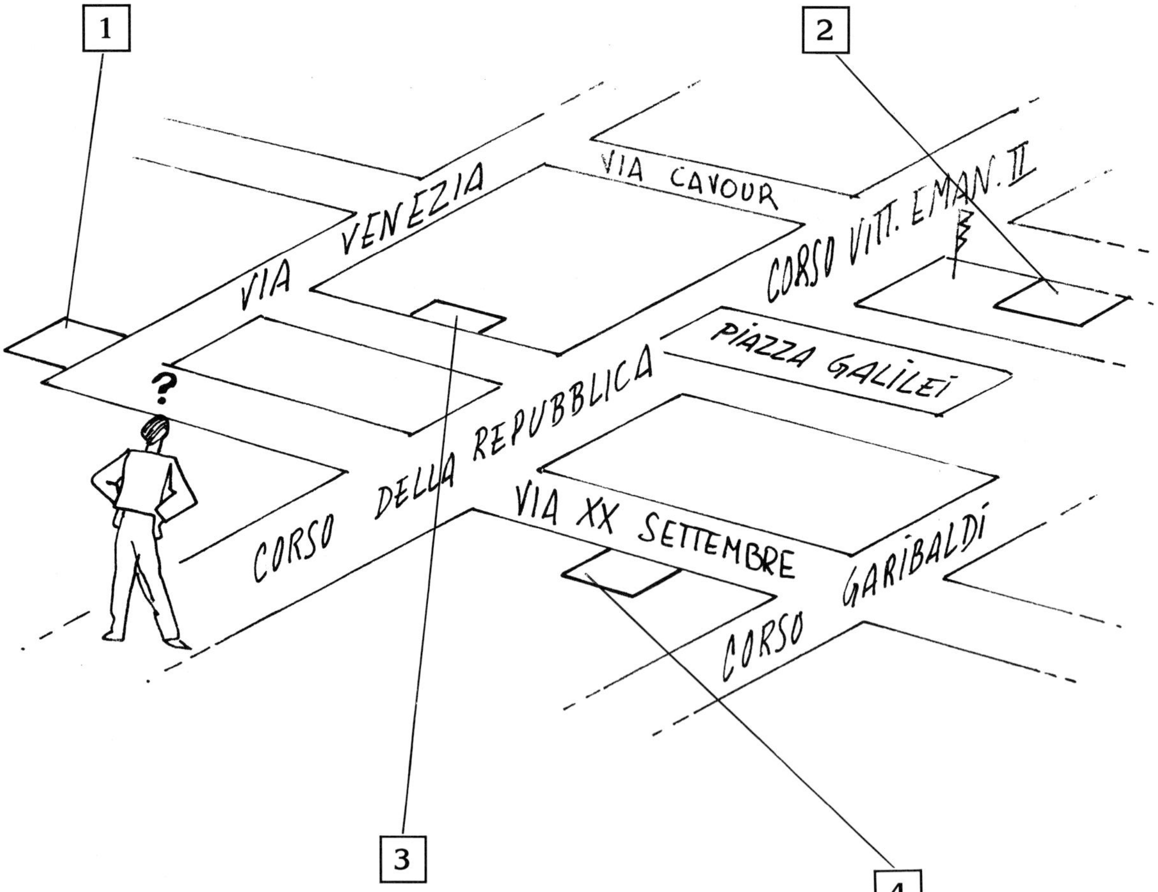

No. 2

Here's a crossword puzzle for you to solve. When you have finished you will find the word for a means of transport in the vertical column.

Definizioni:

1. *L'ultima fermata.*
2. *Senta ..., mi può dire dov'è la fontana di Trevi?*
3. *Domando l'informazione a un ...*
4. *Compro il biglietto dal ...*
5. *Per prendere l'autobus ci vuole il ...*
6. *La fontana è lontano da ...*
7. *Il contrario di destra.*

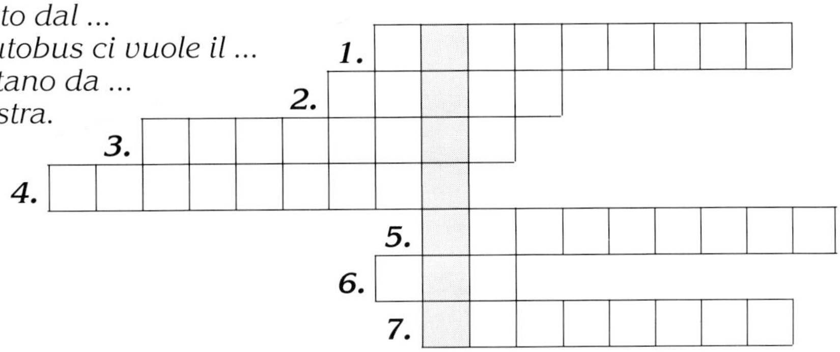

PROVERBIO

LISTEN

Tutte le strade portano a Roma.

All roads lead to Rome

(Answers on page 11 of the booklet)

2.3 DIALOGUE

LISTEN

UNA TELEFONATA

Mr. Moreau phones Mr. Martini, an Italian colleague, to invite him out to dinner.

La sig.ra Martini : *Pronto?*

Il sig. Moreau : *Buongiorno. Vorrei parlare con il signor Martini per cortesia.*

La sig.ra Martini : *Chi lo desidera?*

Il sig. Moreau : *Sono François Moreau, un suo collega francese.*

La sig.ra Martini : *Mi dispiace, mio marito in questo momento non c'è. Vuole lasciar detto qualcosa?*

Il sig. Moreau : *Sì, gli dica che ho telefonato.*

La sig.ra Martini : *Mi ripete il Suo nome per cortesia?*

Il sign.Moreau : *Moreau : Emme - o - erre - e - a - u. E a che ora pensa che tornerà?*

La sig.ra Martini : *Guardi, non so di preciso. Probabilmente fra un'oretta. Se vuole può darmi il Suo numero di telefono e mio marito La richiamerà.*

Il sig. Moreau : *Sì, grazie. Il mio numero è il 48.57.46.15. Gli dica che sono all'hotel Navona e che resterò in albergo fino alle 5.*

L sig.ra Martini : *Va bene, arrivederLa.*

Il sig. Moreau : *Arrivederci.*

....

La centralinista dell'albergo : *Pronto, Hotel Navona. Buongiorno.*

Sig. Martini : *Buongiorno, vorrei parlare con il signor Moreau per cortesia.*

La centralinista : *Attenda in linea, prego. Ecco, Le passo la linea.*

Il sig. Moreau : *Pronto?*

Il sig. Martini : *Pronto, François? Ciao! Sono Andrea.*

Il sig. Moreau : *Ciao Andrea! Come stai?*

Il sig. Martini : *Bene grazie. Quando sei arrivato?*

Il sig. Moreau : *Due giorni fa, e purtroppo resterò solo qualche giorno. Spero che avremo il tempo di andare a cena insieme!*

Il sig. Martini : *Con piacere! per me va bene anche stasera.*

Il sig. Moreau : *Perfetto! Dunque che ora è adesso?*

Il sig. Martini : *Sono quasi le cinque.*

Il sig. Moreau : *Allora ci vediamo alle 8 qui in albergo. Ti va?*

Il sig. Martini : *Benissimo. A stasera alle otto allora.*

LISTEN AND REPEAT

You will find the translation on page 12 of the booklet.

1. The Colosseum
2. St. Peter's Square

1

2

2.3 VOCABULARY

NOUNS

la telefonata — phone call ***(1)***
il/la collega — colleague/associate
il numero di telefono — phone number
la centralinista — operator
la linea — line

---

il messaggio — message
l'elenco telefonico — phone book
il telefono — telephone
la cabina telefonica — phone box
il gettone — token
l'orologio — watch/clock

VERBS

desiderare — to want, require
lasciar detto qualcosa — to leave a message
telefonare (a qualcuno) — to phone
ripetere — to repeat
pensare — to think
tornare — to return/come back
guardare — to watch/look at

---

richiamare— to call back
passare — to pass by/pass

---

fare une telefonata— to call
rispondere al telefono — to answer the phone
riattaccare — to hang up
ricevere — to receive
ripetere lettera per lettera — to spell out

MISCELLANEOUS

pronto! — Hello!
mi dispiace! — I'm sorry!
probabilmente — probably
fra/tra un'ora — in an hour's time
fra un'oretta — in less then a hour (*lit.* in a little hour)
fino alle 5 — until 5
due giorni fa — two days ago
qualche giorno — a few days ***(2)***
sono quasi le 5 — it's almost 5
insieme — together

REMARKS REMARKS REMARKS REMARKS

(1) *The suffix -ata is a common one: "telefono" = phone, telefonata = phone call.*
(2) *"Qualche" is always followed by a singular noun, even though its meaning is plural.*
(3) *In such expressions, the -e of the infinitive can be dropped.*

HOW TO SAY IT

1. TELEPHONING

Pronto, Hotel Navona? — Hello. Is that the Hotel Navona?
Pronto, casa Martini? — Hello. Is that the Martini household?
Pronto, Signor Moreau? — Hello , Mr. Moreau?
Pronto, Andrea? — Hello, Andrea? (Andrew)

2. ASKING IF SOMEONE IS IN

Buongiorno, vorrei parlare con il sig. Martini, per cortesia — Hello. I'd like to speak to Mr. Martini please.
Mi passa il sig. Moreau, per cortesia? — Can you put me through to Mr. Moreau please.
C'è il sig. Moreau? — Is Mr. Moreau there?
Potrei parlare con Andrea? — Could I speak to Andrea?

3. WHO IS IT?

Chi parla? — Who's speaking?
Il suo nome, per cortesia? — Your name, please.
(Il sig. Martini) Chi lo desidera? — Who's asking for him?

4. ANSWERING THE PHONE

Sono io — It's me.
Il signor Martini non c'è — Mr. Martini is not in/here.
Attenda in linea, prego — Hold the line please.

5. LEAVING A MESSAGE

Posso lasciar detto qualcosa? — May I leave a message? ***(3)***
Può dire di richiamarmi? — Can you tell him/her to call me back?
Dica che ha telefonato David — Say that David rang.

6. EXPRESSIONS OF TIME

In questo momento — At the moment
Tra un'oretta — In about an hour
Fino all 5 — Till 5/until 5
Due giorni fa — Two days ago
Resterò qualche giorno — I'm staying a few days.

2.3 ORAL PRACTICE

1. ASKING IF SOMEONE IS IN

LISTEN

Il sig. Martini

- *Vorrei parlare con il sig. Martini, per cortesia.*

Il direttore

- *Vorrei parlare con il direttore, per cortesia.*

Say that you would like to speak to the following people.

Il sig. Martini — Il direttore — La segretaria del sig. Moreau — L'avvocato — L'ingegner Rossi — Il dottor Verde — Andrea — Il responsabile delle vendite — La signora Rossi

2. SPELLING NAMES

LISTEN

(a, b, c, d, e, f....)

LISTEN TO THE EXAMPLE

Moreau

- *emme - o - erre - e - a - u*

Martini

- *emme - a - erre - ti - i - en - i*

Now spell the following names

Moreau — Martini — Jeannot — Dupleix — Goujon — Thomas — Veyrat — Khosrof — Weber.

And now try to spell your own name.

(See Grammar, A)

3. GIVING A PHONE NUMBER

LISTEN

640.11.26

- *Il mio numero è 6.4.0. - 1.1. - 2.6.*

These are all numbers you have. Say them.

640.11.26 — 48.57.46.15 — 54.03.27 — 79.95.84 — 43.96.17.92

Now give your own phone number.

4. TELLING THE TIME

LISTEN

Sono le 16.30

- *Sono le quattro e mezzo*

Sono le 12

- *È mezzogiorno!*

Give the following times, as in the model.

Sono le 16.30 — Sono le 12 — Sono le 14.15 — Sono le 13 — Sono le 22.45 — Sono le 15.20 — Sono le 21.30 — Sono le 11.55

Now say what time it is at the moment.

(See Grammar, K.4.)

5. THE FUTURE OF VERBS IN -*ARE*

LISTEN

Il sig. Martini arriverà fra un'ora (io)

- *Arriverò fra un'ora*

Continue as in the model

Il sig. Martini — io — noi — Marco e Anna — voi — la signora Rossi — tu — il direttore — i turisti — io — il ragazzo inglese — noi.

(See Grammar, L.8.)

6. THE FUTURE OF "TO BE" AND "TO HAVE"

LISTEN

Il signor Martini avrà un'ora di ritardo

- *Il signor Martini sarà in ritardo di un'ora*

Change the sentences as in the model.

Il signor Martini avrà un'ora di ritardo — Io avrò un'ora di ritardo — Loro avranno un'ora di ritardo — Tu avrai un'ora di ritardo — Noi avremo un'ora di ritardo — Beatrice avrà un'ora di ritardo — Voi avrete un'ora di ritardo.

(See Grammar, L.8.)

7. PRONUNCIATION

LISTEN AND REPEAT

Questo - qualcosa - quando - qualche - dunque - quasi - cinque - qui.

WHERE WOULD YOU LIKE TO EAT?

In Italy, eating is not merely a question of physical need. It is something of a religious experience, in its timing, its ingredients and the quantities consumed. When it comes to eating, no question about it: the Italians are dreadfully conservative, both about what they eat, and how they eat it.

For the great majority of Italians firmly believe, (and they are not the only nation to cherish this delusion), that you can only eat really well in their own country. Without wishing to delve too deeply into the subconscious, this is perhaps the result of filial rather than national pride. Deep down, many Italians are firmly convinced that only their own "mamma" really knows how to cook. In the minds of these perpetual children, anything else is just a substitute, and to regain their lost paradise, they should ideally always do as their mother told them: which means, broadly, eating more or less the same thing. Could this be why these "children" are still at home with their "mamma" even when they are over thirty? Or is it the other way round? To find the real reason, we would have to undertake complex sociological or psychological research. Better get back to the table!

The idea of eating "on the hoof" is repellent to most Italians. They would far rather go home, to eat with all the accompanying rituals of "primo piatto" and

"secondo piatto", all liberally washed down with copious quantities of wine (it should not be forgotten that the Italians and the French vie with each other for the coveted title of greatest wine-drinkers in the world.)

Faced with this concept of eating, it is easy to understand why fast-food has met with such limited success in Italy. These days, you do find a few outlets in the major city centres, but only patronised by foreigners, or by youngsters eager to try anything new. There are several things against fast-food: it is not pasta, it is eaten without ceremony, it is very rarely served with wine, and the American-style coffee on offer is, when you consider what Italians are used to, little short of a crime against humanity.

All this said, there is a great variety of places to eat out, ranging from the "tavola calda", a sort of self-service snack-bar where you pay before you eat, to smart restaurants, by way of the "trattoria", a small restaurant traditionally offering "casalinga" food, "home-cooking" in short, unpretentious and reasonably priced. However, as we all know, such traditions are dying out, and "trattorie" are becoming as expensive as restaurants. These can be quite expensive, especially as there is a cover charge as well as the service to add to the bill, which is nearly always "à la carte", as fixed-price menus are unusual. Of course it is possible to find, well off the beaten track, country restaurants where the tourist can have a really enjoyable meal without spending a fortune. In this type of restaurant, where it is always advisable to book, they often serve fixed-price menus.

Foreigners are often surprised that restaurants can be distinguished more by their decor and prices than for the differences in the food they serve. Generally speaking, except for one or two dishes found everywhere, the food retains a strongly regional flavour. When used, as most English-speaking people are, to the huge diversity of restaurants to be found in even relatively small towns, the limited choice of "exotic" restaurants is particularly striking: hardly any Chinese, or Indian, which we all take for granted. These would be too far from "mamma"'s cooking to be anything other than fundamentally alien and alienating to most Italians, who cannot, for instance, forgive the Chinese for making them eat in their restaurants without bread!

2.3 TAKE-A-BREAK

No. 1

LISTEN

Complete the following sentences using the information you hear on the tape.

1. Il signore si chiama ....

2. Il numero del signor Rossi è ....

No. 2

What time is it?

Example - **È mezzogiorno (sono le dodici)**

1. ....

2. ....

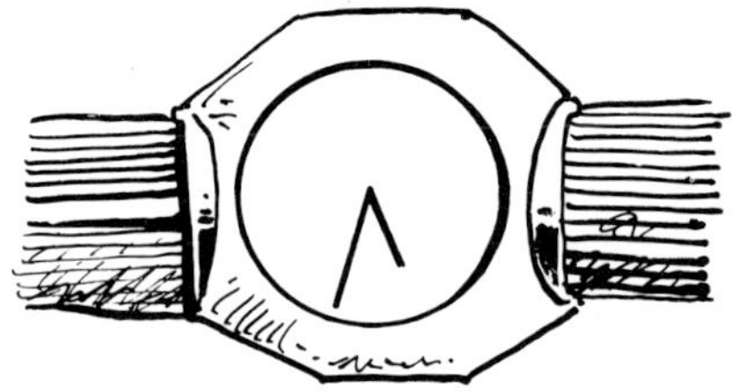

3. ....

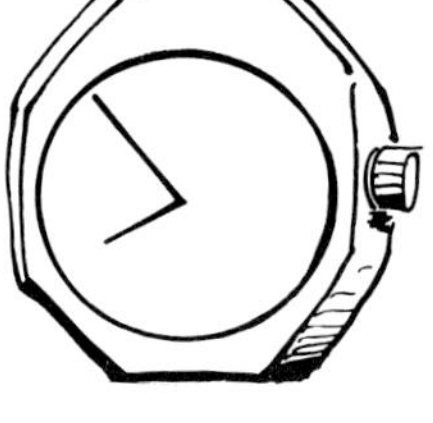

4. ....

5. ....

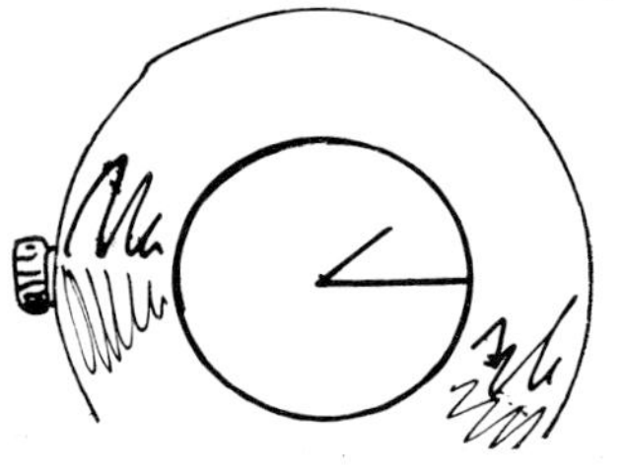

6. ....

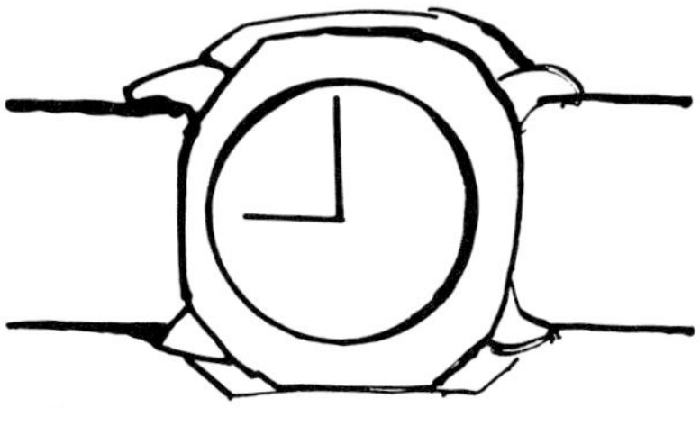

7. ....

No. 3

Consult Mr. Rossi's diary and then answer the questions that follow.

AGENDA

Lunedì. Ore 17 : Andare dal dentista

Martedì. Ore 10 : Telefonare all' avvocato

Mercoledì. Ore 18 : Prenotare i biglietti per il Teatro

Giovedì. Ore 15 : accompagnare Sandra alla Stazione

Venerdì. Ore 12 : aprire il nuovo conto in Banca

Sabato Ore 12 : Prendere l'aperitivo con Mario e Franca

Domenica Ore 17 : richiamare Franca

Che cosa farà il signor Rossi questa settimana?
Lunedì ....
Martedì ....
Mercoledì ....
Giovedì ....
Venerdì ....
Sabato ....
Domenica ....

PROVERBIO

LISTEN

Le ore del mattino hanno l'oro in bocca (lit., Morning hours have gold in their mouths.)

The early bird catches the worm.

(Answers on page 13 of the booklet)

2.4 DIALOGUE

LISTEN

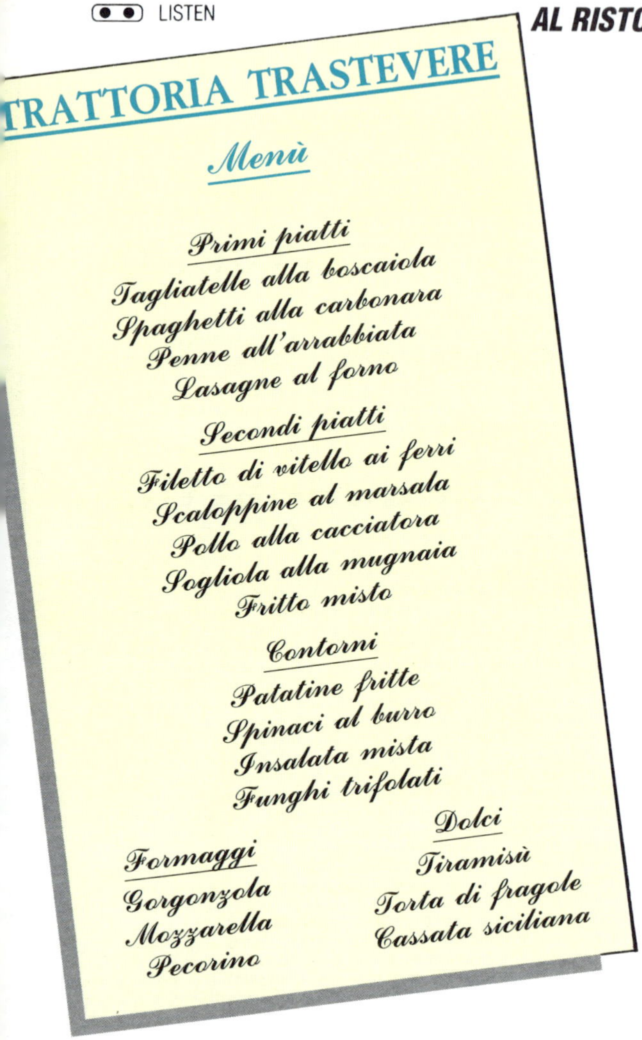

François Moreau and Andrea Martini are having dinner at a typical restaurant in the part of Rome known as Trastevere.

AL RISTORANTE

Andrea : *Ci può portare il menù, per favore?*

Cameriere : *Subito, eccolo.*

Andrea : *Grazie.*

François : *Ho una fame da lupi, e tu?*

Andrea : *Anch'io ho un certo appetito, e in questo ristorante, vedrai, si mangia benissimo. Vediamo un po'che cosa c'è di buono.*

François : *Che cosa prendi di primo?*

Andrea : *Non lo so ancora: sono indeciso tra le tagliatelle alla boscaiola e le penne all'arrabbiata.*

François : *Come sono le tagliatelle alla boscaiola?*

Andrea : *Buonissime! Con la panna, i funghi e i piselli.*

François : *Ah no, i funghi non mi piacciono molto, preferisco prendere le lasagne.*

Andrea : *Io invece credo proprio che prenderò le tagliatelle.*

François : *E di secondo, prendiamo carne o pesce?*

Andrea : *Io prendo la carne, sicuramente: il pesce non mi piace, però se a te piace qui lo fanno benissimo.*

François : *Allora quasi quasi prendo una sogliola con contorno di insalata mista.*

Andrea : *E io un filetto al sangue con contorno di spinaci. E da bere, che cosa preferisci?*

François : *Vino, naturalmente! Il rosato ti piace?*

Andrea : *Sì, mi piace, allora ordiniamo una bottiglia di rosato e mezza minerale.*

LISTEN AND REPEAT

You will find the translation on page 14 of the booklet

1. A typical restaurant
2. An inn sign
3. Assortment of cold meat and wines
4. A plate of "gnocchi" (dumplings)
5. Spaghetti with shellfish and a carafe of white Roman wine

Il Sasso
di Dante
RISTORANTE "Sasso di Dante"

PINOT NERO
Chardonnay
di Oslavia
Vino da tavola
1986
3

4

RASPO DE UA
2

5

2.4 VOCABULARY

NOUNS

il ristorante — restaurant
il menù — menu ***(1)***
la fame — hunger
l'appetito (m) — appetite
il primo — first course
la panna — cream
il fungo — mushroom
i piselli (m/pl) — peas
il secondo — second/main course
la carne — meat
il pesce — fish
la sogliola — sole
il contorno — side dish of vegetables
l'insalata (f) — salad
il filetto — filet
il sangue — blood
gli spinaci (m/pl) — spinach
il vino (rosso, bianco, rosato) — wine (red, white, rosé)
l'acqua minerale (f) — mineral water ***(2)***
il forno — oven
il vitello — veal
la scaloppina — veal cutlet
il pollo — chicken
il fritto misto — fried fish
le patatine fritte — chips
il formaggio — cheese
il dolce — dessert, pudding
la torta di fragole — strawberry cake

---

la bottiglia — bottle
la sete — thirst
il conto — bill
la mancia — tip
la pasta — pasta
la minestra — soup
la verdura — vegetables
la frutta — fruit
la carne (di vitello, di manzo, di maiale) — meat (veal, beef, pork)

---

la bistecca — steak
il pomodoro — tomato
la cottura — cooking, as in "cooking-time"
ben cotto — well-cooked
arrosto — roast
fritto — fried
il condimento — seasoning
il sale — salt
il pepe — pepper
l'olio(m) — oil
l'aceto(m) — vinegar
la senape — mustard ***(3)***

VERBS

portare — to bring
prendere — to take/have
piacere — to be pleasing ***(4)***
credere — to believe
ordinare — to order
essere indeciso — to be undecided
avere una fame da lupi — to be as hungry as a hunter
avere un certo appetito — to be quite hungry
si mangia benissimo — the food is wonderful (lit., one eats very well)

---

pagare — to pay
scegliere — to choose

ADVERBS

proprio — really
sicuramente — surely
quasi quasi — nearly ***(5)***
naturalmente — naturally
mezzo — half

HOW TO SAY IT

1. ASKING FOR THE MENU

Ci può portare il menù, per favore? — Can you bring us the menu, please?
Mi porta il menù, per cortesia? — Can you bring me the menu, please?

2. WHAT DISHES ARE AVAILABLE?

Che cosa c'è di buono? — What's especially good?
Che cosa c'è di primo? — What first courses are there?
Che cosa c'è di secondo? — What main courses are there?
Che dolci avete? — What puddings have you got?
Che cos'è il piatto del giorno? — What's today's special dish?

3. ASKING ABOUT A PARTICULAR DISH

Che cos'è la sogliola? — What is sole?
Che cosa sono le tagliatelle alla boscaiola? — What are "tagliatelle alla boscaiola"?
Com'è la sogliola? — What's the sole like?
Come sono le tagliatelle all boscaiola? — What are the "tagliatelle alla boscaiola" like?

4. COMMENTING ON A DISH

È buonissimo! — It's really good!
È squisito! — It's delicious!
È cattivo! — It's awful!
Mi piace molto — I like it very much.
Non mi piace affatto — I don't like it at all.

5. BEING UNDECIDED

Sono indeciso tra la carne e il pesce — I haven't decided between meat and fish.
Quasi quasi prendo una sogliola — I think I might have sole.

REMARKS REMARKS REMARKS REMARKS

(1) Menus in Italy are generally à la carte, but there are exceptions, such as tourist menus, (menù turistico). — (2) If you order mineral water, it will normally be carbonated. To get uncarbonated water, you will have to specify it: "acqua minerale naturale". — (3) Mustard is not widely used in Italy. You will have to order it especially. — (4) "Piacere" is used to mean "like" when expressing a taste or preference. "Amare" expresses affection,(see Grammar L.16) — (5) Repetition is often used for emphasis, as here, to stress uncertainty.

2.4 ORAL PRACTICE

1. INDIRECT OBJECT PRONOUNS

MI, TI, GLI, LE, CI, VI, GLI

LISTEN

La cameriera porta il menù
Al sig. Rossi • Gli porta il menù
Alla sig.ra Rossi • Le porta il menù

Using pronouns say who the waiter brings the menu to.
Al sig. Rossi — Alla sig.ra Rossi — A noi — A me — A te — A voi — A Franco — A Maria — A Roberto e Marco — A Carlo e Gianna — A Franco e Marina — A lui.

(See Grammar, E.1.)

2. THE VERB "PIACERE"

LISTEN

La carne • Mi piace molto la carne
Le tagliatelle • Mi piacciono molto le tagliatelle.

Make* "piacere" *singular or plural as in the model.
La carne — Le tagliatelle — il pesce — Le lasagne — Il vino rosso — La sogliola — Gli spinaci — I piselli — La pizza — I funghi — L'inslata — Le penne all'arrabbiata.

(See Grammar, L.16)

3. SAYING WHAT THERE IS

LISTEN

Che cosa c'è di buono?
L'arrosto di vitello • C'è l'arrosto di vitello
Le lasagne • Ci sono le lasagne

Continue as in the model, putting the verb into the singular or the plural, as necessary:
L'arrosto di vitello — Le Lasagne — Le tagliatelle alla boscaiola — La sogliola — La minestra di verdura — I funghi fritti — Gli spaghetti al pomodoro — Le patate fritte — Il filetto al pepe — Gli spinaci.

(See Grammar, L.1.)

4. SUPERLATIVE ADJECTIVES

LISTEN

Il pesce è molto buono.
• Sì, è buonissimo
La carne è molto buona
• Sì, è buonissima
Gli spaghetti sono molto buoni
• Sì, sono buonissimi
Le lasagne sono molto buone
• Sì, sono buonissime

Answer as in the model.
Il pesce è molto buono — La carne è molto buona — Gli spaghetti sono molto buoni — Le lasagne sono molto buone — I piselli sono molto buoni — Il filetto è molto buono — La pizza è molto buona — Il dolce è molto buono — La minestra è molto buona — Le tagliatelle sono molto buone — Il vino è molto buono. (See Grammar, H.2.)

5. WHAT IS THERE TO EAT?

LISTEN

Il primo • Che cosa c'è di primo?
Il formaggio • Che cosa c'è di formaggio?

Ask the appropriate questions as in the model.
Il primo — Il formaggio — Il secondo — L'antipasto — Il contomo — La frutta — Il dolce

6. VERBS ENDING IN *-GARE*: PAGARE

LISTEN

Pagare il conto (io) • Pago il conto
(tu) • Paghi il conto

Continue conjugating, as in the model.
io — tu — noi — il sig. Moreau — Franco e Mario — voi — Lei — io — la sig.ra Rossi — noi — tu — lui — voi. (See Grammar, L.6.)

7. PRONUNCIATION

LISTEN AND REPEAT

Menù - città - caffè - nazionalità - società - però - prenderò - perché - cioè - può.

THE TYRANNY OF PASTASCIUTTA

You have been invited to lunch? Best beware, then: in Italy, it pays to be punctual. There are two reasons. Firstly, remember that nearly all Italians have virtually no breakfast ("prima colazione"). It is not hard to understand that by lunch-time, people are frenzied with hunger. Secondly, meal-times are strictly adhered to in Italy, ruled by their first, and most vital, component: pasta.

Yes, indeed, there are no two ways about it: Italian food is superb, and yet for most people there, it seems that "eating" in fact means "eating pasta", which would seem rather restrictive, no matter how much one might like it ordinarily.

And how does this mania control meal-times? it is perfectly simple: usually, a meal will start with "pastasciutta", which has a very precise cooking-time; overcooked it becomes the startlingly red nightmare that slops out of the tins labelled "spaghetti" from British supermarkets. But in Italy, properly cooked pasta is "al dente", that is to say cooked to the exact moment for it to be just slightly firm to the tooth. So, when the fateful cry "A tavola!" summons the hungry hoards to the table, it is vital you hold out your plate immediately, before bidding the company a cheering "Buon appetito!"

"Pastasciutta" holds complete sway over Italian minds, it rules their agenda and their habits. It is accompanied by the ritual "fondina" (soup-plate): to serve pasta on a dinner-plate in Italy would be like serving sherry in a tooth-mug.

Talking of pasta, have you ever wondered why the Italians use the word "pastasciutta", which means "dry pasta"? It is to distinguish it from "pasta in brodo", in soups, or stock. "Minestrone" - the name simply means "big soup" - is the exact opposite of what most nations understand a soup to be: it is full of short bits of pasta, specially designed for the purpose, and is almost thick enough to stand a spoon in. This does not prevent it from being utterly delicious.

Leaving aside any reservations about the ubiquitous pasta, you will find that Italian cooking can be very varied: there is a rich array of meat dishes, of vegetables, many different cheeses and cooked meats, a good choice of fish and of sea-food. Just to make your mouth water, think of "carpaccio", thin slices of raw meat garnished with lemon wedges, of "melanzane alla parmigiana" (aubergines with parmesan), the famous cheese making its presence well and truly felt, or of the many dishes of vegetable and sea-food fritters, ("fritto misto", "scampi fritti"...) This list is entirely subjective, and in no way exhaustive.

One more thing. This business about "first course" and "second course" and sometimes even "third course" leads quickly to this conclusion: Italians eat huge amounts. It is quite staggering, considering the tons of pasta gobbled up each year by the Italian population, that they are not particularly obese. Recent theories even defend the cult of "pastasciutta" in the name of some "dieta mediterranea", rather forgetting that previously, before the Italians took to large-scale meat-eating, (modelling themselves after the last war on the Americans), the sheer bulk of the first course could be amply justified: it was usually the only course.

2.4 TAKE-A-BREAK

No. 1 LISTEN

Indicate on the menu the dishes chosen by the two people.

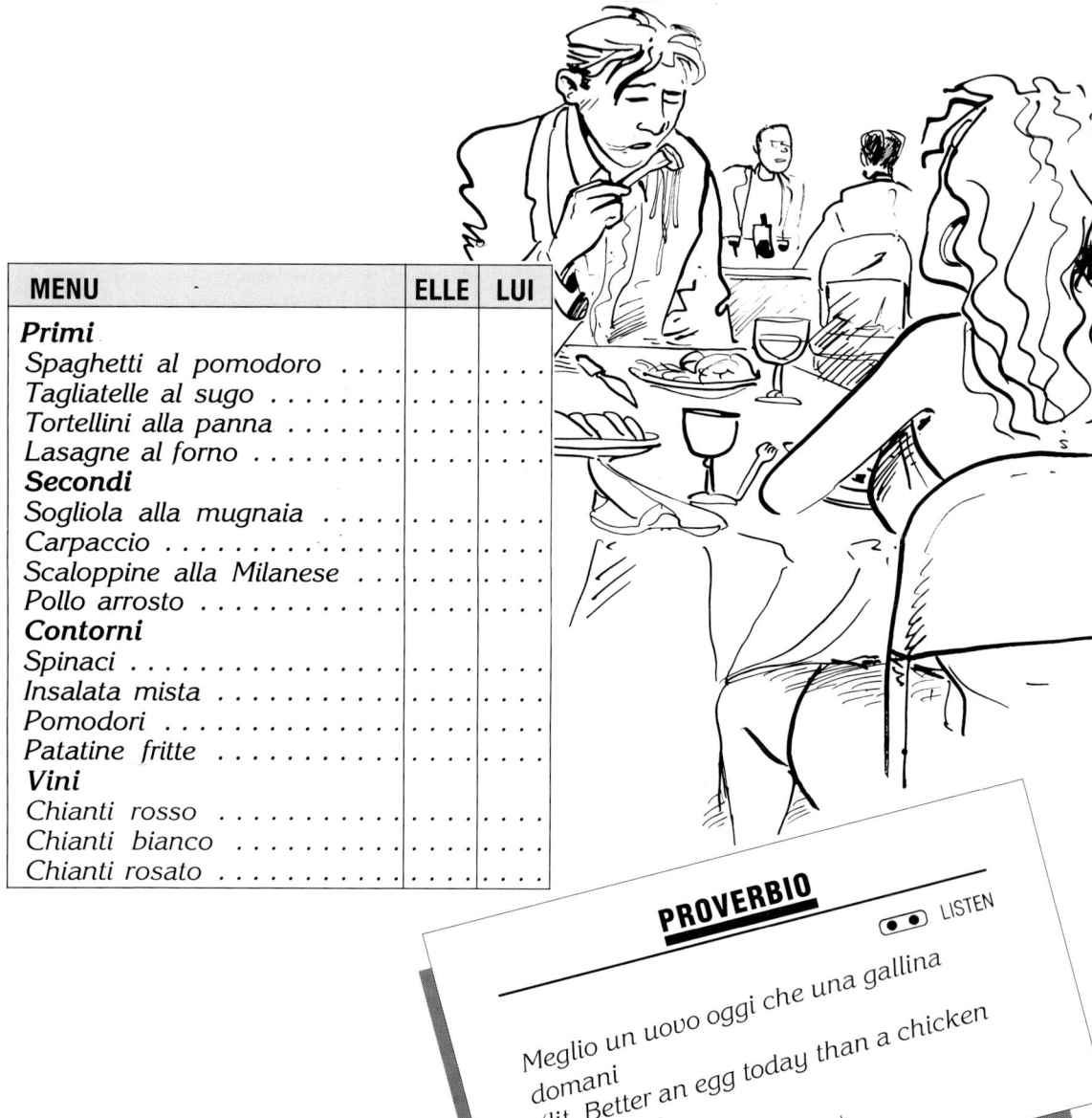

MENU	ELLE	LUI
Primi		
Spaghetti al pomodoro	. . . .	. . . . .
Tagliatelle al sugo	. . . .	. . . . .
Tortellini alla panna	. . . .	. . . . .
Lasagne al forno	. . . .	. . . . .
Secondi		
Sogliola alla mugnaia	. . . .	. . . . .
Carpaccio	. . . .	. . . . .
Scaloppine alla Milanese . . .	. . . .	. . . . .
Pollo arrosto	. . . .	. . . . .
Contorni		
Spinaci	. . . .	. . . . .
Insalata mista	. . . .	. . . . .
Pomodori	. . . .	. . . . .
Patatine fritte	. . . .	. . . . .
Vini		
Chianti rosso	. . . .	. . . . .
Chianti bianco	. . . .	. . . . .
Chianti rosato	. . . .	. . . . .

PROVERBIO

LISTEN

Meglio un uovo oggi che una gallina domani
(lit. Better an egg today than a chicken tomorrow)

A bird in the hand is worth two in the bush.

No. 2

Match each object to its name and put the corresponding number in the box.

COLTELLO ☐	FORCHETTA ☐	CUCCHIAIO ☐
CUCCHIAINO ☐	BOTTIGLIA ☐	BICCHIERE ☐
PIATTO ☐	TOVAGLIOLO ☐	TOVAGLIA ☐
SEDIA ☐		
PANE ☐		
FRUTTA ☐		
SALE ☐		
PEPE ☐		
MENÙ ☐		

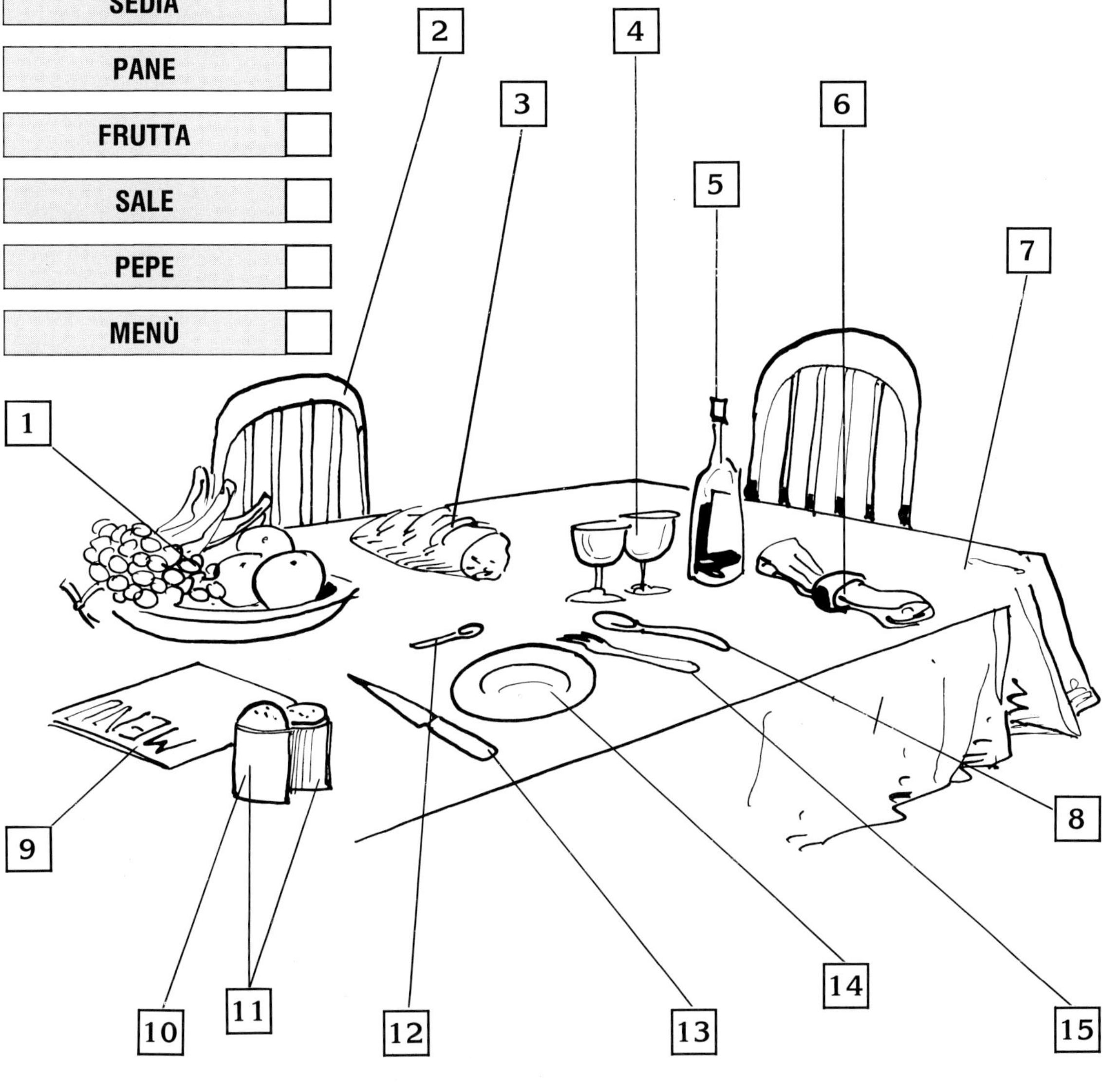

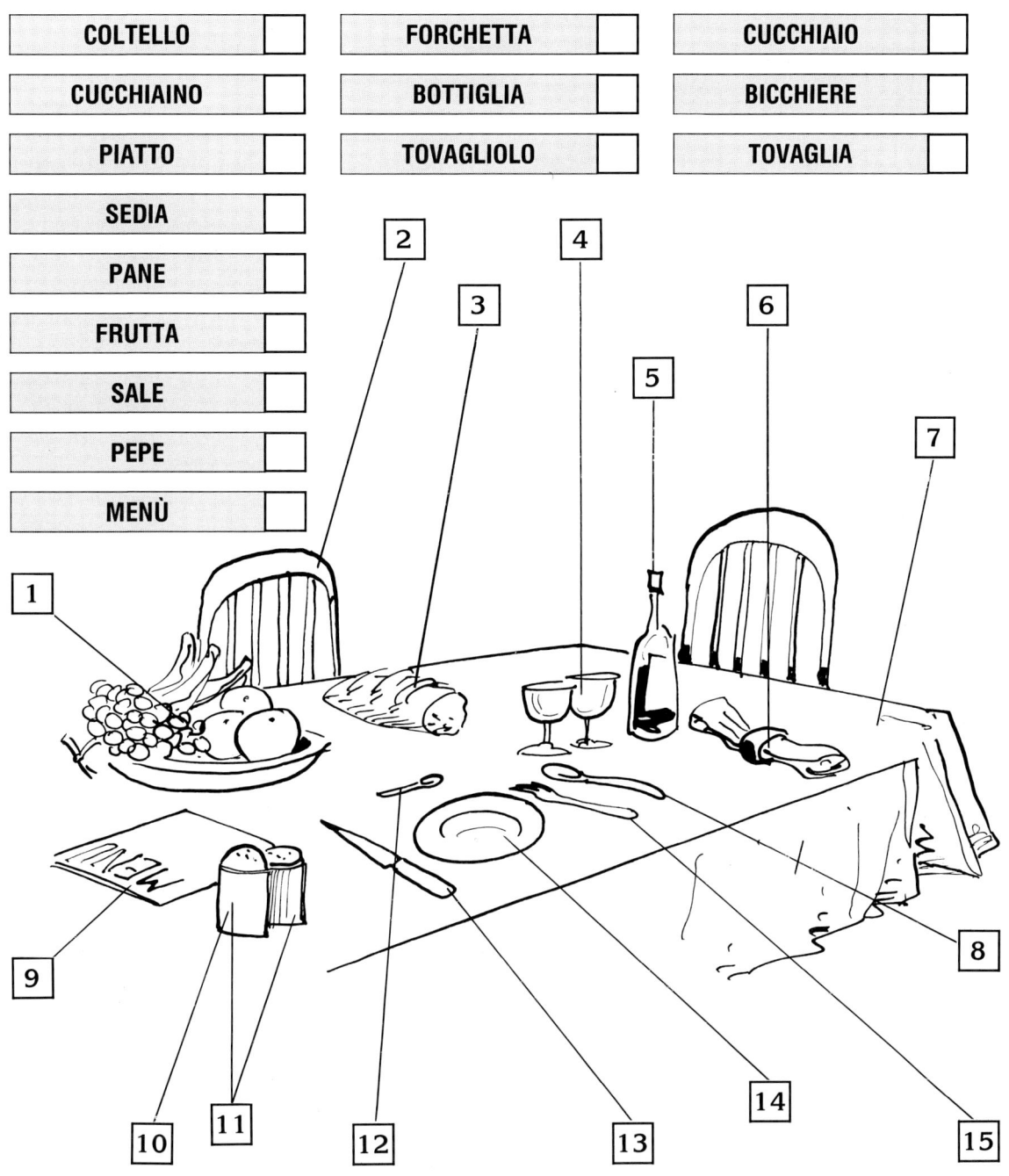

(Answers on page 15 of the booklet)

2.5 DIALOGUE

LISTEN

PARTENZA!

Mr. Moreau is at Rome's Termini Station where he is buying a ticket back to Paris.

L'altoparlante : *L'espresso 712 proveniente da Perugia per Napoli è in arrivo al binario 18. Carrozze di prima classe in coda.*

Allo sportello della biglietteria della stazione.

Sig. Moreau : Buongiorno, vorrei un biglietto per Parigi.

L'impiegata : *Andata e ritorno?*

Sig. Moreau : *No, sola andata.*

L'impiegata : *Di prima o di seconda classe?*

Sig. Moreau : *Di prima.*

L'impiegata : *Che treno vuole prendere? Perché lo sa che per il Palatino deve avere la prenotazione del vagone letto?*

Sig. Moreau : *Ma a che ora parte il Palatino? Perché io vorrei partire oggi stesso.*

L'impiegata : *Guardi, se non ha già la prenotazione del vagone letto non lo può prendere oggi. La prenotazione bisogna farla almeno 12 ore prima della partenza.*

Sig. Moreau : *Ma ci sarà un altro treno!*

L'impiegata : *Certamente! C'è il Napoli Express che parte tra un'ora. Quello lo può prendere perché la prenotazione del vagone letto non è obbligatoria.*

Sig. Moreau : *Ah! Benissimo. Però, corro il rischio di non trovare posto?*

L'impiegata : *Eh si, dipende un po'dal periodo, ma in genere in prima classe si trova.*

Sig. Moreau : *Comunque a che ora arriva a Parigi?*

L'impiegata : *Alle 8 della mattina.*

Sig. Moreau : *Ma sì, mi faccia il biglietto per il Napoli Express. Quanto costa?*

L'impiegata : *190,000 lire.*

Sig. Moreau : *Eccole 200,000 lire.*

L'impiegata : *Ecco a Lei 10,000 lire di resto.*

Sig. Moreau : *Mi scusi, da che binario parte il treno?*

L'impiegata : *Dal binario 11.*

Sig. Moreau : *La ringrazio.*

LISTEN AND REPEAT

You will find the translation on page 16 of the booklet.

1. Trinità dei Monti (Rome)
2. The gardens of the Palazzo Farnese
3. Piazza Navona

2

3

2.5 VOCABULARY

NOUNS

la partenza — departure
l'altoparlante (m) — loudspeaker
l'espresso (m) — express train
l'arrivo (m) — arrival
il binario — platform (*lit.* rail)
la carrozza — coach (train)
la classe — class
la coda — tail, end
la biglietteria — ticket office
l'andata (f) — one-way ticket
il ritorno — return ticket
il treno — train
il vagone — carriage
il vagone letto — sleeper
il posto a sedere — seat
il periodo — period/time
il resto — change (money)

---

la stazione — station
la coincidenza — (train) connection
la cuccetta — berth/couchette
un vagone ristorante — restaurant car
il diretto — through train
il rapido — fast train
il locale — local train
il viaggiatore — traveller

VERBS

partire — to leave, depart
correre il rischio di — to run the risk of
dipendere (da) — to depend on
fare il biglietto — to take a ticket

MISCELLANEOUS

costare — to cost
oggi stesso — this very day
almeno — at least
in genere — in general
comunque — however
prenotazione obbligatoria — reserved seats only

HOW TO SAY IT

1. BUYING A TRAIN TICKET

Vorrei un biglietto di andata e ritorno per Roma — I'd like a return ticket to Rome.
Vorrei prenotare una cuccetta sul treno per Parigi — I'd like to reserve a sleeping berth on the Paris train.

2. ASKING WHICH PLATFORM THE TRAIN IS LEAVING FROM

Scusi, da quale binario parte il treno per Parigi? — Excuse me, which platform is the train for Paris leaving from?

3. ARRIVALS

A che ora arriva a Parigi? — What time does it arrive in Paris?
A che stazione arriva il treno? — Which station does it arrive at?

4. KINDS OF TRAINS

È un treno diretto? — Is it a through train?
Bisogna cambiare ? — Is it necessary to change?
C'è la coincidenza? — Is there a connection?
È un locale? — Is it a local train?
È un espresso? — Is it an express?
È un rapido? — Is it a fast train?

5. ASKING HOW MUCH IT COSTS

Quanto costa? — How much does it cost?
Quanto costa la prenotazione? — How much does a reservation cost?
Quanto costano i biglietti? — How much are the tickets?
Quanto costa il supplemento rapido? — What is the surcharge on a ticket for the express?

6. MORE QUESTIONS ABOUT TRAINS

Quanti treni ci sono per Parigi? — How many trains are there for Paris?
C'è solo un treno diretto al giorno? — Is there only one through train per day?
A che ora è il prossimo treno per Londra? — At what time is the next train for London?

2.5 ORAL PRACTICE

1. BUYING A TRAIN TICKET

LISTEN

Andata e ritorno - Parigi
• Vorrei un biglietto di andata e ritorno per Parigi.

Buy the following kinds of tickets.
Andata e ritorno (Parigi) — Solo andata (Milano) — Prima classe (Monaco) — Seconda classe (Bologna) — Andata e ritorno (Bruxelles) — Solo andata (Roma).

(See Grammar, F)

2. ASKING HOW MUCH IT COSTS

LISTEN

Il vagone letto
• Quanto costa il vagone letto?
I biglietti
• Quanto costano i biglietti?

Continue asking how much things cost.
Il vagone letto — I biglietti — La prenotazione — La prima classe — Le cuccette — La seconda classe — Il taxi — Gli alberghi — Le sigarette — Una birra — Due caffè.

(See Grammar, G.2)

3. WHICH PLATFORM.....?

LISTEN

Da che binario parte il treno per Parigi? (11)
• Il treno per Parigi parte dal binario 11

Continue answering as in the model.
Da che binario parte il treno per Parigi? (11)
Da che binario parte il treno per Londra? (8)
Da che binario parte il treno per Roma? (3)
Da che binario parte il treno per Bologna? (6)
Da che binario parte il treno per Venezia? (4)

(See Grammar, F)

4. MAKING RESERVATIONS

LISTEN

Vagone letto/1ª classe/Parigi
• Vorrei prenotare un vagone letto in 1ª classe per Parigi.

Continue making reservations as in the model.
Vagone letto/1ª classe/Parigi — Due cuccette/2ª classe/Roma — Un posto.— 2ª classe/Venezia — Una cuccette/2ª classe/Londra — Un posto/1ª classe/Milano.

5. THE VERB "DIPENDERE (DA)"

LISTEN

Il periodo • Dipende dal periodo
La gente • Dipende dalla gente
I ragazzi • Dipende dai ragazzi
Le situazioni • Dipende dalle situazioni

***Continue as in the model, using the appropriate form of the preposition* "da".**
Il periodo — La gente — I ragazzi — Le situazioni — Il tempo — La sig.ra Rossi — Il momento — I treni — L'orario — Il ristorante — Le persone — L'ora.

(See Grammar, F.)

6. THE PRONOUN CI (= THERE)

LISTEN

Andiamo alla stazione?
• Sì, ci andiamo

***Answer, using the pronoun* "ci".**
Andiamo alla stazione — Andiamo al ristorante? — Arriviamo a Parigi? — Restiamo in albergo? — Siamo al capolinea? — Ritorniamo alla biglietteria? — Restiamo a Roma?

(See Grammar, E.2.)

7. PRONUNCIATION

LISTEN AND REPEAT

Periodo - binario - vorrei - partenza - obbligatorio - prima - un altro treno - corro il rischio

YOUR ATTENTION PLEASE, THE TRAIN IS ABOUT TO LEAVE...

During the fascist era, Mussolini was known as the "man who made the trains run on time". Since no one inherited Il Duce's singular gift, it must be admitted that in modern Italy the trains are not always on time.

It would be wrong to generalise, of course: most of the trains on the main international lines are punctual. There are still, though, particular cases, "bad" lines. The notorious Napoli Express, linking Paris and, as its name implies, Naples, is unquestionably one of the worst lines in Europe: in both directions, it regularly notches up an hour or so's delay. There is moreover a definite link between geographical location and the pctuality of the train service: in the north, the trains are generally on time, but the further south you go, the more the opposite is true. So, a bit of patience is called for, and, if there is a connection to catch, it is better to leave a good, wide margin of error.

It should be stressed that to make up for any delays, the Italian railways have much lower fares than many other European countries, plus many special rates: for return tickets, tourist tickets etc.

On the other hand, the local trains can be maddeningly slow, and the imposing titles given to the trains: "rapidi", "diritti", better still "direttissimi", "expressi" and others, are frequently deceptive. There is in some cases a

supplement to pay, notably on the InterCity trains, which are indeed fast and reliable. There is perhaps a moral here: speed and respect for the time-table constitute an exception to the rule, and must therefore be paid for.

Yet despite the delays, travelling by train in Italy can still be a most enjoyable experience. The first joy is, as always, the coffee. For maximum enjoyment, take an overnight train. In the morning, awakened by the jingle of the little bell and the aroma of real coffee, you will quickly forget the discomfort of the night.

And then, to a foreigner, the very names of some of the lines are thrillingly romantic. Think of the Palatino, the Galilée, both of which have their particular charm. But above all the others, the Orient Express is surely the most evocative. It has to be, with Venice as its last Italian destination. The legendary Venice, ultimate dream of all Europe. You board the train in the London drizzle, midnight in Paris, a sweet sleep as you thunder through the Alps, to be awakened crossing the Po valley, by this same little bell jingling in your ears as you eagerly await your first Italian coffee. Then, of course, it is off to the buffet-car for a cappucino and brioche. Then, from the comfort of the bar, or your own compartment, you pass through towns each with its own associations: Verona, with "Romeo and Juliet" and its festival of song held each year in its famous arena, Vincenza, the town closely associated with that great architect of the Renaissance, Palladio, Padua, the birthplace of Shakespeare's Shrew as well as of the illustrious Saint Anthony, patron saint of all things lost.

At Mestre, you leave the mainland, and your train plunges into the lagoon (metaphorically speaking, luckily for you), towards the islands, towards adventure, towards Venice... A brief, spectral, crossing, the train seemingly transformed into a great "traghetto"(1) and there you are at Venice station. In front of the station, the Gran Canale sweeps away, its "vaporetti"(2) awaiting you at the landing stage ready to bear you ever onward. It is here that you realise that the this is not a mere railway line: it is a pathway to dreams.

This might well remind you that the first railway to be built in Italy was no vulgar, speculative venture; created in the Kingdom of Naples, the Napoli-Portici line was only intended as a convenient way of whisking their gracious majesties to their country palace. Perhaps that is why train journeys in Italy have retained a sort of carefree gaiety.

(1) ferry, (2) lit. small steamers

2.5 TAKE-A-BREAK

LISTEN

TINTARELLA DI LUNA

(B. de Filippi - F. Migliacci)
Sung by Mina
With permission of Edizioni Musicali/Edizioni Curci

Abbronzate, tutte chiazze,
Pelli rosse un po' paonazze
Son le ragazze che prendono il sol
Ma ce n'è una
Che prende la luna

Ritornello

Tintarella di luna
Tintarella color latte
Tutta notte sopra al tetto
Sopra al tetto come i gatti
E se c'è la luna piena
Tu diventi candida
Tintarella di luna
Tintarella color latte
Che fa bianca la tua pelle
Ti fa bella tra le belle
E se c'è la luna piena
Tu diventi candida
Tin, tin, tin,
Raggi di luna
Tin, tin, tin,
baciano te
Al mondo nessuna è candida come te

Tintarella di luna
Tintarella color latte
Tutte notte sopra al tetto
Sopra al tetto come i gatti
E se c'è la luna piena
Tu diventi candida

Moon-tanned Girl

Brown and blotchy
Red-skinned and purply
Are the girls who get the sun
But there is one
Who "gets the moon"

Refrain

Moon-tanned girl
Milk-tanned girl
All night on the roof-top
On the roof like a cat
And if the moon is full
You become white
Moon-tanned girl
Milk-tanned girl
Makes your skin gleam white
And makes you beautiful among the beautiful
And if the moon is full
You become snow-white
Tin, tin, tin
Moon-beams
Tin, tin, tin
Kiss you
No-one in the world is as white as you

Moon-tanned girl
Milk-tanned girl
All night on the roof-top
On the roof like a cat
And if the moon is full
You become snow-white.

Figures of Speech

AVERE UN DIAVOLO PER CAPELLO
(lit. *to have a devil for every hair*)
To be in a towering rage

ESSERE ALL'OSCURO DI TUTTO

To be completely in the dark

SPUTARE IL ROSPO

(lit. *to spit out a toad*)
To spit it out!

AVERE UN CERVELLO DA GALLINA
(lit. *to have the brain of a chicken*)
To be bird-brained

2. WRITTEN PRACTICE

2.1

WRITE OUT IN FULL: *1.000, 2.000, 1.560, 730, 2.820, 14.000, 21.700, 100.000, 1.000.000 (numbers are written all as one word, except for millions)*

....

....

TRANSLATE : *Attenda un attimo, per cortesia! — Si accomodi alla cassa. — Ci vuole il libretto degli assegni.*
I'd like to know what the exchange rate for the Italian lira is. — I'd like to change £500 — Do you take international credit cards? — Thank you, sir.

2.2

COMPLETE WITH lo, la, li, le : *Mario Rossi ....conosco bene. — Il caffè,.......................................prendo ristretto. — La fontana di Trevi,....................... vedo domani. — I biglietti, ...compro dal tabaccaio. — Le informazioni,.........................domando a un pasante. — La città,....................visito oggi. — I soldi,...................cambio in banca.*
TRANSLATE: *Ritorni indietro. — Scenda al capolinea. — Domandi a un passante. — Aspetti un momento!*
Turn right! — Take bus number 35. — Go straight on. — Cross the square. — Go over the lights.

2.3

PUT EACH INFINITIVE INTO THE FUTURE, MAKING IT AGREE WITH THE SUBJECT: *Io (domandare) ....la direzione. — Lui (prendere) ....l'appuntamento. — Noi (dormire) ....all'hotel. — Tu (andare) ....a Roma. — Voi (avere) ....molto tempo. — Loro (essere) ....in ritardo. — Io non (potere) ....venire. — Voi (dovere) ....cenare con noi.*
TRANSLATE: *Pronto chi parla? — Posso lasciar detto qualcosa? — Gli dica di richiamarmi fra un'ora.*
I'd like to speak to Mr. Moreau. — Hello, Robert. it's me. — I'm sorry. The director is not here today.

2.4

REPLACE EACH PHRASE IN BRACKETS WITH AN INDIRECT PRONOUN: (mi, ti, gli, le, Le, ci, vi, gli):

Io ....telefono (a Roberto). — Lui ....parla (a me). — L'ingegner Rossi .... prenota le camere (a voi). — Il signor Marchi ....domanda un' informazione (all'impiegata). — Signora, ...posso offrire un caffè? (a Lei). — Signor Bauer, ...posso offrire un caffè? (a Lei). — Il cameriere ....porta il menù (a loro). Per cortesia, ...porta il menù (a noi).
TRANSLATE: *Di contorno ci sono gli spinaci. — A Roma ci sono molti ristoranti caratteristici. — Come pesce c'è la sogliola.*
First, there's spinach. — For the second course there's roast veal. — Today there are mushrooms. — To drink there's red wine and white wine.

2.5

PUT EACH INFINITIVE INTO THE CORRECT FORM OF THE PRESENT: *Il sig. Rossi (pagare) .... con un biglietto da 100.000 lire. — Tu (cercare) ....la stazione. — Noi (pagare) ....con un assegno. — Voi (cercare) ....una segretaria bilingue. — Io (pagare) ....il conto dell'albergo. — Loro (cercare) ....un albergo vicino alla stazione. — Che cosa (tu-cercare)................?*
TRANSLATE: *È possibile prenotare una cuccetta? — Quanto costa il vagone letto? — A che ora arriva a Roma?*
A return ticket for Rome. — From which platform is the train leaving? — I'd like a first-class ticket. — The connection is in Turin.

(Answers on page 36 of the booklet)

MORE VOCABULARY

DRINKS

acquavite(f) — brandy
alcoolici(m/pl) — alcoholic drinks
amaro(m) — bitters
analcoolici(m/pl) — nonalcoholic drinks
bevande(f) — drinks
cognac(m) — cognac
digestivo(m) — "digestif" (usu. spirits after a meal)
gazzosa(f) — fizzy drink
gin(m) — gin
grappa(f) — Italian brandy
liquore(m) — liqueur
moscato(m) — muscatel
spremuta di limone(f) — fresh lemon juice
spremuta d'arancia(f) — fresh orange juice
spumante(m) — sparkling wine
succo di frutta(m) — fruit juice
succo di pomodoro(m) — tomato juice
vodka(f) — vodka
whisky(m) — whisky

FOOD

cibo(m) — food
albicocca(f) — apricot
ananas(m) — pineapple
anguria(f) — watermelon
banana(f) — banana
ciliegia(f) — cherry
fico(m) — fig
fragola(f) — strawberry
lampone(m) — raspberry
mandarino(m) — mandarine
mela(f) — apple
melone(m) — melon
mirtillo(m) — bilberry
mora(f) — blackberry
pera(f) — pear
pesca(f) — peach
prugna(f) — plum
ribes(m) — redcurrant
uva(f/sing) — grapes
verdura(f/sing) — vegetables
aglio(m) — garlic
basilico(m) — basil
carciofo(m) — artichoke
carota(f) — carrot
cavolo(m) — cabbage
cece(m) — chick pea
cipolla(f) — onion
fagiolino(m) — green bean
fagiolo(m) — bean
finocchio(m) — fennel
lenticchia(f) — lentil
melanzana(f) — aubergine
menta(f) — mint
peperone(m) — pepper (veg., not spice)
porro(m) — leek
prezzemolo(m) — parsley
zucchino(m) — courgette
cacciagione(m) — game
capriolo(m) — venison
cinghiale(m) — wild boar
fagiano(m) — pheasant
lepre(f) — hare
pernice(f) — partridge
quaglia(f) — quail
animali da allevamento(m/pl) — farm animals
anatra(f) — duck
bue (m.plur.:buoi) — ox, oxen
capra(f) — goat
cavallo(m) — horse
coniglio(m) — rabbit
gallina(f) — hen
maiale(f) — pig
mucca(f) — cow
oca(f) — goose
pecora(f) — sheep
pollo(m) — chicken
toro(m) — bull
pesce(m) — fish
acciuga(f) — anchovy
anguilla(f) — eel
carpa(f) — carp
luccio(m) — pike
merluzzo(m) — cod
nasello(m) — hake
pescespada(m) — swordfish
salmone(m) — salmon
sardina(f) — sardine
tinca(f) — tench
tonno(m) — tuna
frutti di mare(m/pl) — seafood
aragosta(f) — lobster
gamberetto(m) — shrimp
gambero(m) — crayfish
granchio(m) — crab
muscolo(m) — mussel
ostrica(f) — oyster
scampo(m) — prawn
vongola(f) — clam
molluschi(m/pl) — mulluscs
calamaro(m) — squid
polpo(m) — octopus
seppia(f) — cuttlefish
tavola(f) — table
bicchiere(m) — drinking glass
coltello(m) — knife
cucchiaino(m) — small spoon
cucchiaio(m) — spoon
forchetta(f) — fork
piatto(m) — plate
posate(f/pl) — cutlery
tovaglia(f) — tablecloth
tovagliolo(m) — napkin

COLD MEATS

prosciutto(m) — ham (*crudo* — uncooked, *cotto* — cooked)
salame(m) — salami
coppa(f) — brawn
pancetta(f) — bacon
pancetta affumicata(f) — smoked bacon
lardo(m) — lard/bacon-fat

WEIGHTS

grammo(m) — gramme
etto(m) — a hundred grammes/ hectogramme
mezzo etto(m) — fifty grammes
due etti(m.pl) — two hundred grammes
un chilo(m) — a kilogramme
mezzo chilo(m) — half a kilo
due chili(m.pl) — two kilos
un litro(m) — a litre
mezzo litro(m) — half a litre
quintale(m) — 100 kilos
tonnellata(f) — tonne

EATING OUT

ristorante(m) — restaurant
trattoria(f) — restaurant (less formal)
tavola calda(f) — snack bar
pizzeria(f) — pizza house
self-service(m) — cafeteria
paninoteca(f) — sandwich bar
birreria(f) — beer house
bar(m) — bar
mensa aziendale(f) — company canteen
mensa studentesca(f) — students' canteen

2. TEST YOURSELF

1. REPLACE EACH PHRASE WITH THE APPROPRIATE OBJECT PRONOUN

(A Paolo)...*telefono alle 5*
(Il documento)...*restituisco domani.*
(I franchi) ....*cambierò in banca.*
(La prenotazione) ....*faccio subito.*
(Alla segretaria) ....*lascio il mio numero di telefono.*
(A noi) ....*piace il caffè ristretto.*
(Le tagliatelle) ....*mangio volentieri.*
(Ai corsisti) .... *do l'appuntamento alle 10.*

2. USE EITHER "TRA" OR "FA" ACCORDING TO THE MEANING

Sono arrivato a Milano due giorni ....
Il treno per Roma partirà ....*un'ora.*
Ho telefonato a Carlo 10 minuti ....
Gli ritelefonerò ....*10 minuti.*
Ho prenotato le camere una settimana ....
Andrò a Roma ....*un anno.*
Mi sono sposato 10 anni ....
Il signor Marchi arriverà ....*un attimo.*

3. GIVE THE OPPOSITE OF EACH WORD

sempre..
simpatico..
il primo...
grande..
caldo..
l'andata...

bello...
facile ....
buono...
lontano ....
forte...
davanti ....

4. WHAT WOULD YOU SAY IF YOU WANTED....

to change 100 marks in a bank ....
to know how long it took to get to the station ....
to know the time ....
the waiter to give you a menu ....
to know how much a ticket costs ....
to tell someone " he's not in" ....

5. ONLY ONE SENTENCE IN EACH SET IS CORECT. CAN YOU FIND IT?

A. *Per aprire un conto bisogna un documento* .... ☐
B. *Per aprire un conto ci vuole un documento* .... ☐
C. *Per aprire un conto ci vuole avere un documento*.................................... ☐

A. *Vado a comprare il biglietto* .... ☐
B. *Vado comprare il biglietto* .... ☐
C. *Vado da comprare il biglietto* .... ☐

A. *Le lasagne mi piace molto* .... ☐
B. *Le lasagne me piace molto* .... ☐
C. *Le lasagne mi piacciono molto*.. ☐

A. *Quanto costa le cuccette?* .... ☐
B. *Quanto costano le cuccette?* .... ☐
C. *Quante costano le cuccette?* .... ☐

6. MATCH EACH QUESTION TO ITS ANSWER

A. *Al capolinea.*
B. *Due giorni fa.*
C. *Vino, naturalmente!*
D. *Di niente!*
E. *Eccolo!*

1. *Da bere, che cosa preferisci?*
2. *Ha il passaporto?*
3. *A che fermata devo scendere?*
4. *Grazie mille!*
5. *Quando sei arrivato?*

(Check your answers on page 38 of the booklet)

IN BOCCA AL LUPO

Mrs. Piper-Sharp had scarcely turned on her heels before Lucia burst into his office, giggling.

"Ambrogio, avresti dovuto vederla quando è arrivata; sembrava fuori di testa. Cosa ti ha chiesto quella pazza.?"

"Mah…Non me lo sarei immaginato. Voleva l'opzione su In bocca al lupo. Sai, la solita cosettina sulla mafia."

Lucia burst out laughing.

"Ti tocca leggerlo, allora".

Ambrogio gave a muffled cry; he sank, moaning, onto his desk, and hid his head in his hands.

"Non, dai, Lucia! Per carità. Fammi un favore. Leggilo tu. Così mi fai un riassunto ."

Lucia pouted.

"Nemmeno per sogno," she retorted. "Lo sai che sono impegnatissima. Poi basta darci un' occhiata, no?"

"Portamelo, almeno, se sei ancora la mia assistente."

He had resumed the distant formality of a manager aware of his responsibilities, scrupulously observing the niceties of rank.

Lucia shot him a murderous glance.

"Così sei ancora più insopportabile."

"You're never satisfied".

"And you never know when to draw the line. And as for your summary, you can do it yourself. It's kind enough of me to fetch your book."

She left the room, slamming the door behind her. Ambrogio smiled. All things considered, these multilingual squabbles were not without their charm. If English was good for coolly sardonic epigrammatic concision, Italian was so much more physical and theatrical.

Lucia returned and flung onto his desk a book whose title - in blood-red letters - stood out fiercely against the yellow background.

"Enjoy yourself!" she said, sticking out her tongue.

Ambrogio chortled when he read the author's name: ANONIMO. It could hardly be anything else, when the "onorata società" was under discussion. He skimmed over the blurb on the cover: the anonymous author *was described as a famous journalist who had taken it on himself to put his pen - and his pen only - at the disposal of a certain Mr. S, (as in "sicario"), so that he could write his confessions - the confessions of a professional killer about to retire. He wanted to reveal what he knew of certain matters which had dominated the headlines, not only in Italy, but throughout the world. Mr. S maintained that he was in no way associated with the Mafia. All his life, he had worked freelance, refusing to be subject to any one organisation, since market forces worked so much in his favour, and enabled him to charge immense fees for his services. He prided himself on a speed and efficiency which left little scope for his competitors.*

Mr. S's punters were, from what he said, worthy politicians and financiers: a prestigious clientèle perfectly willing to pay hand over fist for the services of a man on whose professionalism they could confidently rely. Mr. S sang the praises of his clients - discreet, extremely correct, very obliging, polite without being obsequious. Throughout his life, he had only ever encountered one bad payer; if the latter had lived to regret it; no one was sorrier than Mr. S. His job was a thankless one, and the competition often disloyal. He could not allow malicious gossip to be spread about him, such as his letting people fleece him without turning a hair.

But in every respect, Mr. S was beyond reproach. Devoted to his job, which he considered a sacred vocation, he had not hesitated to sacrifice himself to complete asceticism in order to accomplish what he felt to be a laudable task. There was only one cause for regret in this glittering career: the secrecy which he was obliged to observe. As an educated man, he was fully aware of the historical importance of some of the affairs he was involved in; as a practical man, he kept quiet about them. He sometimes felt that he was the hand of justice, the sword of fate or of some supreme order, simply carrying out on earth what was ordained in the annals of time. Such an idea was clearly attractive, but he nonetheless suffered a sharp sense of frustration , which had induced him to take up his pen, or rather, someone else's, to leave to posterity certain edifying anecdotes.

Ambrogio could not help smiling as he read this. He recognised Magagnati's house-style: Blood! Shock! Horror! and, in the end, hot air. it was not surprising that the Piper-Sharp woman had fallen for it: it was consoling to think that she, like anyone else, could put her head into the jaws of the wolf.

That very evening, Ambrogio had scarcely had time to hang up his coat, put down his briefcase, open it and take out, amongst other papers, Anonimo's volume, when, once again, the phone rang. Of course, he could always pretend that he was not in yet, or that he had already gone out again - it was after all, after eight. Wasn't he allowed any kind of private life? But his sense of duty always won in the end.

He noticed, through the bay window of the sitting room, great flakes of snow drifting onto the balcony. It lay there like a rug, getting thicker every minute, muffling the sounds outside. The reflection of the street-lamps in it cast enough light into the room for him to see by. He lifted the receiver.

"Pronto, Ambrogio?..."

It was the same strange voice as the day before, just as abrupt. Ambrogio did not bother to reply, simply putting his hand over the mouthpiece.

"Lo so che sei tu. Dammi retta. Ti sei messo in bocca al lupo."

Ambrogio was startled.

"Un momento. Chi parla?"

He was shouting to no avail. It had gone dead. This time, there had been no crackling on the line: the caller had seemed terrifyingly close.

To be continued . . .

AVE MARIA

UNIT 3

3.1 DIALOGUE

LISTEN

ALLA RINASCENTE

The Clerici are a Neapolitan couple. They are shopping in a department store.

Al reparto "abbigliamento donna"

La commessa : *In che cosa posso servirLa?*

La sig.ra Clerici : *Vorrei vedere una gonna a pieghe.*

La commessa : *Ha già visto qualcosa che Le piace?*

La sig.ra Clerici : *Sì, quella gonna bianca che è in vetrina. È di seta?*

La commessa : *Sì, è di pura seta leggerissima. Vuole provarla?*

La sig.ra Clerici : *Sì, ma vorrei sapere prima quanto viene.*

La commessa : *Questo modello viene 180.000 lire, e esiste anche in nero e in azzurro.*

La sig.ra Clerici : *Va bene, allora la provo.*

La commessa : *Che taglia porta?*

La sig.ra Clerici : *La 44.*

La commessa : *Ecco, questa è la Sua taglia. Per provarla si accomodi in cabina.*

La sig.ra Clerici : *Come mi sta?*

Il marito : *Bene, ma mi sembra un po'lunga.*

La commessa : *La lunghezza non ha importanza: si può sempre accorciare.*

La sig.ra Clerici : *Sì, però forse è anche un po'larga. Quasi quasi provo la taglia più piccola.*

La commessa : *Ecco la 42.*

Il marito : *Ah, sì, questa ti sta molto meglio dell'altra!*

La sig.ra Clerici : *Sì, questa mi va bene. È proprio la mia misura.*

Il marito : *Allora che cosa fai, la prendi?*

La sig.ra Clerici : *Sì, ho deciso.*

La commessa : *Mentre Le faccio il pacchetto si accomodi pure alla cassa.*

Al reparto "abbigliamento uomo"

Il sig. Clerici : *Vorrei vedere una camicia sportiva, con le maniche lunghe.*

Il commesso : *Benissimo. Abbiamo parecchi modelli, tutti di puro cotone. Questa qui a quadretti, per esempio. Le piace?*

Il sig. Clerici : *Non è male. Ma non mi piacciono i bottoncini sul colletto.*

Il commesso : *Allora c'è questo modello senza bottoncini, che esiste anche a righe e a tinta unita.*

Il sig. Clerici : *Questa qui a righe quanto viene?*

Il commesso : *72.000 lire.*

Il sig. Clerici : *Però! è un po'cara...*

Il commesso : *Sì, ma la qualità è ottima. Ci sono modelli più economici ma non sono di puro cotone.*

Il sig. Clerici : *Mi ha convinto. La prendo.*

LISTEN AND REPEAT

You will find the translation on page 18 of the booklet.

1. The Bay of Naples
2. The centre of Naples

1

2

3.1 VOCABULARY

NOUNS

il reparto — department
l'abbigliamento (m) — clothing
la donna — woman
l'uomo (pl.: gli uomini) — man
il commesso, la commessa — assistant
la gonna — skirt
la vetrina — shop-window
la seta — silk
il modello — model/style
la taglia — size/fit
la cabina — fitting-room
la lunghezza — length
la misura — size
il pacchetto — package
la camicia — shirt
la manica — sleeve
il cotone — cotton
il bottone — button
il bottoncino — small button
il colletto — collar
la qualità — quality

---

il colore — colour
il grande magazzino — department store
il negozio — shop
l'acquisto(m) — purchase
la camicetta — blouse
il vestito — (woman's) dress/(man's) suit

ADJECTIVES

bianco — white
leggero/pesante — light/heavy ***(1)***
largo/stretto — loose/tight
sportivo/elegante — casual/smart
parecchi — several
caro/economico — expensive/cheap
azzurro — blue
blu — dark blue***(2)***
nero — black
rosso — red
verde — green
grigio — grey
giallo — yellow
rosa — pink ***(2)***
viola — purple ***(2)***
marrone — brown ***(2)***
classico/di moda — classic/fashionable

VERBS

servire — to serve
provare — to try on
esistere — to exist
sembrare — to seem
accorciare/allungare — to shorten/to lengthen
decidere — to decide
convincere — to convince

MISCELLANEOUS

a pieghe — pleated
a quadretti — checked
a righe — striped
a tinta unita — plain, self-coloured
di lana — wool
di cotone — cotton
di seta — silk
per esempio — for example
forse — perhaps
senza — without
meglio (di) — better (than) ***(3)***
più (di) — more (than) ***(4)***
questo — this
quello — that

HOW TO SAY IT

1. I'D LIKE TO SEE.....

Vorrei vedere la gonna bianca a pieghe che è in vetrina — I'd like to see the white pleated skirt that is in the window.
Vorrei vedere una camicia sportiva con le maniche lunghe — I'd like to see a casual shirt with long sleeves.

2. COMMENTING ON THE CLOTHES

Questa gonna mi sembra un po'lunga — This skirt seems a bit long to me.
Forse è anche un po'larga — Maybe it's a bit too wide, too.
È un modello di ottima qualità — It's a top quality item.
È propio la mia misura — It's exactly my size.
Mi va bene — It fits me
Mi sta bene — It suits me
Non mi sta bene — It doesn't look good on me.

3. COMPARING

Questa gonna è più bella di quella — This skirt is more attractive than that one.
Questa camicia è meno cara dell'altra — This shirt is less expensive than the other one.
Questa ti sta molto meglio dell'altra — This looks much better on you than the other one.

4. PRICE, QUALITY AND SIZES

Quanto viene quella gonna? — How much does that skirt cost?
Questo modello viene a 60.000 lire — This model costs 60.000 lire.
Costa 42.000 lire — It costs 42,000 lire.
La qualità è ottima — It's top quality.
Porto il 44 — I wear size 44. ***(5)***
È una 42 — It's a size 42.

5. SAYING WHAT'S BEEN DECIDED

Ho deciso, la prendo — I've decided. I'll take it.
Mi ha convinto — You've convinced me.
Va bene, allora la provo — Alright, then, I'll try it on.

REMARKS REMARKS REMARKS REMARKS

*(1) This means "heavy", but can also mean "warm" for clothing.— **(2)** Invariable.— **(3)** See Grammar, H.1. — **(4)** See Grammar, H.1. — **(5)** In Italy, the standard European sizes are used.*

3.1 ORAL PRACTICE

1. "QUEL/QUELLA"

LISTEN

La gonna • Di che colore è quella gonna?
Il vestito • Di che colore è quel vestito?

Continue asking questions, using "quel" or "quella".

La gonna — Il vestito — La camicetta — Il modello — La cravatta — La valigia — La camicia — Il vestito — La gonna.

(See Grammar, D.2.)

2. "QUESTO.QUESTA"

LISTEN

Gonna/corta • Questa gonna mi sembra un po' corta.
Vestito/stretto • Questo vestito mi sembra un po' stretto.

Form sentences using "questo" or "questa".

Gonna/corta — Vestito/stretto — Camicetta/larga — Modello/caro — Colletto/largo — Lana/pesante — Cotone/leggero — Taglia/grande.

(See Grammar, D.2)

3. COMPARING

LISTEN

Gonna/bella • Questa gonna è più bella di quella.
Vestito/caro • Questo vestito è più caro di quello.
Camicie/leggere • Queste camicie sono più leggere di quelle.
Modelli/economici • Questi modelli sono più economici di quelli.

Continue making comparisons, as in the model.

Gonna/bella — Vestito/caro — Camicie/leggere — Modelli/economici — Camicetta/stretta — Modello/elegante — Vestiti/classici — Cravatta/sportiva — Ristorante/caro.

(See Grammar, H.1.)

4. THE PAST TENSE

LISTEN

Oggi compro una gonna
• Ieri ho comprato una gonna
Oggi bevo un caffè
• Ieri ho bevuto un caffè
Oggi finisco alle 8 • Ieri ho finito alle 8

Continue as in the model

Oggi, compro una gonna — Oggi bevo un caffè — Oggi finisco alle otto — Oggi telefono a Claudio — Oggi firmo il contratto — Oggi ripeto l'esercizio — Oggi non dormo — Oggi spedisco la lettera.

(See Grammar, L.7.)

5. THE PAST TENSE AGAIN...

VERBS OF MOTION

LISTEN

Sei già andato alla stazione?
• No, non ci sono ancora andato.

Continue answering in the negative, using the pronoun "ci".

Sei già andato alla stazione? — Sei già ritornato a Roma? — Sei già salito al quinto piano? — Sei già stato a Napoli? — Sei già andato in ufficio? — Sei già stato in quel ristorante?

(See Grammar, L.7.)

6. ...AND AGAIN

A FEW IRREGULAR VERBS

LISTEN

Prendere la macchina (io).
• Ho preso la macchina
Decidere subito (tu) • Hai deciso subito

Change to the past tense, as in the model.

Prendere la macchina (io) — Decidere subito (tu) — Chiudere la porta (noi) — Vedere la gonna in vetrina (la sig.ra Clerici) — Scrivere la lettera (voi) — Leggere la posta (io) — Fare una telefonata (tu).

(See Grammar, L.7.)

HOW ABOUT A LITTLE DISCOUNT...

You fancy a spot of shopping? Now's your chance: Italy is a consumer's paradise. Not least because everything stylish, creative, fashionable is to be found there, all represented by great names known throughout the world: Armani, Valentino, Capucci, Versace, Missoni, for fashion; Pomellato and Bulgari for jewellery; Ferragamo and Fratelli Rossetti for shoes; Trussardi for leatherware; many of them , Armani, Gucci, Cerruti, Trussardi, Versace, Capucci, for perfume as well.

Fashion is not all. Italy is an equally important centre for design, for elegance in every domain. Alessi springs to mind, his prestigious tableware meriting a place in New York's Museum of Modern Art . Or Barilla, the pasta not to be missed, the pasta to eat with reverence.

There is no point listing all the famous brand-names which can be found in capital cities throughout the world. Of course, it does not come cheap, everything being "pura seta", "di puro cotone", "di vero cuoio", etc. Real jewellery has to be gold. The whole notion of fake jewellery is indecent or, presumably, French, since "bijouterie" is the name given to shops selling imitation jewellery. "Proper" jewellery shops are called "gioiellerie". As for Italian shoes, they need no introduction. The Italians, of course, would never dream of wearing anything but

leather, but that does not prevent them making large numbers of cheap, synthetic shoes for export, especially to the third world.

It is possible to buy exquisite things without paying the earth, by shopping at Rinascente, Italy's biggest chain-store. Based in Milan, it is something between Harrods and C & A. The nearest thing Italy has to Woolworths, (also Milan-based), is La Strada, which sells everything, including food. You can often find examples of very attractive design here too, within everyone's price-range. Upim is a similar chain-store.

But it is possible to shop for even less. The best thing is to visit those markets which specialise almost entirely in clothing. That is where you have to go to snap up the bargains. Of course, the atmosphere is very different from that of the luxurious shops named above. Here, you thread your way through the crowd, elbowing the others aside, to reach the various "branchetti" (stalls) and look at, and feel, the wares. If something takes your fancy, do not hesitate to ask for "un po'di sconto" (a little discount). It is perfectly normal in Italy, not only in the markets but even in shops, especially during the sales - this goes for clothes, but also for china, furniture, records, books, electical goods, etc. In fact, it is an old business practice that goes back to the days before prices were marked, as well as being a game and a social convention. It is a way of humanising a business transaction, of making it more personal.

But observe the system well: it is not just to establish a warmer relationship, it is really that each customer is demanding special, individual treatment. Like the use of "Lei", this practice reveals something aristocratic, anti-democratic, which can often be seen in Italians (like their refusal to queue). It goes with the feeling of having more rights than the next man. Getting a "sconto" gives the satisfaction of paying less, but added to this purely financial satisfaction is the sense of having received more favourable treatment than the others, of having been "puì forbo" (sharper), in short of having been treated as one deserves, namely better.

But away with these physchoanalytical musings. Before the shops all close, have a think: is there anything you need? Food shops are closed on Wednesday afternoon and all day Sunday, and nothing is open after eight in the evening (later in the South). Just about all you can find is milk in a milk-bar or cigarettes sold by a street vendor without a licence.

3.1 TAKE-A-BREAK

No. 1

LISTEN

Indicate which of the two articles of clothing in each drawing is the one chosen by the cutomer.

1	A	B

2	A	B

PROVERBIO

LISTEN

Chi più spende, meno spende.
(lit. He who spends more, spends less)

For want of a nail, the horse was lost.

3	A	B

No. 2

What's missing in the second drawing? List the ten items. (There is vocabulary to help you on page 145.)

1

2

(Answers on page 19 of the booklet)

3.2 DIALOGUE

LISTEN

DAL DOTTORE

Mr. Clerici does not feel very well, so he has made an appointment to see the doctor.

La segretaria : *Buongiorno, signor Clerici. Ha un appuntamento?*

Sig. Clerici : *Sì, alle 6. Sono un po' in anticipo…*

La segretaria : *Il dottore è ancora in visita. Si accomodi nella sala d'attesa.*

Sig. Clerici : *Va bene, grazie.*

La segretaria : *Sul tavolino ci sono delle riviste, e c'è anche il giornale di oggi, se Le interessa.*

Sig. Clerici : *Molto gentile.*

....

La segretaria : *Signor Clerici, prego! tocca a Lei: si accomodi in studio.*

Il dottore : *Buongiorno, Signor Clerici, allora, che cosa c'è che non va?*

Sig. Clerici : *Buongiorno, dottore. Guardi, da qualche giorno non sto molto bene. Ho mal di gola e un po' di tosse e quando mi sveglio ho sempre mal di testa.*

Il dottore : *Ha la febbre?*

Sig. Clerici : *Credo di no.*

Il dottore : *Potrebbe essere un inizio di influenza. Ha già preso qualche medicina?*

Sig. Clerici : *Solo un po' di aspirina, ma non mi ha fatto niente.*

Il dottore : *Vediamo un po' quanto ha di pressione.*

Sig. Clerici : *Forse ho la pressione bassa. Mi sento piuttosto debole in questo periodo.*

Il dottore : *No, la pressione è normale. La sua debolezza è dovuta probabilmente a un po' di fatica. Lavora molto?*

Sig. Clerici : *Beh sì, ultimamente ho avuto moltissimi impegni di lavoro e ho dormito poco.*

Il dottore : *Senta, Le prescrivo queste compresse: ne prenda due al giorno dopo i pasti principali. E la sera prenda un cucchiaio di questo sciroppo.*

Sig. Clerici : *Per quanto tempo devo seguire la cura?*

Il dottore : *Secondo me una settimana dovrebbe bastare. Ma ci vuole anche un po' di riposo! Ritorni martedì prossimo se vede che non va meglio.*

Sig. Clerici : *Grazie mille, dottore.... ArrivederLa.*

La segretaria : *Signor Clerici! Aspetti! Ha dimenticato di prendere la ricetta!*

Sig. Clerici : *Ah, già! Che distratto! …*

LISTEN AND REPEAT

You will find the translation on page 19 of the booklet.

1. Spacca Napoli (Old Naples) 2. The sea-front 3. Selling shell-fish 4. Fire-works and lottery tickets for sale

IL MATTINO
CORRIERE DI NAPOLI

2

'a Maraviglia
72
'o Capitone
32
the big-Headed eel
75
43
in edicola
e in libreria
Tombola Napoletana
a popular tradition
Buon divertimento
'o Capitone
32
the big-Headed eel
e Zzizze
28
Le tette
the Tits

4

3.2 VOCABULARY

NOUNS

Il dottore — doctor
la visita — visit/doctor's rounds
la sala d'attesa — waiting room
la rivista — magazine
il giornale — newspaper
lo studio — consulting-room/chambers etc. ***(1)***
la gola — throat
la tosse — cough
la testa — head
la febbre — fever/temperature
l'influenza(f) — flu
la medicina — medicine
l'aspirina(f) — aspirin
la pressione — blood pressure
la debolezza — weakness
la fatica — fatigue
l'impegno(m) — obligation/thing to do
la compressa — tablet
il pasto — meal
il cucchiaio — spoon
lo sciroppo — syrup
la cura — treatment/care
la ricetta — prescription ***(2)***

---

il medico — doctor
la farmacia — pharmacy
il/la farmacista — pharmacist
il raffreddore — a cold/chill
l'antibiotico — antibiotic
la supposta — suppository

VERBS

interessare — to interest
stare bene/male = sentirsi bene/male — to feel well/ill
aver mal di gola — to have a sore throat
svegliarsi — to wake up
aver mal di testa — to have a headache
dormire — to sleep
prescrivere — to prescribe
seguire — to follow
bastare — to be enough
dimenticare — to forget

---

ammalarsi — to fall ill
guarire — to get better
curare — to look after/to cure

ADJECTIVES

basso — low
debole — weak
normale — normal
distratto — distracted/ absent-minded

MISCELLANEOUS

tocca a Lei — it's your turn
ultimamente — lately
secondo me — according to me
due volte al giorno — twice a day
dopo i pasti — after meals
prima dei pasti — before meals
credo di no — I believe not
credo di si — I believe so
ah già! — ah, yes!

HOW TO SAY IT

1. WHOSE TURN IS IT?

Tocca a Lei — It's your turn!
Tocca a me! — It's my turn!
Tocca a Claudio! — It's Claudio's turn!

2. SAYING HOW YOU FEEL

Non me sento molto bene — I don't feel well.
Mi sento un po' debole — I feel a bit weak.
Sto male — I feel ill
Ho il raffreddore — I have a cold
Ho l'influenza — I have 'flu
Ho mal di testa — I have a headache
Ho mal di schiena — I have backache
Ho mal di denti — I have toothache
Ho mal di gola — I have a sore throat
Ho mal di stomaco — I have stomach ache.
Sto bene — I feel well
Sono in piena forma — I'm in top shape

3. EXPRESSING AN OPINION

Secondo me — According to me
Per me — For me
A mio avviso (a mio parere) — In my opinion
Credi di sì— I believe so
Credi di no — I believe not
Potrebbe essere l'influenza — It could be the flu

4. HOW MANY TIMES

Tre volte al giorno — three times a day
Una volta alla settimana — once a week
Due volte al mese — twice a month
Una volta all'anno — once a year

5. THE EFFECTS OF TREATMENT

Non mi ha fatto niente — It had no effect on me.
Mi ha fatto bene — It made me feel better
Mi ha fatto male — It harmed me/it made me ill

REMARKS REMARKS REMARKS REMARKS

***(1)** This is the consulting-room for doctors, lawyers, etc., otherwise, "ufficio" is the usual word for "office". — **(2)** This is also the word for "recipe". — **(3)** "Male" drops the final -e in expressions such as "ho mal di testa".*

3.2 ORAL PRACTICE

1. "POTERE/DOVERE/VOLERE"

FOLLOWED BY AN INFINITIVE: THE POSITION OF OBJECT PRONOUNS

(● ●) LISTEN

Per la tosse, posso darLe questo sciroppo.
● *Per la tosse, Le posso dare questo sciroppo.*
Quando lo devo prendere?
● *Quando devo prenderlo?*

Change the following by moving the pronoun, as in the model.
Per la tosse, posso darLe questo sciroppo — Quando lo devo prendere? — Non voglio farlo — Non lo posso dire — Non la voglio vedere — Devo prenderle 3 volte al giorno — Li posso comprare domani — Le supposte, non le voglio prendere — La camera, la devo prenotare. (See Grammar, E.4)

2. THE PRONOUN "NE"

(● ●) LISTEN

Hai molti amici? ● *Sì, ne ho molti*
Hai molte cravatte? ● *Sì, ne ho molte.*

Answer the following, using* "ne" *in the same way.
Hai molti amici? — Hai molte cravatte? — Hai molti vestiti? — Hai molte valigie? — Fumi molte sigarette? — Guardi molti film? — Compri molte riviste? — Prendi molte medicine? — Scrivi molte lettere? (See Grammar, E.2.)

3. THE PARTITIVE del, dello, dell', dela, dei, degli, delle

(● ●) LISTEN

Il vino rosso ● *Vorrei del vino rosso.*
Lo sciroppo per la tosse ● *Vorrei dello sciroppo per la tosse*

Say what you would like, using partitives.
Il vino rosso — Lo sciroppo per la tosse — Le compresse per il raffreddore — Gli antibiotici — Le riviste francesi — I francobolli da 600 lire — Le buste — La carta da lettere — Le cartoline — I giornali.
(See Grammar, B.2.)

4. THE PREPOSITION "DA" (PLACE)

(● ●) LISTEN

Il dottore
● *Vado dal dottore*
L'avvocato
● *Vado dall'avvocato.*

Say where you are going, using the preposition* "da" *and the article when necessary.
Il dottore — L'avvocato — Roberto — Il medico — La segretaria — L'architetto — I miei amici — Le mie amiche — La sig.ra Rossi — Il direttore — Gli amici di Mario.
(See Grammar, F.)

5. AND "DA" (TIME)

(● ●) LISTEN

Lavorare qui/2 anni
● *Lavoro qui da due anni*
Abitare a Roma/il 1° agosto
● *Abito a Roma dal 1° agosto*

Form sentences by using* "da" *as in the model.
Lavorare qui/2 anni — Abitare a Roma/il 1° agosto — Parlare l'italiano/qualche mese — Vivere in Francia/molti anni — Conoscere la sig.ra Clerici/poco tempo — Essere sposato/12 anni — Non stare bene/qualche giorno.
(See Grammar, F.)

6. AGREEMENT WITH THE OBJECT PRONOUN

IN THE PAST TENSE

(● ●) LISTEN

Hai preso la medicina?
● *Sì, l'ho presa?*

Answer the following, making sure that the past participle agrees with the object.
Hai preso la medicina? — Hai letto il libro — Hai seguito la cura? — Hai cambiato i dollari? — Hai scritto le cartoline? — Hai preso l'appuntamento? — Hai fatto gli esercizi? — Hai ripetuto le frasi?
(See Grammar, E.3.)

THE STATE OF THE MEDIA

You enjoy reading? You will not be disappointed in Italy. The "edicole" (kiosks) offer a myriad of newspapers and magazines, among them journals such as "L'Espresso", "Il Mondo", "L'Europeo", in the style of America's Time Magazine and Newsweek. Unlike Britain, but like Germany and the United States, Italy has no national newspapers; all its press is regional, although some papers are sold throughout the country.

But rest assured that with a few local exceptions, and one or two pages dedicated to local culture, the papers are all in standard Italian and not dialect: "La Stampa" from Turin is not in Piedmontese, the "Corriere della Sera" is not in Milanese any more than the "Giorno" or the "Repubblica" are in Roman.

The multi-faceted Italian press covers an extraordinarily wide spectrum; the dailies named above are not the only ones: in the whole of Italy there are about 80. Cities and even small towns have their own daily papers. Political parties are not to be left out ("Il Popolo" for Christian Democrats, "L'Unità" for Communists, "Avanti" for Socialists). There is even the "Secolo" from Genoa, which must be the only major European daily paper to pride itself on being a paper for the 19th century! Sporting journals, fashion

magazines, fine art reviews, women's magazines, special interest publications (philately, pornography, cross-words - something for everyone) comics, scientific journals: a huge choice. Italy has even created a luxury magazine, F.M.R., aimed at an elite readership, which now boasts American and French editions.

Despite this, as publishers often complain, Italians do not read much, even less than the French and British. That explains why so few copies are sold, the struggle many journals have in maintaining their readership, and the lengths they go to to lure the public. Rare are the magazines which do not try to entice the potential reader by one of the two following methods: either titillating cover-photos, with at least "donnine nude" (naked girls), or gifts: very often, you buy your favourite magazine at a stand and find it comes in a plastic wrapper enclosing something extra: a tourists' guide, a road map, a pocket diary, even a paperback novel. They stop at nothing to encourage Italians to read.

But television (la "Tivù") is the great problem. In Italy, according to where you live and the size of your set, you can receive up to 18 or 20 channels. Independent television reigns supreme. There is a state company, the RAI, which is alive and kicking, showing quality programmes and co-producing excellent films. But the independent companies soon discovered the secret of success: buy in the cheaper telefilms, show them throughout the day, with a liberal sprinkling of commercials.

This can be taken to horrific extremes. Films, serials, broadcasts continually interrupted by adverts (a normal film, of 1hr. 40 mins, lasts at least an hour longer), usually without any form of transition between the film and the break. The same advert occurs several times during the film and by the end, the viewer will certainly recall the advert better than the plot of the unfortunate film.

As a direct consequence, for many Italians the day is broken up, you could say shattered, by television. They eat to it, watch it after eating, go to sleep in front of it. Watching what? Everything. Never mind what, in the end it is a matter of "guardare un po'di Tivù" (watching a bit of telly). A serious disease has struck down part of the Italian population: tele-addiction.

3.2 TAKE-A-BREAK

No. 1

LISTEN

Listen to the patients tell the doctor what is wrong with them. Then under each medicine write down the name of the ailment it treats.

1. .... **2.** ....

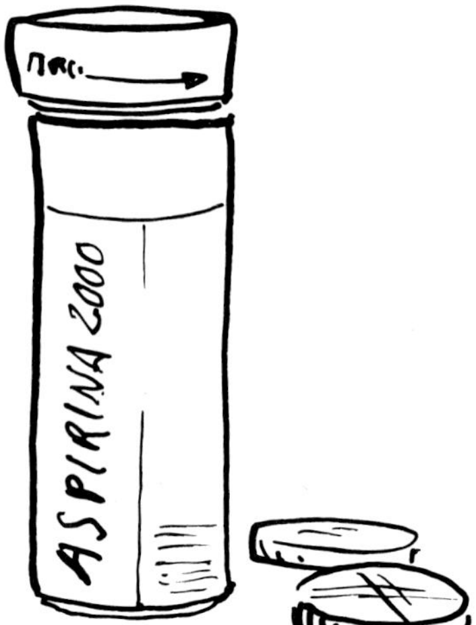

3. .... **4.** .... **5.** ....

No. 2

The human body. Match each part of the body to its name by putting its number in the box.

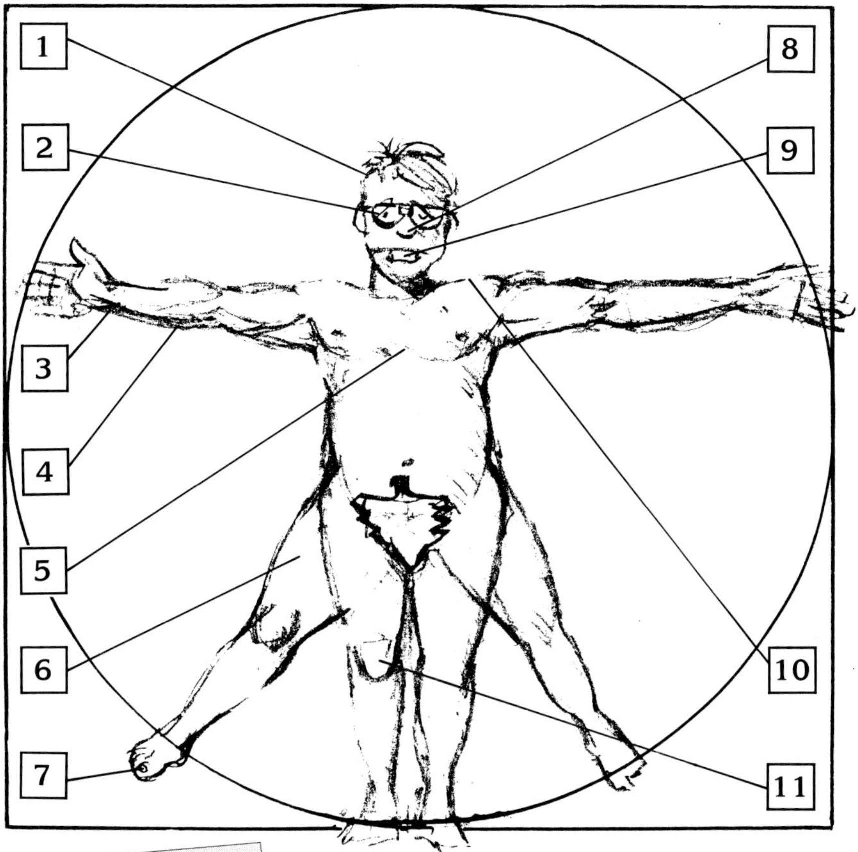

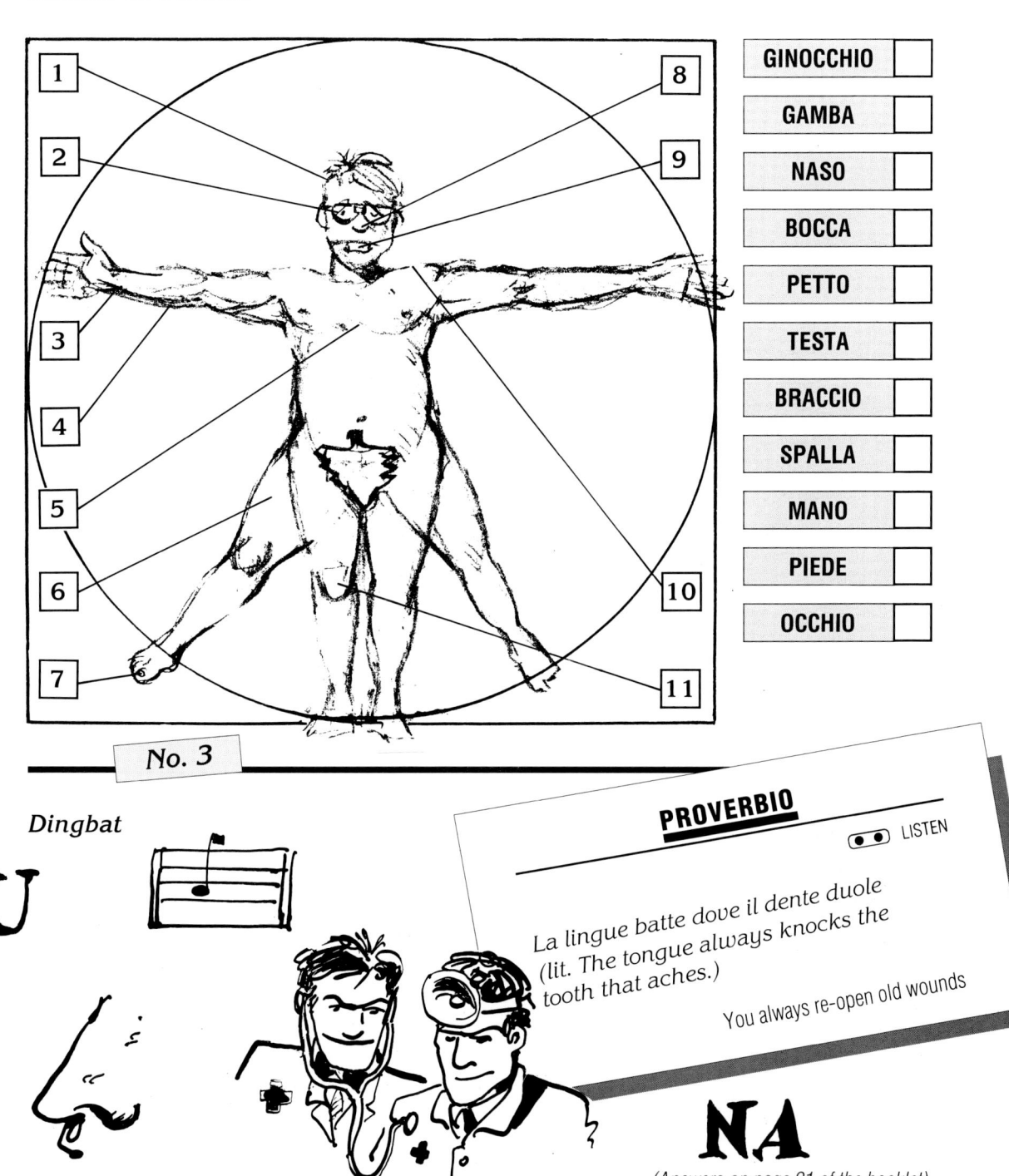

GINOCCHIO	
GAMBA	
NASO	
BOCCA	
PETTO	
TESTA	
BRACCIO	
SPALLA	
MANO	
PIEDE	
OCCHIO	

No. 3

Dingbat

NA

PROVERBIO

LISTEN

La lingue batte dove il dente duole
(lit. The tongue always knocks the tooth that aches.)

You always re-open old wounds

(Answers on page 21 of the booklet)

3.3 DIALOGUE

LISTEN

SPETTACOLI

The Clerici are making plans for the evening.

Lui : *Che ne dici di uscire stasera?*

Lei : *Sì, usciamo! Non ho proprio voglia di stare a casa. Che cosa mi proponi di bello?*

Lui : *Andiamo a ballare!*

Lei : *Ma sei matto! Proprio tu che non hai mai messo piede in una discoteca!*

Lui : *Sto scherzando, naturalmente! Se ti va, potremmo andare al cinema o a un concerto...*

Lei : *No, a un concerto non mi va. L'ultima volta, ti ricordi, mi sono annoiata da morire! Piuttosto potremmo guardare che cosa c'è a teatro.*

Lui : *Ho già guardato sul giornale e non c'è praticamente niente. Quasi tutti i teatri sono chiusi per ferie.*

Lei : *E al cinema che cosa danno?*

Lui : *Ma, l'unico film che vale la pena e che non abbiamo ancora visto è "Il Nome della rosa".*

Lei : *Ah, il film tratto dal romanzo di Umberto Eco! Sarei curiosa di vederlo perchè ho letto il libro e mi è piaciuto molto. Chi è il regista?*

Lui : *È un francese, Jean-Jacques Annaud. Il protagonista è Sean Connery, quello che è diventato famoso con la serie di James Bond.*

Lei : *Ah, già, è un bravissimo attore...*

Lui : *Guarda però che il film è un po' lungo.*

Lei : *Andiamo allo spettacolo delle otto allora. Non vorrei andare a letto troppo tardi. In quale cinema lo danno?*

Lui : *Al Cannon Odeon. Non è troppo lontano. Se ci sbrighiamo facciamo in tempo: il film comincia alle 20.10.*

Lei : *Va bene. Mi preparo in due minuti e ceneremo dopo il film.*

Lui : *Non più di due minuti, mi raccomando... Altrimenti rischiamo di arrivare a film già cominciato. Lo sai che odio perdere le prime scene!*

Lei : *Sarò pronta in un attimo!*

LISTEN AND REPEAT

You will find the translation on page 21 of the booklet.

Naples:
1. A statue
2. A traditional home
3. Neighbourliness

1

2

3

3.3 VOCABULARY

NOUNS

lo spettacolo — show
la discoteca — discotheque
il cinema — the pictures/cinema ***(1)***
il concerto — concert
il teatro — theatre
le ferie (f.pl) — holidays ***(2)***
il film — film ***(1)***
il romanzo — novel
il libro — book
il regista — film director
il protagonista — main actor
la serie — series ***(3)***
l'attore/l'attrice — actor/actress
la scena — scene

---

il programma — programme
la serata — evening (as a length of time)
la commedia — comedy
la tragedia — tragedy
il dramma — drama
lo scrittore/la scrittrice — writer

ADJECTIVES

curioso — curious
famoso — famous, well-known
bravo — talented/good

---

violento — violent
psicologico — psychological
drammatico — dramatic
brillante — brilliant

VERBS

uscire — to go out
proporre — to propose/ suggest ***(4)***
ballare — to dance
scherzare — to joke
ricordarsi — to remember
annoiarsi — to be bored
divertirsi — to enjoy oneself
diventare — to become
andare a letto — to go to bed
sbrigarsi — to hurry
fare in tempo — to make it/get there in time
prepararsi — to get ready
mi raccomando — I mean it
rischiare — to risk
odiare — to hate
amare — to love
essere pronto — to be ready

MISCELLANEOUS

stare a casa — to stay at home ***(5)***
mettere piede — to set foot
avere voglia — to feel like/want
vale la pena — it's worth (while)
essere matto — to be crazy
da morire — to death (lit. to die)
altrimenti — otherwise
tardi/presto — late/early
andare a teatro — to go to the theatre
" *al cinema* — to the cinema
" *al concerto* — to a concert
" *in campagna* — to the country
" *in montagna* — to the mountains
" *al mare* — to the sea

HOW TO SAY IT

1. GOING OUT

Che ne dici di uscire? — What about going out?
Andiamo a ballare? — Shall we go dancing?
Ti va di andare al cinema? — Do you feel like going to the cinema?
Potremmo andare a teatro! — We could go to the theatre!
Hai voglia di andare a un concerto? — Do you feel like going to a concert?
Usciamo insieme stasera? — Shall we go out together this evening?

2. FINDING OUT WHAT'S ON

Che cosa c'è a teatro? — What's on at the theatre?
Che cosa danno al cinema? — What are they showing at the cinema?
In quale cinema danno questo film? — Which cinema are they showing that film?
Che film danno alla televisione? — What films are they showing on TV?
Quanto dura lo spettacolo? — How long does the show last?
A che ora comincia (finisce) il film? — What time does the film start (end)?

3. TALKING ABOUT ENTERTAINMENT

Lo spettacolo mi è piaciuto molto — I liked the show a lot.
Il protagonista è un bravissimo attore — The main charactor is a very good actor.
Il regista è un francese — The director is a Frenchman.
Lo spettacolo è stato un po' lungo — The show lasted a bit too long.
È stato molto interessante — It was very interesting.
È stato molto noioso — It was very boring.
Non mi è piaciuto affatto — I didn't like it at all.
È una discoteca di moda — It's a fashionable disco.

4. HURRYING UP

Presto! — Hurry up! ***(6)***
Sbrigati! — Hurry up! Be quick!
Se ci sbrighiamo facciamo in tempo — If we hurry, we'll make it in time. ***(7)***
Facciamo in fretta! — Let's hurry up.

REMARKS REMARKS REMARKS REMARKS

(1) *Invariable (See Grammar C.3.)* — ***(2)*** *"Ferie" (always plural) is used for "paid leave".* — ***(3)*** *Invariable.* — ***(4)*** *See Grammar L.8.* — ***(5)*** *"Casa" means both "house" and "home".* — ***(6)*** *Literally, this means "Soon!"* — ***(7)*** *Both verbs, (unlike English), are in the present tense.*

3.3 ORAL PRACTICE

1. REFLEXIVE VERBS IN THE PAST

LISTEN

Lei si annoia al concert

• *Lei si è annoiata al concerto*

Continue putting the sentences in the past.

Lei si annoia al concerto — Io mi diverto molto — I signori Clerici si preparano in due minuti — Tu ti preoccupi per niente — Laura si sente male — Noi ci vediamo spesso — Maria e Francesca si sbagliano — Il ragazzo si scusa.

(See Grammar, L.7.)

2. THE VERB "PIACERE" IN THE PAST

LISTEN

Il film

• *Il film mi è piaciuto*

La commedia

• *La commedia mi è piaciuta*

Say that you liked the following.

Il film — La commedia — Lo spettacolo — La tragedia — Il romanzo — La serata — Il libro — La carne — Il concerto — La scena — La discoteca — Il programma.

(See Grammar, L.7.)

3. "TO BE" IN THE PAST

LISTEN

Il film - lungo.

• *Il film è stato lungo*

La commedia - interessante

• *La commedia è stata interessante*

Form sentences as in the model.

Il film/lungo — La commedia/interessante — Il concerto/noioso — La scena/violenta — L'attore/bravissimo — La serata/divertente — Il viaggio/bello — Il lavoro/pesante — Lo spettacolo/simpatico.

(See Grammar, L.7.)

4. THE INTERROGATIVE FORM "CHI"

LISTEN

Il regista

• *Chi è il regista?*

Gli attori

• *Chi sono gli attori?*

Continue asking questions in this way.

Il regista — Gli attori — Il protagonista — L'autore — Le attrici — L'attore — Il direttore — I protagonisti — Il presidente — I responsabili.

(See Grammar, G.2.)

5. RELATIVE PRONOUN "CHE"

LISTEN

Il regista ha fatto il film - Il regista è molto bravo

• *Il regista che ha fatto il film è molto bravo*

Ho visto lo spettacolo - Lo spettacolo è lungo

• *Lo spettacolo che ho visto è lungo*

Combine the two sentences into one by using "che".

Il regista ha fatto il film/Il regista è molto bravo — Ho visto lo spettacolo/Lo spettacolo è lungo — Il ragazzo compra il giornale/Il ragazzo è americano — Ho letto il libro/Il libro è di Umberto Eco — La signora parla con il direttore/La signora è la moglie del sig. Rossi — Ho comprato una gonna/La gonna è bianca.

(See Grammar, G.1.)

6. THE VERB "USCIRE"

LISTEN

Io

• *Esco dall'ufficio alle 5*

Noi

• *Usciamo dall'ufficio alle 5*

Conjugate* "uscire" *as in the model.

Io — Noi — Il direttore — Tu — La segretaria — Voi — Noi — I signori Clerici — Io — Claudio — Francesco e Marco — Il responsabile — Voi.

(See Grammar, L.6.)

THE SHOW GOES ON!

Everybody knows that Italy gave birth to opera. This is no accident. Quite apart from the obvious musicality of the language, bear in mind two other vital common factors: Italians like to fill any given space with sound, (they seem almost afraid of silence), and they have a highly developed sense of theatre.

There is no need to dwell much on the subject of noise. Be it in full-blown opera or everyday conversation, Italians manifest impressive vocal chords. Italian, with its strongly marked rhythms and precise phrasing, is infinitely more resonant than English. The streets, bars, trains ... any public place is always bursting with noise, and this is without taking the traffic into account, with its incessant hooting ever more in evidence the further south you go.

But bear in mind too, most people's attitude to noise in Italy: radios and televisions blaring away, ostentatious public displays of friendship, rowdy enthusiasm of fans (especially at football matches): these are all well documented. As always, it is dangerous to generalise: the Romans, Neapolitans, Venetians or Sicilians are not all noisy in the same way.

Even more flagrant is the Italians' sense of theatre. Once outside the immediate family circle, Italians are constantly showing off. This is never more true than in matters of dress. They have retained this peculiarly Mediterranean taste for display, gorgeously arrayed whenever the opportunity arises. Their extreme love of finery has, in fact, given quite a boost to the Italian ecomony at the moment, since economic growth has allowed them to indulge this fancy in a most creative way. While the "Mediterranean look" is often rather sleazy, Italian style is the benchmark for elegance throughout Europe and the States. Look at the success of Italian couture throughout the world, (including Paris), and at the notices it gets in the specialist press.

Refinement may be the keynote of Italian fashion, but that does not mean that it satisfies the native population's love of drama and display. Italians are famous for taking everything to extremes: wild verbal exaggeration; fanciful embroidering of the truth (so very different from British reticence); monstrous obscenities flung about so casually that they become commonplace banalities. Indeed, fear of passing unnoticed occasionally may even induce them to overstep the strict bounds of good taste.

Other things are also in marked contrast to their tasteful dress, like the heavy make-up, (influenced by the "average bad taste" shown on the omnipresent television), the overpowering perfumes, and the excessive jewellery, with some women decked up like Christmas trees.

Their love of display naturally finds expression in the family home. Apart from being comfortable, practical, and attractive, the "casa", be it a house or a flat, has a specific role to play: it must set the scene. This "home as film-set" aspiration has certainly contributed to the flowering of Italian design, as much appreciated throughout the world as Italian fashion.

In any event, it should be remembered that however much people enjoy the opera and theatre, the show is also going on in the street, in each individual, and that everyone, with apologies to Dante, is playing a part in some "Divina Commedia".

3.3 TAKE-A-BREAK

No. 1

LISTEN

Circle* [V] *if the statement is "vero" (true), or* [F] *if it is "falso"(false).

1. *Carla vuole vedere un film nuovo* .... V F
2. *A Carla non piacciono i film gialli* .... V F
3. *Carla è indecisa tra una commedia all'italiana e un vecchio western* V F
4. *Alla fine vanno a vedere "C'era una volta il West"* .... V F

No. 2

Anagram. The following two clues will give you, respectively, the names of a famous film director and his favourite actor.

1. *Lei mi offende, Ric!*
2. *Maestro, rimani con la "L".*

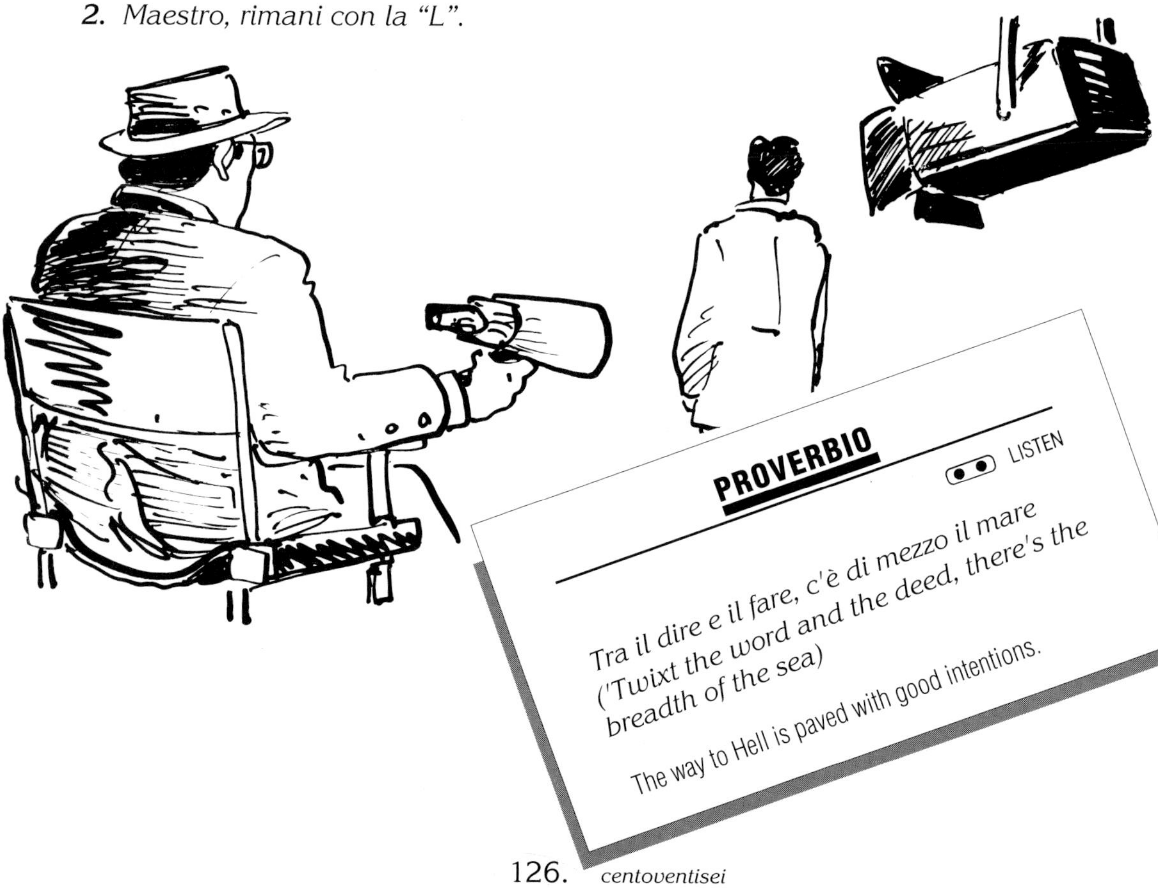

PROVERBIO

LISTEN

Tra il dire e il fare, c'è di mezzo il mare
(*'Twixt the word and the deed, there's the breadth of the sea*)

The way to Hell is paved with good intentions.

No. 3

Match each kind of film (as shown in the separate drawings) with its name.

1. *Comico*
2. *Giallo*
3. *Western*
4. *Drammatico*
5. *Fantascienza*
6. *Sentimentale*

A [ ]

B [ ]

C [ ]

D [ ]

E [ ]

F [ ]

3.4 DIALOGUE

LISTEN

PETTEGOLEZZI

Mario and Luisa Clerici are chatting as they leave the cinema.

Luisa : *Hai visto chi c'era nella fila davanti alla nostra?*
Mario : *No. Perché? Chi c'era?*
Luisa : *Ma dai! Tu non vedi mai niente! Era la signora Calvi, sai, quella del quarto piano...*
Mario : *La signora Calvi ... È quella signora che ha divorziato due anni fa?*
Luisa : *Esatto, quell'antipatica, che non mi saluta mai quando ci incontriamo per strada.*
Mario : *E allora?*
Luisa : *Non hai visto se era con qualcuno.*
Mario : *Io, a dire il vero, non ho visto proprio nessuno, e poi in fondo sono affari suoi, no?*
Luisa : *Con te non si può proprio parlare...*
Mario : *So benissimo che non la puoi soffrire ma a me sembra una persona a modo.*
Luisa : *Figurati! Si da un sacco di arie e si veste in un modo ridicolo per la sua età.*
Mario: *Quanti anni avrà?*
Luisa : *Avrà almeno cinquantacinque anni...*
Mario : *Beh, non li dimostra.*
Luisa : *Per forza, non hai visto come è truccata?*
Mario : *Sarà, comunque è una bella donna.*
Luisa : *Bella, lei?*
Mario : *Io le trovo un certo fascino.*
Luisa : *Per carità!*
Mario : *Ma non si è risposata recentemente?*
Luisa : *Sì, tre mesi fa, e pensa che ha sposato un uomo che avrà almeno vent'anni più di lei...Un grande industriale napoletano, ricchissimo, naturalmente...*
Mario : *Ma sai veramente tutto!*

LISTEN AND REPEAT

You will find the translation on page 23 of the booklet.

1. A religious procession
2. A game of "scopa".
3. Women in Naples.
4. Gesturing
5. Reading the newspaper
6. Teenagers

2

3

4

6

3.4 VOCABULARY

NOUNS

il pettegolezzo — gossip
la fila — row/line
l'età(f) — age
il fascino — appeal/fascination
l'industriale — industrialist

---

il divorzio — divorce
il matrimonio — marriage/matrimony
il trucco — make-up
il rossetto — lipstick
il profumo — perfume
il rimmel — mascara
la crema di bellezza — beauty cream

VERBS

divorziare — to divorce
salutare — to greet
incontrarsi — to meet/run into
soffrire — to suffer
darsi delle arie — to give oneself airs
vestirsi — to dress (oneself)
dimostrare — to show/demonstrate
sposarsi — to get married
risposarsi — to remarry
non poter soffrire qualcuno — to be unable to stand someone
dimostrare l'età — to show one's age
truccarsi — to put on make-up

ADJECTIVES

ridicolo — ridiculous
truccato — wearing make up
napoletano — Neapolitan
ricco — rich

---

povero — poor
agiato — comfortably off

MISCELLANEOUS

ma dai! — come on!
esatto! — exactly!
qualcuno — someone
nessuno — no-one
a dire il vero — to tell the truth
sono affari miei (suoi ecc.) — it's my (his etc.) own business
una persona a modo — a decent person
un sacco di — a heap/load of
per forza! — of course!
comunque — however
per carità! — for pity's sake!
recentemente — recently

HOW TO SAY IT

1. PROBABILITY

Avrà almeno 45 anni — She must be at least 45 years old. ***(1)***
Avrà 20 anni più di lei — He must be 20 years older than her.
Sarà uscito — He must have gone out.
Dormirà ancora — He must still be sleeping.

2. ...AGO

Ha divorziato 2 anni fa — She was divorced 2 years ago.
Si è risposata 3 mesi fa — She remarrried 3 months ago.
Ho visto Franco due ore fa — I saw Franco two hours ago.
Sono arrivato due minuti fa — I arrived two minutes ago.

3. SOMEONE/NO ONE

C'è qualcuno? — Is anyone there?
Hai visto qualcuno? — Did you see anyone?
No, non c'è nessuno — No, there's no one.
No, non ho visto nessuno — No, I didn't see anyone.

4. SOMETHING/NOTHING

C'è qualche cosa di bello? — Is there something nice?
No, non c'è niente — No, there's nothing.
Hai visto qualcosa di bello? — Did you see anything nice?
No, non ho visto niente — No, I didn't see anything.

5. COMMENTING ON OTHER PEOPLE

Quella signora è antipatica — That lady is horrible.
A me sembra simpatica — She seems nice to me.
Non la posso soffrire — I can't stand her.
È una persona a modo — She's a decent person.
Si da un sacco di arie — She is full of herself.
È una bella donna (è un bell'uomo) — She's a beautiful woman. (He's a handsome man.)
Si veste male — She dresses badly.
Ha un certo fascino — She has a certain appeal/charm.

6. A FEW EXCLAMATIONS

Dai! — Come on! *Ma dai!* — Come now! *Figurati!* — Not at all! *Per carità!* — For pity's sake!

REMARKS REMARKS REMARKS REMARKS

(1) *The future tense is often used to express probability.*

3.4 ORAL PRACTICE

1. ANSWERING IN THE NEGATIVE

USING "NESSUNO"

LISTEN

Ha telefonato qualcuno?
- *No, non ha telefonato nessuno*

Hai visto qualcuno?
- *No, non ho visto nessuno*

Continue answering in the negative.
Ha telefonato qualcuno? — Hai visto qualcuno? — È venuto qualcuno? — Hai incontrato qualcuno? — Hai conosciuto qualcuno? — Hai parlato con qualcuno? — Hai scritto a qualcuno? — Hai salutat o qualcuno? — Hai pensato a qualcuno?

(See Grammar, 1.)

2. ANSWERING IN THE NEGATIVE

USING "NIENTE"

LISTEN

Fai qualcosa stasera?
- *No, non faccio niente*

Continue answering in the negative.
Fai qualcosa stasera? — Prendi qualcosa? — Mangi qualcosa? — Bevi qualcosa? — Desideri qualcosa? — Vedi qualcosa? — Senti qualcosa? — Compri qualcosa? — Dici qualcosa?

(See Grammar, I.)

3. ...AGO

LISTEN

Quando sei arrivato?
- *due mesi*
- *Sono arrivato due mesi fa.*

Answer each question as indicated.
Quando sei arrivato?/due mesi — Quando hai visto Claudio?/un'ora — Quando sei ritornato?/una settimana — Quando hai cominciato a lavorare?/quattro anni — Quando ti sei sposato?/ 12 anni — Quando hai telefonato?/due minuti.

(See Grammar, F.)

4. PROBABILITY

USING THE FUTURE TENSE

LISTEN

Forse dorme ancora
- *Dormirà ancora.*

Forse è uscito
- *Sarà uscito.*

Change the sentences as in the model.
Forse dorme ancora — Forse è uscito — Forse lavora ancora — Forse è ritomato — Forse ha telefonato — Forse è in vacanza — Forse ha 40 anni — Forse è al cinema — Forse non può venire.

(See Grammar, L.8.)

5. HOW MUCH/HOW MANY

LISTEN

Claudio ha 5 cravatte
- *Quante cravatte ha?*

Maria ha molti vestiti
- *Quanti vestiti ha?*

Continue asking questions in this way.
Claudio ha 5 cravatte — Maria ha molti vestiti — La signora Calvi ha 55 ani — Il sig. Clerici ha due macchine — La valigia ha una sola chiave — Quel ragazzo ha molti libri — L'albergo ha quaranta stanze — Il sig. Bauer ha mille dollari.

(See Grammar, G.2.)

6. THE IMPERFECT

"ESSERE" and "AVERE"

LISTEN

Sono occupato
- *Ero occupato*

Ho mal di testa
- *Avevo mal di testa*

Change the following sentences from the present to the imperfect.
Sono occupato — Ho mal di testa — Sono in vacanza — Siamo in vacanza — Abbiamo un appuntamento — Hai un appuntamento — Siete in ritardo — Loro sono in anticipo — Hanno la chiave — Avete il libro — Ho 20 anni — Sono al bar.

(See Grammar, L.9.)

DIVORCE, ITALIAN STYLE

Always a favourite topic, in conversation as well as in films and plays, (notably the famous Italian comedies by writers such as Dario Fo), divorce in fact was only introduced in Italy in 1969, and did not become legal until the referendum in 1974. It is, in short, quite a recent phenomenon, and in a country where Catholicism is the state religion, it constituted in its way a real revolution. The law was fought tooth and nail by the Church, and ended up as a mere toe dipped in the water: divorce is allowed only after five years of separation - a long time by any standards. So you need to think hard before committing yourself to marriage, Italian style!

Even though attitudes and the laws have changed, the family is still the keystone of Italian society, and Italians still divorce less and marry more than many of their European partners. Marriage is still seen as a sound investment, which most young people aspire to. There is the same contradiction often seen in the U.K.: religion is on the wane, the churches are empty, yet most couples still chose to marry in church, which, since both countries have an established church, constitutes a legal marriage. In the cities, not surprisingly, some couples opt for the registry office ("il municipio") , but elsewhere in Italy this is unusual, and rather daring.

In many cases, marriage also represents young people's best chance of asserting their independence, of being finally

recognised as "grown up" by their parents. Look around: there are many fewer young people living by themselves, in their own homes, than there are, for instance, in the U.K. or France. For many Italian parents, the idea that their little ones might want to spread their wings is absolutely incomprehensible, even offensive. That is why marriage can sometimes seem the only way of leaving the parental nest without appearing ungracious. As with families everywhere, love is closely intertwined with moral blackmail: "how can you think of leaving "tua mamma" when she does so much for you?"

In many of the English-speaking countries, where independence from parents is regarded as a virtue, it can seem that Italian children have a high price to pay for their early morning cup of coffee, their daily "pastasciutta", and their piles of crisp ironing. In fact, the tight hold that parents have on their children is generally welcomed, since the latter feel the advantages far outweigh any inconvenience. You may be surprised to find that many of the Italians you meet, even though over thirty, still live at home, the tendency being to marry later and later.

On careful examination, you see that this system, deeply entrenched in people's minds, is reflected in the language. When an Italian, though happily married for years, speaks of "casa mia", you will soon realise that the "casa" in question is his parents'!

The idea of the family has changed too, of course. Firstly, people have fewer children, and then, on the whole, the family is now reduced to the "nuclear family", of parents and their children. However, the extended family, with its uncles, aunts, cousins and in-laws, the whole clan, is still important, especially in money matters: the extended family forms a network of connections, of influence, of fixers, which can open doors that might otherwise remain tightly closed. Many Italians have greater faith in the effectiveness of a second cousin twice removed than that of some faceless bureaucrat.

This is why the family remains such a force to be reckoned with in Italian society, and it is easy to understand that divorce is not easy in such circumstances. But things are nonetheless different now: it is possible in Sicily to take a girl for a walk without being threatened by her brothers. And should you marry an Italian, you will it is true have to submit to all the family rituals, but on the other hand, you will have gained a "mamma", ready to love and spoil you as much as her other children.

3.4 TAKE-A-BREAK

No. 1 LISTEN

Listen to the descriptions of these people, and pick out the characteristic which is not mentioned.

1. *Maria è ....*

A. *simpatica* C. *riservata*
B. *allegra* D. *depressa*

2. *L'ingegner Verdi è.............*

A. *disonesto* B. *onesto*
C. *serio*

3. *La signora Belli è ....*

A. *dinamica* B. *intelligente*
C. *intraprendente*

4. *Il figlio della signora Carmeli è ...*

A. *affettuoso* C. *maleducato*
B. *vivace* D. *insopportabile*

No. 2

Search out the words hidden in the following puzzle and highlight them. Words can read backwards and forewards, up, down or diagonally, but always in a straight line. Some letters are a part of several, intersecting words.

P	O	S	O	I	O	N	O
S	V	O	L	O	R	A	C
I	I	B	O	U	O	O	I
M	T	R	C	T	R	B	T
P	T	U	C	T	E	E	A
A	A	T	I	C	N	L	P
T	C	T	P	A	C	L	I
I	**P**	**O**	**V**	**E**	**R**	**O**	T
C	F	O	R	T	E	M	N
O	I	O	V	A	R	B	A
G	V	E	C	C	H	I	O

Antipatico - bravo - brutto - caro - cattivo - corti - forte - giovane - nero - noioso - piccolo - ***povero*** *- simpatico - tuoi - vecchio.*

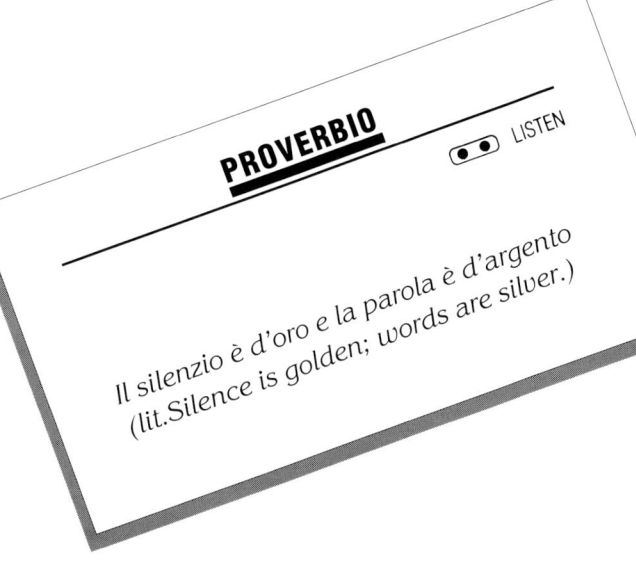

PROVERBIO LISTEN

Il silenzio è d'oro e la parola è d'argento
(lit.Silence is golden; words are silver.)

No. 3

Dingbat

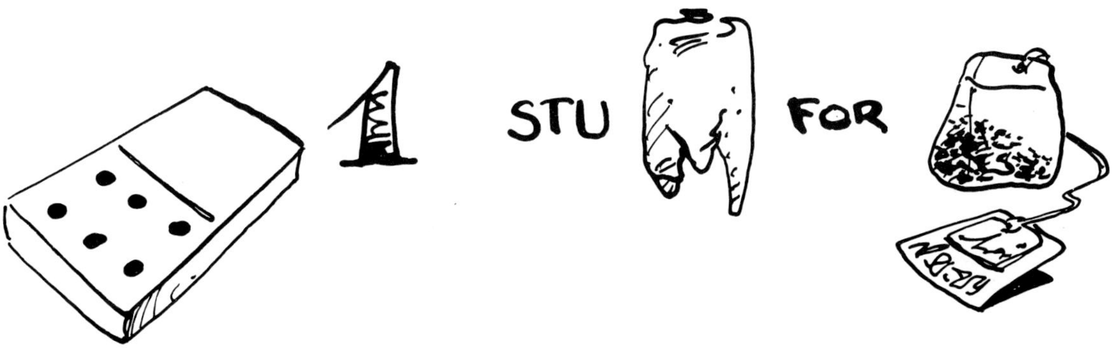

(Answers on page 24 of the booklet)

3.5 DIALOGUE

LISTEN

AFFITTARE UN APPARTAMENTO

The Clerici want to move, so they go and see an estate agent in Naples.

L'agente immobiliare : *Buongiorno. I Signori desiderano?*

Lui : *Buongiorno. Senta, cerchiamo un appartamento in affitto, possibilmente abbastanza grande e vicino al centro.*

L'agente imm. : *Quanti vani dovrebbe avere?*

Lui : *Quattro vani.*

L'agente imm.: *Quindi quattro stanze più i servizi. Va bene. E quanto vogliono spendere d'affitto?*

Lui : *Sulle sette-ottocentomila lire.*

L'agente imm.: *Vediamo un po'. Sì, su questo prezzo ne ho due che potrebbero andare bene : uno è proprio nel centro. L'altro è un po' più decentrato.*

Lei : *Com'è quello in centro?*

L'agente imm.: *Dunque ... Come superficie fa 80m². Non è grandissimo ma è ben disposto. È al settimo piano con ascensore, e ci sono anche la cantina e il box.*

Lei : *In cucina si può mangiare?*

L'agente imm.: *Non credo, perché non è molto spaziosa. Però c'è un bel soggiorno e ci sono i doppi servizi.*

Lui : *E il palazzo di che anno è?*

L'agente imm.: *Degli anni trenta, è un bel palazzo con la portineria e il citofono.*

Lei : *Il riscaldamento è centrale?*

L'agente imm.: *Sì, e le spese di amministrazione non sono troppo elevate.*

Lui : *L'altro appartamento è più grande?*

L'agente imm.: *Sì, è circa 100m², ma è da rinfrescare, mentre il primo di cui vi ho parlato è appena stato rimesso a nuovo.*

Lei : *Ah, e come è esposto il primo?*

L'agente imm.: *Ha un'ottima esposizione : il salotto e una camera da letto sono ad est, e il resto al sud.*

Lei : *Non mi sembra male! Si può visitare?*

L'agente imm.: *Certo. Quando vuole! Anche subito.*

Lui : *Per me va bene. Che ne dici, cara?*

Lei : *Oh, sì. Non vedo l'ora di vederlo!*

Lui : *Ancora una cosa : bisogna versare una cauzione?*

L'agente imm.: *Sì, alla firma del contratto deve pagare il primo mese di affitto e versare due mesi di cauzione più naturalment le spese di agenzia.*

LISTEN AND REPEAT

You will find the translation on page 24 of the booklet

1. Procida
2. The old port of Naples
3. The Posillipo area
4. A 17th century villa
5. Wall of an old building
6. A religious statue on a street corner

1

2

3

4

5

6

3.5 VOCABULARY

NOUNS

l'appartamento(m) — apartment/flat
l'agenzia immobiliare(f) — estate agency
l'agente immobiliare — estate agent
l'affitto(m) — rent
il vano — room
i doppi servizi(m.pl)— kitchen/bathroom ***(1)***
la superficie — floor area
la cantina — basement storage/cellar
il box — garage/parking place
la cucina — kitchen
il soggiorno — living room
il palazzo — building ***(2)***
la portineria — caretaker's lodge
il citofono — intercom
il riscaldamento — heating
le spese di amministrazione — administrative charges
l'esposizione(f) — aspect
il salotto — sitting room
la camera da letto — bedroom
la cauzione — down-payment/ deposit
la firma — signature
il contratto d'affitto — lease
i punti cardinali(m.pl) — cardinal points
est — east
ovest — west
sud — south
nord — north

il trasloco — moving (house)
l'inquilino(m) — tenant
il padrone di casa — owner of the building ***(3)***
il portinaio — caretaker
il termosifone — radiator
l'ingresso(m) — entrance
la finestra — window

ADJECTIVES

decentrato — out of town/in the suburbs
centrale — central
elevato — elevated
spazioso — spacious
luminoso — (with lots of) light/well-lit
buio — dark

VERBS

cercare — to search/look for
affittare — to rent
spendere — to spend (money)
disporre — to have available
rinfrescare — to redecorate
rimettere a nuovo — to do up/renovate
non vedere l'ora (di) — to be unable to wait (can't wait to)
versare — to put down (a deposit)
traslocare — to move

HOW TO SAY IT

1. RENTING AN APARTMENT OR ROOM

Cerco un appartamento in affitto — I am looking for an apartment to rent.
Vorrei affittare una camera ammobiliata per un mese — I'd like to rent a furnished room for a month.
Vorrei affittare un apartamento di tre vani più servizi — I'd like to rent an apartment with three rooms with kitchen and bathroom.

2. ASKING ABOUT APARTMENTS

Quant'è l'affitto? — What's the rent?
Le spese di amministrazione sono comprese? — Are maintenance charges included?
Qual è la superfice? — How big is it? (What's its floor-area?)
Il riscaldamento è centrale (a gas, elettrico, individuale)? — Does it have central heating? (gas, electric, individual)
A che piano è? — Which floor is it?
C'è l'ascensore (il citofono, la portineria)? — Is there a lift (intercom, caretaker's lodge?)
Com'è esposto? — Which way does it face?
Il palazzo di che anno è? — How old is the building?

3. RENTING

Bisogna versare una cauzione? — Is a deposit necessary?
Quanto dura il contratto d'affitto? — How long does the tenancy agreement last?
Ci sono delle spese di agenzia? — Are there any estate-agent's fees?
L'assicurazione è obbligatoria? — Is insurance compulsory?

4. DESCRIBING THE APARTMENT

È un po'decentrato — It's a bit out of town.
È in periferia — It's in the suburbs.
È centralissimo — It's right in the centre.
È ben disposto — It's well arranged.
Le finestre danno sulla strada (sul cortile) — The windows look out onto the street (courtyard).
Ha un'ottima esposizione — It has a first-class aspect.
È un'occasione — It's a bargain.
È da rinfrescare — It needs some redecoration.
È rimesso a nuovo — It's been renovated.
Ci sono i doppi servizi — There are two bathrooms.

REMARKS REMARKS REMARKS REMARKS

(1) "Servizi" covers bathroom, lavatory, kitchen, utility room, and entrance. — (2) You could also say "edificio". — (3) "Proprietario" means the same thing, namely the person who owns the block of flats.

3.5 ORAL PRACTICE

1. THE RELATIVE PRONOUN "CUI"

LISTEN

Vi ho parlato di un appartamento
- *Ecco l'appartamento di cui vi ho parlato*

Ho parlato con una signora
- *Ecco la signora con cui ho parlato*

Change the sentences by using* "cui" *with the prepositions* "di, da, con, a, per" *as in the model.

Vi ho parlato di un appartamento — Ho parlato con una signora — Sono venuto per un motivo — Sono andato da un agente immobiliare — Ho dato il libro a una ragazza — Ti ho parlato di una persona — Sono uscito con un amico.

(See Grammar, G.1.)

2. THE CONDITIONAL

THE VERB "VOLERE"

LISTEN

Io
- *Vorrei affittare un appartamento*

Tu
- *Vorresti affittare un appartamento*

Conjugate* "volere" *as in the model.

Io — Tu — I signori Clerici — Mario — Noi — I nostri amici — Voi — Lei —Io — Marina.

(See Grammar, L.8.)

3. THE CONDITIONAL

THE VERB "POTERE"

LISTEN

Visitare l'appartamento - io
- *Potrei visitare l'appartamento?*

Fare una telefonata - noi
- *Potremmo fare una telefonata?*

Continue forming questions in the conditional.

Visitare l'appartamento/io — Fare una telefonata/noi — Aprire la finestra/tu — Telefonare a Mario/voi — Parlare con il direttore/io — Spedire il curriculum vitae/loro.

(See Grammar, L.8.)

4. THE IMPERSONAL: "SI"

LISTEN

È possibile entrare
- *Si può entrare*

Bisogna firmare
- *Si deve firmare*

Change each sentence as in the model.

È possibile entrare — Bisogna firmare — Non è possibile fumare — Non bisogna prenotare — È possibile pagare in due volte — Non è possibile avere la linea — Bisogna versare una cauzione.

(See Grammar, L.15)

5. ADJECTIVES

LISTEN

È grande l'appartamento?
- *No, è piccolo*

È luminosa la cucina?
- *No, è buia*

Continue answering giving the opposite of the adjective in the question.

È grande l'appartamento? — È luminosa la cucina? — È lungo il corridoio? — È nuovo il palazzo? — È largo l'ingresso? — È divertente lo spettacolo? — È buono il pesce?

6. COMPARISONS

LISTEN

Rapido — Prendere il treno/prendere l'aereo
- *È più rapido prendere l'aereo che prendere il treno*

Make comparisons, as in the model.

Rapido—Prendere il treno/prendere l'aereo — Caro—Mangiare al ristorante/mangiare a casa — Divertente—Andare in vacanza/restare in città — Importante—Essere in buona forma/avere molti soldi.

(See Grammar, H.I)

AN ETERNAL HOME

Looking for somewhere to live? Perhaps we can help you. I would not in all seriousness recommend the notorious "bassi" in Naples. In fact, Naples has not yet solved the acute housing shortage caused by its last earthquake. I would not really recommend industrialised Turin either, not even the centre: fine architecture, but a bit rigid, perhaps.

What are you looking for? A strikingly unusual house? There are some to be had towards Matera, in Basilicate, where you might stumble across a desirable cave dwelling. No? You prefer to move with the times. How about trying further south, in the Puglia? South of Bari, there is the very thing: the "trulli" of Alberobello. These are nothing if not unusual, with conical, stone roofs, topped off with a sort of knob, like the bell on a magician's hat. Unfortunately, the area can hardly described as the hub of European affairs.

You would like something chic, stylish? Go and live in Milan, beside the Navigli; or in a villa on Capri; in Portofino or any other of the quaint little ports frequented by the rich and famous; in a Venetian palazzo on the Gran Canale, which you could turn into a Foundation, like Peggy Guggenheim's; or in one of those wonderful Tuscan houses, half palace half monastery, to be found in, for instance, Fiesole, home of the European Institute (an ideal place to improve the mind); or in an apartment overlooking the Piazza del Campo in Sienna, so you can watch from your windows the

Palio, one of the oldest festivals in the western world.

You are obviously very hard to please. Just for you, and connoisseurs like you, we have one or two quite exceptional items on offer. Come deep into Veneto, on dry land. A Renaissance villa, designed by Palladio himself, for a mere 3,000,000,000 lire, does that interest you? Of course, you would not be allowed to alter anything, but would have to maintain it meticulously, devoting your whole life, as well as your income, to its upkeep. But look at it: would it not be worth it , just to possess such a jewel? Your tastes are more modern? We happen to have on our books the villa Girasole, an extraordinary place built in the 1930s not far from Verona. What is so extraordinary about it? it rotates on an axis, following the sun, hence its name.

You would like something more modest? A piece of advice: leave dry land, leave trains, cars... go to Venice. Take the vaporetto, number 5. The ride is exciting in itself: down the Gran Canale, in front of St. Mark's, across the Arsenal (two hundred years ago, you would have been arrested as a spy), and there you are, at the Fondamenta Nuove. There you catch a vaporetto number 12, which takes you onto the open sea. Ignore Michele and Murano, but stop at Burano. There, in the jostling harlequinade of houses that make up this large, sea-side village, you cannot fail to find your heart's desire. Every single house is a gem - a post-card come to life. Of course you will also have to buy a "moscato", a motor-boat.

What do you mean, that is still not what you are looking for? You were impressed by Pompei, and are looking for something for all time? Well, there are two addresses we can offer. The first is a monument to a people's self-opinion: the Staglieno cemetery in Genoa. The ancient kingdom of Genoa was known as "la Superba". The Staglieno cemetery only dates back to the last century, but is nonetheless a graphic justification of the name. Better than any history book, the statues which decorate the tombs lay before us a remarkable gallery of the nineteenth-century Genoese bourgeoisie. The art nouveau ("liberty" in Italian) tombs are often decorated with macabre jollity, strangely reminiscent of baroque art. Just outside the city, Staglieno is one of the most curious things to see in Genoa.

The other posibility is a place of silence and meditation: San Michele's graveyard, in Venice. The vaporetto number 5 (see above) will take you there. Compared to the overheated bustle of the centre of Venice, San Michele is a haven of peace, the end of the Earth. A dream come true. This must be how Stravinski and Diaghilev saw it, when they chose it as their eternal home.

3.5 TAKE-A-BREAK

LISTEN

L'ITALIANO

(C. Minellono - S. Cutugno)
Sung by Toto Cutugno

Lasciatemi cantare con la chitarra in mano
Lasciatemi cantare, sono un italiano

Buongiorno Italia, gli spaghetti al dente
e un partigiano come Presidente
con l'autoradio sempre nella mano destra
e un canarino sopra la finestra

Buongiorno Italia con i tuoi artisti
con troppa America sui manifesti
con le canzoni, con amore, con il cuore
con più donne, sempre meno suore.

Buongiorno Italia, buongiorno Maria
con gli occhi pieni di malinconia
Buongiorno Dio
lo sai che ci sono anch'io.

Lasciatemi cantare con la chitarra in mano
Lasciatemi cantare una canzone piano
piano

Lasciatemi cantare perché ne sono fiero
Sono un italiano, un italiano vero

Buongiorno Italia che non si spaventa
e con la crema da barba alla menta
con un vestito gessato sul blu
e la moviola la domenica in TV.

Buongiorno Italia con caffè ristretto
le calze nuove nel primo cassetto
con la bandiera in tintoria
e una 600 giù di carrozzeria.

The Italian

Let me sing with my guitar in my hands
Let me sing, I'm an Italian

Good morning Italy, spaghetti al dente
And a freedom fighter as President
With a car radio always at my right hand
And a canary above my window,

Good morning Italy, with all your artists
with too much America in your ads
with songs, love, heart,
with always more women and fewer nuns.

Good morning Italy, good morning Mary
with eyes full of sorrow
Good morning God
You know that I am here too.

Let me sing with my guitar in my hands

Let me sing a song softly, softly.

Let me sing because I'm proud
to be an Italian, a true Italian

Good morning fearless Italy
with mint shaving cream
with a blue chalk-stripe suit
and slow-motion re-plays on Sunday TV.

Good morning Italy with strong coffee
new socks in the top drawer
with a banner at the laundry
and a battered Fiat 600.

NASCERE CON LA CAMICIA

(lit., to be born with a shirt)

To be born with a silver spoon in your mouth.

MANGIARE LA FOGLIA

(lit., to eat the leaf)

To twig onto something

ESSERE UN PALLONE GONFIATO

(lit., to be an inflated balloon)

To be swollen-headed

AVERE L'ACQUA ALLA GOLA

(lit., to have water at your throat)

To be at your last gasp

3. WRITTEN PRACTICE

3.1

FILL IN THE BLANKS WITH "quel/quei/quella/quelle".....*vestito è troppo corto. - ..... camicia è sportiva. - .....pantaloni sono di lana. - .....cravatte sono troppo vivaci. - .....gonna Le sta molto bene. - .....modello è molto elegante.*

TRANSLATE: *Vuole provare la taglia più grande? - Quella di seta è più cara dell'altra. -Il cappotto rosso non ti sta molto bene.*

Mr. and Mrs. Clerici went to Rinascente. - Have you already seen something in the window? - Do you like this shirt, madam? - What's your size?

3.2

ANSWER EACH QUESTION, ALWAYS USING "ne" OR "ci" AS EACH CASE REQUIRES.

Sei andato alla stazione? Sì,..
Conosci molte persone? Sì, ...
Vieni anche tu al ristorante? Sì, ...anch'io.
Quante medicine prendi al giorno? ....molte.
Quando vai dal dottore? ....domani.

TRANSLATE: *Devo prendere questa medicina tré volte alla settimana. - Il dottore mi ha misurato la pressione. - Ho dimenticato di prendere la ricetta.*

Today I have a dental appointment. - There we are, it's my turn now. - I have a headache. - I'm not sure, but I believe so.

3.3

FILL IN THE BLANKS WITH "che" OR "chi": *Il regista ...ha fatto il film è molto famoso. - ...è il protagonista? - ....film danno al cinema? - L'attore ....interpreta il film è un tipo affascinante. - ....ha comprato il giornale? - ....ne dici di uscire stasera? - La commedia ....ho visto ieri mi è piaciuta molto.*

TRANSLATE: *Il film mi è piaciuto molto. - Ti va di andare a teatro? - Sei pronta? - È una bravissima attrice.*

Shall we go out together this evening? - What film is being shown on TV? - I didn't like the concert at all. - I hate going dancing.

3.4

ANSWER THE FOLLOWING QUESTIONS:

Hai visto qualcuno? No, ...
Hai fatto qualcosa di bello? No, ...
Ha telefonato qualcuno? No, ...
C'è qualcosa al cinema? No, ...
C'è qualcuno qui che parla il russo? No, ...

TRANSLATE: *Suo marito ha dieci anni più di lei. - È sempre elegantissima! - Non si trucca mai. - Was there someone with her? - No, there was no-one. - I said nothing. - She remarried six months ago.*

3.5

FILL THE BLANKS WITH "cui" OR "che" AS EACH CASE REQUIRES: *Il film di ....ti ho parlato è uscito ieri. - La ragazza con ....ho cenato è molto simpatica. - L'attore ....preferisco è italiano. - Il libro da.......... è tratto il film è un celebre romanzo di Eco. - Questa è la ragione per ....ti scrivo. - Il cinema ......dà "Il nome della rosa" è in centro. - La signora ....abbiamo incontrato è la vicina del 4° piano.*

TRANSLATE: *L'affitto non è troppo caro. - Il riscaldamento è individuale. - Non vedo l'ora di cambiare casa!*

The Clerici would like to rent a flat. - The building I talked to you about is very modern. - One can eat in the kitchen.

(Answers on page 37 of the booklet)

MORE VOCABULARY

CLOTHING

accappatoio (m) — dressing-gown
berretto (m) — cap
calze (f.pl.) — stockings
calze di nylon (f.pl) — tights
camicia da notte (f) — night-dress
canottiera (f) — vest
cappello (m) — hat
cappotto (m) — coat
cintura (f) — belt
costume da bagno (m) — swimsuit
giacca (f) — jacket
giubbotto (m) — blouson/bomber-jacket
golf (m)— sleeveless pullover
guanti (m.pl.) — gloves
maglietta (f) — T-shirt
mutandine (f.pl.) — pants
ombrello (m) — umbrella
pantaloncini (m.pl.) — shorts
pantaloni (m.pl.) — trousers
pelliccia (f) — fur coat
pigiama (m) — pyjamas
reggiseno (m) — bra
scarpe (f.pl.) — shoes
scialle (f) — shawl
sciarpa (f) — scarf
stivali (m.pl.) — boots

PARTS OF THE BODY

capelli (m.pl.) — hair
faccia (f) — face
viso (m) — face
fronte (f) — forehead
occhi (m.pl) — eyes
naso (m) — nose
bocca (f) — mouth
denti (m.pl.) — teeth
labbra (f.pl.) — lips
mento (m) — chin
orecchi (m.pl) — ears
collo (m) — neck
spalle (f.pl.) — shoulders
braccio (m) — arm
braccia (f.pl.) — arms
gomito (m) — elbow
gambe (f.pl.) — legs
coscia (f) — thigh
ginocchio (m) — knee
polpaccio (m) — calf
mani (f.pl.) — hands
polso (m) — wrist
piedi (m.pl.) — feet
dito (m) — finger
dita (f.pl.) — fingers
schiena (f) — back
petto (m) — chest
seno (m) — breast

SHOPS

calzoleria — shoe shop
calzolaio — shoemaker
drogheria — grocer's shop
droghiere — grocer
farmacia — chemist shop
farmacista — chemist
frutta e verdura — green grocer's shop
fruttivendolo — green grocer
gelateria — ice-cream parlour
gelataio — ice cream maker
gioielleria — jewellery shop
gioielliere — jeweller
latteria — dairy
lattaio — milkman
macelleria — butcher's shop
macellaio — butcher
panetteria — bakery/breadshop
panettiere — baker
pasticceria — cake-shop
pasticcere — pastry-cook
pescheria — fish-shop
pescivendolo — fishmonger
rosticceria — rotisserie (cooked meat dishes)
rosticcere — rotisserie owner
salumeria — prepared pork (salami, ham etc) shop
salumiere — pork butcher

JOBS/PROFESSIONS

elettricista — electrician
fabbro — locksmith
falegname — carpenter
fotografo — photographer
giornalaio — newsagent
idraulico — plumber
meccanico — mechanic
orologiaio — watchmaker
parrucchiere — hairdresser
barbiere — barber

THE HOUSE

ingresso (m) — entrance
corridoio (m) — corridor
stanza (f) — room
camera (f) (da letto) — bedroom
sala da pranzo (f) — dining-room
salone (salotto) (m) — sitting-room
soggiorno (m) — living room
cucina (f) — kitchen
ripostiglio (m) — store-room
balcone /terrazzo (m) — balcony
terrazza (f) — terrace
bagno (m) — bath
gabinetto (m) — lavatory
pavimento (m) — floor
soffitto (f) — ceiling
finestra (f) — window
porta (f) — door

FURNITURE

armadio (m) — wardrobe
tavolo (m) — table
sedia /seggiola (f) — chair
poltrona (f) — armchair
divano/sofà (m) — sofa
scaffale (m) — shelf/bookcase

3. TEST YOURSELF

1. PUT INTO THE PAST TENSE

Dico a Mario di venire ....
Prendiamo l'autobus ....
Bevono una birra ....
La commedia mi piace molto ....
Luisa si annoia al concerto ....
Non faccio niente ....
Scrivo una lettura a Mario...

2. FILL IN THE BLANKS WITH "DI" OR "CHE" AS REQUIRED

Questo vestito è meno caro ....*quello.*
È meglio andare in montagna ....*restare in città.*
È più facile capire ....*parlare una lingua straniera.*
Quest' appartamento è più grande ....*quello.*
Maria è più alta ....*Carlo.*

3. GIVE THE OPPOSITE OF EACH VERB

aprire..
entrare ....
salire ....
ricordare ....
andare ....
divertirsi ....
accorciare ....
cominciare ....
domandare ....
essere in anticipo...............................

4. WHAT WOULD YOU SAY IF YOU HAD TO.........

know the colour of something: ....
say what your size was: ....
say that you didn't feel very well: ....

invite a friend to go out with you: ....
ask what's on at a cinema: ....
ask how much the rent is: ....
ask which floor the apartment is on: ....

5. ONLY ONE SENTENCE IN EACH SET IS CORRECT. CAN YOU FIND IT?

A. *Qui si non può fumare* .... ☐
B. *Qui non si può fumare* .... ☐
C. *Qui non si può di fumare* .... ☐

A. *Le posso dare questo sciroppo* .... ☐
B. *Posso Le dare questo sciroppo* .... ☐
C. *La posso dare questo sciroppo* .... ☐

A. *Questa sera uscio con Francesco* .... ☐
B. *Questa sera uscito con Francesco* .... ☐
C. *Questa sera esco con Francesco* .... ☐

A. *Ha divorziato due anni fa* .... ☐
B. *Ha divorziato fa due anni* .... ☐
C. *Ha divorziato fra due anni* .... ☐

6. MATCH EACH QUESTION TO ITS ANSWER

A. *Molto bene: è proprio la tua misura!*
B. *Solo un po' di aspirina.*
C. *Perché non? Potremmo andare a teatro...*
D. *Non lo so di preciso... forse 45.*
E. *Sulle sette-ottocentomila lire.*

1. *Ha già preso qualche medicina?*
2. *Quanti anni avrà quella signora?*
3. *Quanto vogliono spendere d'affitto?*
4. *Come mi sta questo vestito?*
5. *Che ne diresti di uscire stasera?*

(Check your answers on page 38 of the booklet)

IN BOCCA AL LUPO

That night, Ambrogio found it hard to sleep. These repeated telephone riddles bothered him. He could not imagine what pleasure there was in jokes of such very poor taste. Those two phone calls had opened up an abyss at his feet, and it was all he could do to stop himself hurtling headlong into it. He tried to reason with himself:

"It is inevitable that my name should get about; it could easily have attracted some idiot's attention, here or back in Italy. Someone's just trying to frighten me."

Unfortunately, they were succeeding only too well. The feeling that the caller had moved closer since the day before really worried him. But that was only an impression. And after all, the expression "in bocca al lupo" was the most commonplace of clichés, such as any fool might use. But no argument, however logical, could quiet him. He could look at the book's cover, but not touch it, open it, thumb through it.... He felt that to do so would incur the most dire retribution.

It was far into the night, when the snow was already half-way up the balcony window, that Ambrogio finally fell into a troubled sleep.

Lucia was highly amused next morning by his haggard face, with its deeply ringed eyes.

"Come ti sei ridotto! Ma con chi hai passato la notte? " *and she added, touching his chin:* "Ti sei anche tagliato."

"Lo so. Non c'è niente da ridere."

"Insomma, non si può più scherzare. Sai che ho dato un'occhiata al famigerato "In Bocca al Lupo"?

Ambrogio blenched.

"Ah si?

"Dai, Ambrogio, non fare questa faccia! *I only looked at the index.* Ma forse l'avrai già consultata?"

"No". *Ambrogio assumed a very strait-laced tone:* "Come dicevi tu, sono stato molto occupato questa notte, non ho avuto un minuto da dedicare alle scemenze della Piper-Sharp."

"Allora non avrai visto che uno dei capitoli s'intitola "Gelsi in via Pioppette". A Milano, non abitavi in via Pioppette? Li hai visti, i gelsi, in via Pioppette?"

Ambrogio had indeed lived for several years in this street, via Pioppette; that was in fact the reason that he used to catch the tram opposite the Roman pillars at San Lorenzo: they were only about a hundred yards from his front-door. But never - he was ready to stake his life on it - had he seen any mulberry trees there. Nor anywhere else in Milan, for that matter. Silk-worm rearing was not a common practice in the city-centre. It seemed absurd to entitle the chapter of a book, supposedly based on fact, "The Mulberry trees of the Via Pioppette". Ambrogio felt reassured; his worries crumbled at the thought of such nonsense.

Sitting quietly in his office, he was about to check what Lucia had told him about Anonimo's book, when she called to him:

"La Piper-Sharp al telefono; te la passo? Sai, lupo non mangia lupo."

"Molto divertente."

He lifted the receiver.

"Hello, is that you, Ambrogio darling?"

Mrs. Piper-Sharp sounded strained.

"I'm so sorry to ring you at such an unearthly hour..."

"Not at all, my dear Mrs. Piper-Sharp, it is always delightful to hear from you."

Ambrogio always felt a little thrill of satisfaction when he demonstrated his powers of empty flattery.

"As you know, I mentioned yesterday that book, you recall, "Into the jaws of the wolf" *or something of the sort. Well, I'm afraid I was just a tiny bit premature. You know how it is. Anyway, I've realised that the book does not in fact interest us. I just thought I'd let you know so that you can offer it to other British publishers. I really am most frightfully sorry. I had really wanted so much to do it."*

"Ma va' a quel paese"*, thought Ambrogio. He added, aloud: "Please, think nothing of it. These things happen. I understand perfectly. Another time, no doubt."*

At least he would not have to read it in order to talk about it: that was something. What did intrigue him, however, was the unmistakably anxious note in Mrs. Piper-Sharp's voice.She was not usually given to haste, nor to apologising, and certainly not to doing other publishers favours! Such a conciliatory attitude on her part was all the more surprising.

He picked the book up again. There really was a chapter "Gelsi in via Pioppette" *. He looked at it, and immediately realised his mistake: it was not about mulberry trees - or* gelsi *- in the via Pioppette, but bankers. Or, to be more precise, one particular banker: the controvertial Dottor Gelsi, financial wizard and shady businessman. He had been unlucky enough to cross that road once in his life....and lose it there. A patrol of* vigili urbani, *on their nightly beat, had found his body hanging from a tree at the corner of the via Pioppette and the Piazza Vetra. It had been winter, and the mist thick enough for the policemen to mistake his body at a distance for a plastic bag, requiring investigation. Through Anonimo's obliging pen, M.S. was able to make the following comments on the whole affair:*

"Nessuno si stupì di una così squallida fine. Tutti sapevano delle traversie che aveva conosciuto il banchiere Gelsi, dei complotti in cui era stato coinvolto, delle colpe di cui si era macchiato. Però ci si aspettava una morte più discreta, una sparizione nel nulla, qualcosa che non destasse scalpore. Infatti, la cosa fu subito messa a tacere. Pochi giornali riferirono la notizia, e quelli che lo fecero le dedicarono appena un piccolo trafiletto. Chiaramente, i mandanti dell'omocidio volevano dare l'esempio, mandare una specie di ammonimento a certe persone di cui non farò i nomi. Insomma, tutto sarebbe andato a buon porto se non ci fosse stato un inghippo: qualcuno della zona aveva visto tutto."

To be continued . . .

UNIT 4

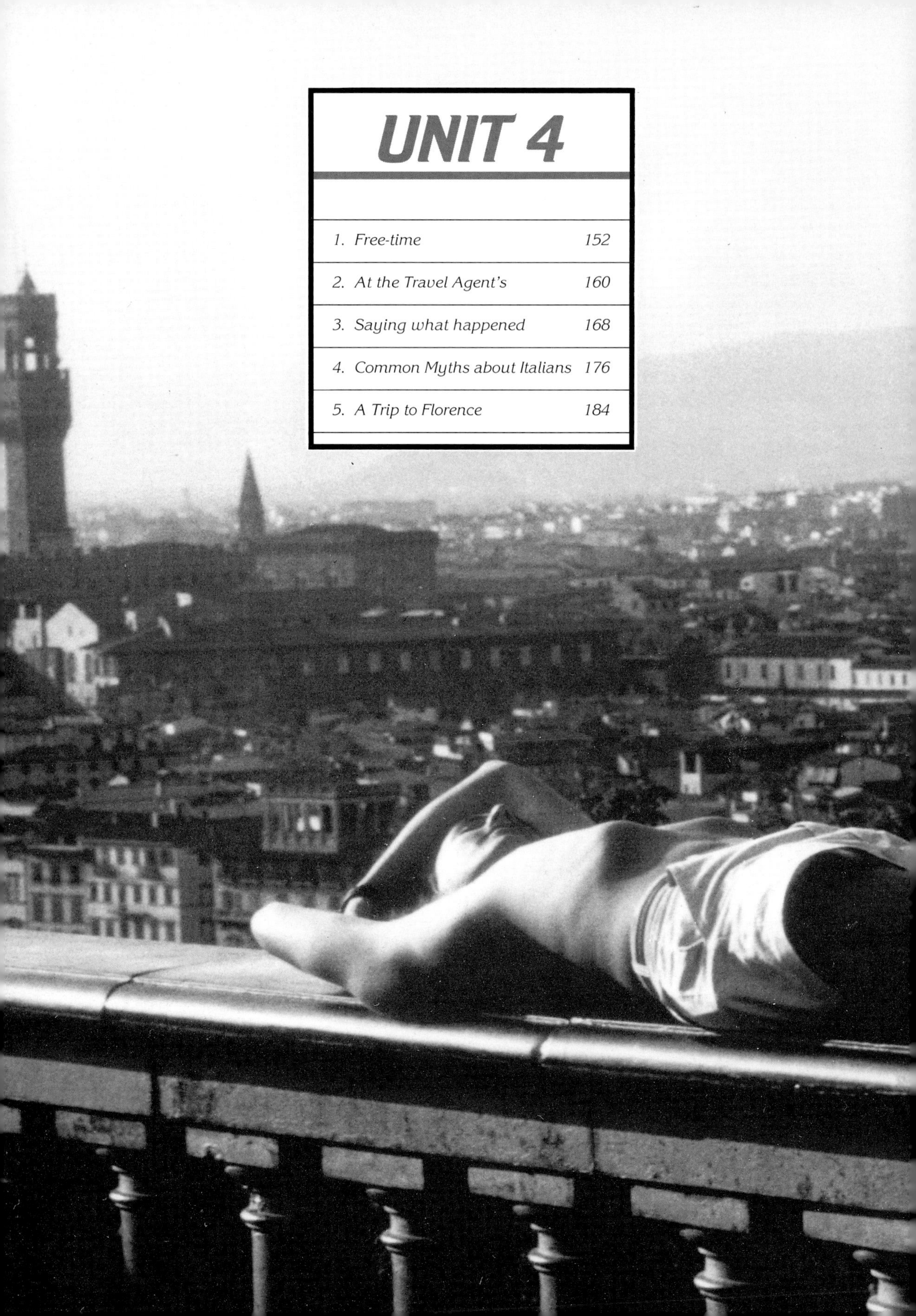

4.1 DIALOGUE

LISTEN

TEMPO LIBERO

We are in Florence. Mrs. Gili has invited Mrs. Rizzi to tea.

Signora Gili : *Ieri sono andata a iscrivere mia figlia a un corso di nuoto.*

Signora Rizzi : *Anche mia figlia fa nuoto. Va in piscina due o tre volte alla settimana.*

Signora Gili : *E Suo figlio?*

Signora Rizzi : *Mio figlio invece non è per niente sportivo, ma suona molto bene il violino.*

Signora Gili : *Davvero? Ah, la musica non è il nostro forte. In famiglia siamo tutti stonati! Però la mia figlia maggiore fa danza classica.*

Signora Rizzi : *Ma guarda! Anch'io quando ero giovane facevo danza e sognavo di diventare una grande ballerina!*

Signora Gili : *E come mai non ha continuato?*

Signora Rizzi : *Eh! I miei genitori non approvavano la mia scelta. Ma è sempre stato un mio grande rimpianto.*

Signotra Gili : *A volte è difficile essere genitori! Me ne rendo conto adesso che i miei figli stanno crescendo...*

Signora Rizzi : *Non me ne parli!*

Signora Gili : *Gradisce un'altra tazza di tè, signora?*

Signora Rizzi : *Grazie volentieri.*

Signora Gili : *Allora, avete poi deciso che cosa farete questo fine settimana?*

Signora Rizzi : *Come al solito andremo in montagna. Mio marito è un appassionato di sci.*

Signora Gili : *Noi, invece andremo in campagna dai miei.*

Signora Rizzi : *E per le vacanze che cosa fate?*

Signora Gili : *Non abbiamo ancora un programma preciso. Ci piacerebbe fare un viaggio...*

Signora Rizzi : *Noi volevamo andare in Sicilia : non ci siamo mai stati e sarebbe un'occasione per andare un po' alla spiaggia e nello stesso tempo fare anche del turismo.*

Signora Gili : *Perché non viene con me domani all'agenzia? Potremmo intanto informarci sui viaggi organizzati e farci un'idea dei prezzi.*

Signora Gili : *Con piacere.*

LISTEN AND REPEAT

You will find the translation on page 27 of the booklet.

Florence: the Badia church is in the foreground with the Bargello Museum behind.

4.1 VOCABULARY

NOUNS

il tempo libero — free time
il corso — class
il nuoto — swimming
la piscina — swimming pool
il violino — violin
la musica — music
la danza (classica, moderna) — dance (ballet, modern)
la ballerina — ballerina
la scelta — choice
il rimpianto — regret
il fine-settimana — weekend
l'appassionato/a — enthusiast/lover of (dance etc.)
lo sci — skiing
la vacanza — holiday
l'occasione (f) — opportunity
la spiaggia — beach
il turismo — tourism
l'agenzia (f) — agency
il viaggio organizzato — package holiday
la famiglia — family
i genitori — parents
i miei (i tuoi, i suoi, ecc .) — my (your, his etc.) relations
il padre — father
la madre — mother
il figlio maggiore — oldest son
il figlio minore — youngest son
il fratello — brother
la sorella — sister
il suocero — father-in-law
la suocera — mother-in-law

---

l'hobby (m) — hobby
lo sport — sport
il tennis — tennis
la vela — sailing
la ginnastica — gymnastics
l'equitazione (f) — horse riding
la scherma — fencing

VERBS

iscrivere (si) — to enrol/register
suonare (uno strumento) — to play (an instrument)
essere stonato — to sing off-key
sognare — to dream
approvare — to approve
rendersi conto — to realise
crescere — to grow
informarsi — to get information
farsi un'idea — to get an idea

---

fare sport — to do sport
chiacchierare — to chat
recitare (un ruolo) — to play (a role)
giocare (a) — to play (a game)

MISCELLANEOUS

per niente — not at all
davvero? — really?
non è il mio forte — It's not my strong point
come mai...? — how come?
gradisce una tazza di tè? — would you like a cup of tea? ***(1)***

HOW TO SAY IT

1. TALKING ABOUT SPORT

Mia figlia fa nuoto — My daughter goes swimming. ***(2)***
La mia figlia maggiore fa danza — My oldest daughter does ballet.
Mio marito è un appassionato di sci — My husband loves skiing.
Mia sorella gioca a tennis — My sister plays tennis.
Mio fratello fa vela — My brother goes sailing
Io non so sciare (nuotare, giocare a tennis, ecc.) — I can't ski (swim, play tennis, etc.) ***(3)***
I miei figli fanno molto sport — My children do a lot of sport.

2. ASKING SOMEONE IF THEY ENJOY SPORT

Fa qualche sport? — Do you do any sport? (informal)
Lei fa dello sport? — Do you do sport? (formal)
Che sport fa? — Which sports do you do?
Quale sport preferisce? — Which sport do you prefer?

3. TALKING ABOUT HOBBIES

Il mio hobby è la musica (la lettura, la fotografia) — My hobby is music (reading, photography.)
Suono il violino (il piano, la chitarra, la tromba) — I play the violin (piano, guitar, trumpet).

4. LEISURE TIME

Che cosa farete questo fine-settimana? — What are you doing this weekend?
Per le vacanze, che cosa fate? — What are you doing for the holidays?
Che programmi ha per le vacanze, signora? — What plans do you have for your holiday, Mrs. X/madam?

5. DESCRIBING YOUR HOLIDAY PLANS

Se farà bel tempo andrò al mare ***(4)*** — If the weather is nice, I'll go to the sea.
Come al solito andremo in montagna (in campagna) — As usual, we're going to the mountains (into the country).
Non abbiamo ancora un programma preciso — We haven't made definite plans yet.
Ci piacerebbe fare un viaggio — We'd like to take a trip.
Noi volevamo andare in Sicilia — We wanted to go to Sicily.

REMARKS REMARKS REMARKS REMARKS

(1) *"Gradire" means literally "to enjoy".* — ***(2)*** *For possessives without the article, see Grammar, D.1.* — ***(3)*** *Literally, "I don't know how to".* — ***(4)*** *In this kind of sentence, the two verbs are either both in the present or in the future.*

4.1 ORAL PRACTICE

1. THE IMPERFECT

LISTEN

Che cosa facevi quando eri giovane? - giocare a tennis

- *Quando ero giovane giocavo a tennis.*

Che cosa facevi ieri alle 5? - bere il tè

- *Ieri alle 5 bevevo il tè*

Continue answering the questions as in the model.

Che cosa facevi quando eri giovane? / giocare a tennis — Che cosa facevi ieri alle 5? / bere il tè — Che cosa faceva la signora Rizzi quando era giovane? / fare danza — Che cosa faceva Marco quando era piccolo? / andare in piscina — Che cosa facevano Claudio e Filippo ieri alle 8? / cenare — Che cosa facevi ieri alle 3? / leggere il giornale — Che cosa facevate quando eravate bambini? / suonare il violino

(See Grammar, L.9)

2. PRESENT PROGRESSIVE

STARE with GERUND

LISTEN

Io-mangio

- *Sto mangiando*

Lui-legge

- *Sta leggendo*

Put the verb in the present progressive

Io-mangio — Lui-legge — Noi-finiamo — Tu-scrivi — Voi-guardate la televione — Io-scherzo — Loro-bevono il tè — Lei-fuma una sigaretta — Noi-facciamo colazione — Tu-dici la verità — Lei-chiacchiera con una signora.

See Grammar, L.13.)

3. FUTURE CONDITIONAL USING "se"

LISTEN

Se fa bel tempo vado al mare

- *Se farà bel tempo andrò al mare.*

Put the sentences into the future.

Se fa bel tempo vado al mare — Se ho tempo vengo da te — Se posso ti telefono alle 8 — Se vieni ti diverti sicuramente — Se piove non usciamo — Se fa brutto tempo restate a casa.

(See Grammar, L.8)

4. POSSESSIVES

WITH MEMBERS OF THE FAMILY

LISTEN

Sorella

- *Questa è mia sorella*

Genitori

- *Questi sono i miei genitori*

Form sentences as in the model. Pay attention to the article used before the possessive adjective.

Sorella — Genitori — Marito — Moglie — Fratello — Padre — Figli — Madre — Figlie — Sorelle — Fratelli — Figlio.

(See Grammar, D.1)

5. I'D LIKE TO....

LISTEN

Fare un viaggio

- *Mi piacerebbe fare un viaggio.*

Continue saying that you would like to do the following things.

Fare un viaggio — Andare a sciare — Uscire con te — Suonare uno strumento — Visitare Firenze — Andare in Sicillia — Conoscere bene l'Italia — Giocare bene a tennis.

6. SAYING THE OPPOSITE

LISTEN

Mio figlio è sportivo

- *Il mio, invece, non è per niente sportivo.*

Mia moglie è stonata.

- *La mia, invece, non è per niente stonata.*

Continue as in the model.

Mio figlio è sportivo — Mia moglie è stonata — Il mio appartamento è grande — La mia macchina è veloce — La mia camera è spaziosa — La mia cucina è moderna — I miei genitori sono severi.

(See Grammar, L.)

FREE TIME

Free time is not the same as leisure time. On the contrary, one of the many facets of Italian life to-day is the increasing popularity of moonlighting. That is why many Italians, despite the official shorter working-day, are actually working more than ever. The phenomenon of the "secondo lavoro", with office clerks turning bricklayer, electrician, accountant, working, in short, in any number of ways totally unrelated to their normal job, is reckoned to involve as much as 40% of the working population.

It is a parallel world, one which is known about, even quantified, (there are attempts to include it in the statistics showing the nation's wealth), but which is run on different lines: nothing in writing, no legal safeguards, (though sometimes a moonlighter reports his underground employer, who is then liable to heavy penalties), no social security...but no taxes to pay either. It is undisputed that this sector, free from the strikes and absenteeism which dog the official sector, functions perfectly well, and, it is generally agreed, contributes usefully to the nation's wealth. Some people would go as far as to say that it is a key element in Italy's economic expansion.

Do not make the mistake, however, of thinking that these pioneers of free enterprise are so busy beavering in the moonlight that they never have any time to enjoy themselves. Quite the contrary: the Italians' talent for having a good time is renowned, and especially their love of all kinds of celebrations .

One of the main entertainments of Homo Italicus , and one which is transformed into a mass-celebration, is "calcio" (football); essentially a male domain, it has many of the features of a religious rite. There was even an old song, in which a woman lamented: "La domenica, mi lasci sempre sola", ("you always desert me on Sundays"). Every "partita" is sure of attracting ardent support from spectactors who are dedicated "tifosi" (fans) of one or other of the teams. With television and radio, it is, of course, possible to follow the match at home, but whether it is with noisy bands of "tifosi", or alone at home, the "partita" is an important event on Sunday afternoons in Italy. So just imagine what it is like when the Italian national team is participating in the European cup! Fervour is turned to delirium, as the players enshrine the Hope of the Nation.

This frantic passion for football has given rise to "Totocalcio", like the football pools in the U.K. and elsewhere. It is followed with the same close interest, with vast numbers of people, many of whom would not normally dream of betting, joining in, in the vague hope of winning one of the huge prices.

Who can tell where the Italians got this passion for gambling, and for sporting events which lend themselves to the form of tribal jubilation beloved of the "tifosi"? Some might say that they inherited it directly from the Ancient Romans, who loved both gaming and the games in the circus. While on the subject of games, it should not be forgotten that certain card games are also very popular, such as "scopa".

But "calcio", sport in general, cards, whatever, are not enough to distract Italians' attention from the thousand and one "feste" that punctuate the year. Traditional feast-days, of historic or religious origin, such as the Carnivals of Venice, Viareggio or Ivrea, Sienna's Palio, Venice's Feast of the Redeemer; humbler festivals, more akin to village fetes, where there is eating and drinking on a grand scale: free gnocchi, sausages, fish, wine: one such is the famous Sagra del Pesce, which takes place every year in Camogli, on the Ligurian Riviera, where fish are fried in an enormous pan kept on the quayside.

All these lively "feste", whether traditional or recent, have this in common: they are all celebrated with the maximun gaiety and high spirits, everybody joining in, united in their determination to have a really wonderful time!

4.1 TAKE-A-BREAK

No. 1 LISTEN

Check off all the sports mentioned in the taped conversations

EQUITAZIONE ☐

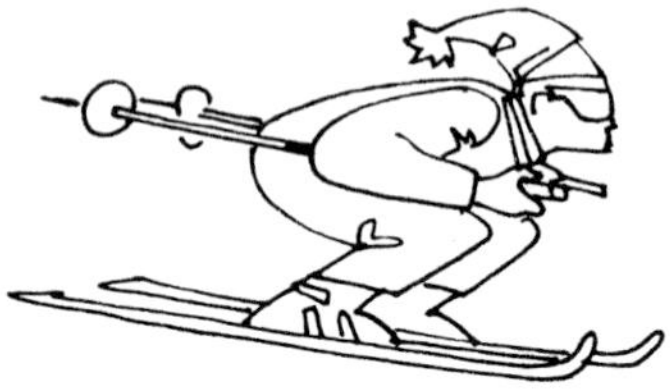

SCI ☐

JUDO ☐

PALLACANESTRO ☐

CALCIO ☐

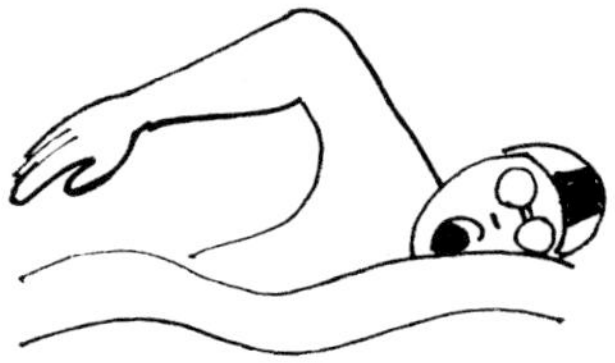

NUOTO ☐

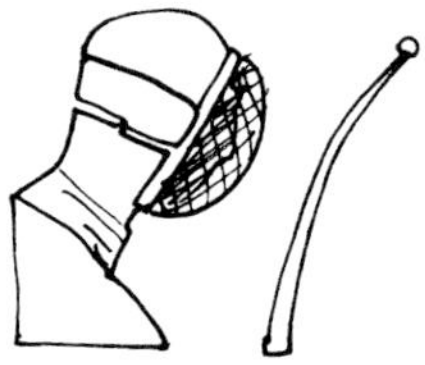

SCHERMA ☐

VELA ☐

CICLISMO ☐

DANZA ☐

TENNIS ☐

PATTINAGGIO ☐

No. 2

Match each drawing with the missing object. *1. Racchetta* ***2.*** *Pallone* ***3.*** *Sci* ***4.*** *Fioretto* ***5.*** *Cavallo* ***6.*** *Pattini* ***7.*** *Bicicletta* ***8.*** *Vela*

PROVERBIO

LISTEN

L'ozio è il padre dei vizi
(lit., Idleness is the father of all vices)

The Devil finds work for idle hands.

(Answers on page 28 of the booklet)

4.2 DIALOGUE

LISTEN

ALL' AGENZIA DI VIAGGI

GIRO DELLA SICILIA

1° giorno : Arrivo a Palermo. Sistemazione in autopullman. Visita di Segeste e Selinunte. Nel pomeriggio visita della zona archeologica. In serata si raggiunge Agrigento. Pernottamento in hotel.

2° giorno : Visita della Valle dei Templi. Escursione panoramica lungo la costa nel pomeriggio. Dopo cena visita ai monumenti illuminati.

3° giorno : Partenza per Catania. All'arrivo visita della città. In serata partenza per Taormina.

4° giorno : Visita di Taormina e del teatro. Nel pomeriggio partenza per l'Etna, dove si potranno ammirare la zona dei crateri e i campi di lava.

5° giorno : Siracusa. Visita della città e pomeriggio a disposizione.

6° giorno : Proseguimento per Messina. Giro della città. Nel pomeriggio partenza per Palermo.

7° giorno : In mattinata visita del chiostro di Monreale. 2ª colazione in albergo e trasferimento all'aeroporto.

Mrs. Rizzi and Mrs. Gili have arranged to meet at a travel agent's to get information on a package tour of Sicily.

L'impiegato : *Viaggi organizzati in Sicilia? Ma naturalmente! Abbiamo diverse formule, da una settimana o da 15 giorni, o anche di più se vuole.*

Signora Rizzi : *No, no. Una settimana va bene. Però non vorrei rimanere fissa in un posto. Vorrei visitare un po' di tutto...*

L'impiegato : *Guardi questo giro della Sicilia, per esempio : è molto vario. Eccole il dépliant dettagliato.*

Signora Rizzi : *Grazie, me ne dia due, per cortesia.*

Signora Gili : *Vediamo...sì...Il primo giorno nel pomeriggio c'è una visita della zona archeologica a Segeste e a Selinunte.*

Signora Rizzi : *Oh! Si visita Agrigento e c'è anche una visita ai monumenti illuminati, dopo cena...*

Signora Gili : *Non è male! Si visita anche Taormina, che deve essere splendida!*

Signora Rizzi : *Ma la cosa che mi attira di più, è l'escursione all'Etna.*

Signora Gili : *Ah sì! Ho sentito dire che è impressionante!*

Signora Rizzi : *Insomma, che cosa ne pensa? Mi sembra un viaggio magnifico!*

Signora Gili : *E un po' caro, però...*

L'impiegato : *No, non lo è, se Lei considera che gli alberghi in cui soggiornerete sono tutti di prima categoria, con piscina e aria condizionata, e il prezzo è per la pensione completa.*

Signora Rizzi : *In effetti è vero.*

Signora Gili : *Comunque grazie, Lei è stato molto gentile. Rifletteremo e torneremo per prenotare, eventualmente.*

LISTEN AND REPEAT

You will find the translation on page 28 of the booklet.

Sicily:
1. A religious festival in Capizzi
2. Taormina beach
3. Greek ruins in Selinunte
4. Agrigento

2

4.2 VOCABULARY

NOUNS

l'agenzia (f) di viaggi — travel agent's
la formula — formula
il dépliant — brochure
la visita — visit
la sistemazione — arrangement
la zona archeologica — archaeological site
il pernottamento — a night's stay
l'escursione (f) — excursion
la costa — coast
il monumento — monument
il cratere — crater
la lava — lava
il proseguimento — the continuation (of the tour)
il giro della città — tour of the city
il chiostro — cloister
il trasferimento — transfer
l'aria condizionata — air conditioning
la pensione completa — full board

---

la guida — guide
il circuito — circuit/tour
l'itinerario (m) — route/itinerary
la cartina geografica — map
la piantina della città — town-plan
il vulcano — volcano
l'isola (f) — island
la penisola — peninsular
la mezza pensione — half board
l'autopullman (il pullman) — coach
il campaggio — camp-site
l'ufficio del turismo (m) — tourist office

ADJECTIVES

diverso — different/diverse ***(1)***
uguale — the same
vario — various
dettagliato — detailed
illuminato — well lit (floodlit)
splendido — splendid
impressionante — impressive
magnifico — magnificent

VERBS

rimanere fisso — to stay in one place
raggiungere — to reach
ammirare — to admire
considerare — to consider
soggiornare — to stay
riflettere — to think over/reflect

MISCELLANEOUS

anche di più — even more
me ne dia due — give me two (of them)
non è male! — it's not bad!
di prima categoria — first class/five-star
a disposizione — available
in serata — during the evening
in mattinata — during the morning
in giornata — during the day
nel pomeriggio — during the afternoon
1ª colazione — breakfast ***(2)***
2ª colazione — lunch ***(2)***

HOW TO SAY IT

1. SAYING WHERE AND WHEN YOU WANT TO GO

Vorrei andare in Sicilia — I'd like to go to Sicily.
Vorrei visitare la zona archeologica — I'd like to visit the archaeological site.
Vorrei partire durante le vacanze di Natale (di Pasqua) — I'd like to go during the Christmas (Easter) holidays.
Vorrei partire d'estate (d'inverno, in autunno, in primavera) — I'd like to go in the summer (winter, autumn, spring)
Vorrei restare a Taormina per 15 giorni — I'd like to stay 15 days in Taormina. ***(3)***

2. ASKING ABOUT PACKAGE TOURS

Che cosa comprende il prezzo? — What does the price include?
Di che categoria è l'albergo? — What category of hotel is it?
Sono previste delle escursioni? — Are any excursions planned?
I trasferimenti sono in treno o in pullman? — Are the trips by train or by coach?

3. AT THE TOURIST OFFICE

Mi può dare una piantina della città — Can you give me a plan of the city?
Quali sono gli orari dei musei? — What are the opening-hours of the museum?
Qual è il giorno di chiusura dei musei? — What is the museums' closing-day?

4. DESCRIBING WHERE PLACES ARE

L'albergo è a 10 chilometri dall'aeroporto — The hotel is 10 kilometres from the airport.
Siracusa è nel sud della Sicilia — Syracuse is in the south of Sicily.
Enna e Caltanisetta sono nell'interno — Enna and Caltanisetta are inland.
Taormina è sulla costa — Taormina is on the coast.

5. GIVING AN OPINION

Mi sembra un itinerario magnifico — Its seems to be a marvellous itinerary
Sono posti bellissimi — They are really beautiful places.
È un'escursione interessantissima — It's an extremely interesting excursion.

REMARKS REMARKS REMARKS REMARKS

(1) *This means both "different" and "several". —* ***(2)*** *You will hear these terms mainly in hotels. "Lunch" is normally called "pranzo". —* ***(3)*** *"durante" is used for a period of time, (the summer, the holidays,) "per" for a length (a week, two years).*

4.2 ORAL PRACTICE

1. SAYING HOW MANY YOU WANT

LISTEN

Mi dia un dépliant, per cortesia
- *Me ne dia uno, per cortesia*

Mi dia una piantina, per cortesia
- *Me ne dia una, per cortesia*

Continue as in the model.
Mi dia un dépliant, per cortesia — Mi dia una piantina, per cortesia — Mi dia due cartoline, per cortesia — Mi dia 10 francobolli, per cortesia — Mi dia una busta, per cortesia — Mi dia due pacchetti di sigarette, per cortesia.

(See Grammar, E.3.)

2. ACCEPTING SOMETHING

OBJECT PRONOUNS

LISTEN

Le do un depliant?
- *Si, me lo dia.*

Le do una piantina?
- *Si, me la dia.*

Answer "yes", as in the model.
Le do un dépliant? — Le do una piantina? — Le do i francobolli? — Le do le buste? — Le do il giornale? — Le do gli orari dei musei? — Le do la cartina dell'isola? — Le do l'orario dei treni? — Le do i nomi degli alberghi? — Le do la ricevuta?

(See Grammar, E.4)

3. SAYING IT'S IN FRONT OF....

LISTEN

Dov'è la spiaggia? - albergo
- *La spiaggia è davanti all'albergo*

Continue answering in this way.
Dov'è la spiaggia? / albergo — Dov'è la fermata dell'autobus? / tabaccaio — Dov'è il museo? / ufficio del turismo — Dov'è la casa? / farmacia — Dov'è l'albergo? / stazione?

(See Grammar, F.)

4. SAYING IT'S A LONG WAY AWAY

LISTEN

L'albergo è vicino al centro?
- *No, è lontano dal centro*

Continue answering in this way.
L'albergo è vicino al centro? — L'albergo è vicino alla stazione? — Il museo è vicino all'ufficio del turismo? — La casa è vicino al mare? — La spiaggia è vicino al campeggio? — L'albergo è vicino alla fermata dell'autobus?

(See Grammar, F.)

5. INDEFINITE QUANTITIES

LISTEN

Ho passato alcuni giorni a Taormina
- *Ho passato qualche giorno a Taormina*

Change the sentences by replacing "alcuni" with "qualche".
Ho passato alcuni giorni a Taormina — Ho comprato alcune riviste — Ho visitato alcuni musei — Ho conosciuto alcune persone — Ho spedito alcune cartoline — Sono andato in alcune agenzie — Ho chiesto alcune informazioni — Ho visitato alcune città.

(See Grammar, I.)

6. THE SUPERLATIVE

LISTEN

Il pullman è moderno?
- *Sì, è modernissimo!*

L'escursione è interessante?
- *Sì, è interessantissima!*

Answer the questions by using the superlative, as in the model.
Il pullman è moderno? — L'escursione è interessante? — Il viaggio è bello? — La formula è cara? — La guida è brava? — I trasferimenti sono corti? — Le spiaggie sono belle? — La ragazza è giovane? — Gli italiani sono simpatici?

(See Grammar, H.2.)

THE LENGTH AND BREADTH OF THE BOOT

The Italians have always been intrepid travellers. It was true of the past: everybody has heard of the Venetian, Marco Polo, of the Genoese, Christopher Columbus, and of the Florentine, Amerigo Vespucci, who graciously bequeathed his name to the New World. It is true of the present: of all the European Community, it is the Italians who travel the most outside their own frontiers. But they also travel widely within them: trips to lap up the culture, to eat the local delicacies, to take the waters, the Boot of Italy is trampled along its whole length and breadth, its country inns bursting every Sunday with trippers.

This delight in visiting their own country is made all the easier by an extensive network of motorways, one of the oldest, (first started by Mussolini for military purposes), and largest in Europe. The Po Valley especially has been criss-crossed by a veritable spider's web of motorways, considerably reducing the travelling time between the different regions.

What is the reason for all this to-ing and fro-ing, round and round their own country, up and down the same mountains (there are so many of them! Italy must be the European country best endowed with tunnels and viaducts)? It's perfectly simple: Italy is overflowing with beautiful things, both natural and man-made, with certain place-names, like Capri and Venice, casting their spells way, way beyond Italy's frontiers.

More than one kind of journey can be made in Italy. Geographically,

you can go from the "African" droughts of Sicily, to the "Swiss" lushness of the Alps. Linguistically, three of the great European language groups are to be found in Italy: Italian itself, of course, which comes from Latin, along with Sard and the French spoken in the Val d'Aosta; there is German in the Alto Adige, (the High Tyrol, as the Austrians call it); and there is too a Slavonic-speaking group, centred on the famous frontier town of Trieste and its surrounding area.

Last but not least, there are the journeys through time. So many cities, starting with Rome, so many places of all kinds in Italy, lead the traveller back into the past. Think of Rome, Pompeli, Herculaneum, Etruscan Tuscany, the magnificent complex of early Christian and mediaeval churches and chapels at Santo Stefano in Bologna, Florence and the Renaissance, the Roman remains scattered throughout the country...

The region with the most dramatic "time-warp" is also the most exotic: Sicily. This is partly because it is separated from the main-land, partly because of its climate, (the sirocco blows straight from the Sahara, often laden with sand) but also because of the island's troubled history. Sicily has been Greek, Byzantine, Arab, Norman, and each conqueror left different traces on the countryside and new strata in the minds of the Sicilians. So it is that Sicily is the most "Greek" of all Western European countries, with temples at Agrigento, Segeste and Selinunte and amphi-theatres at Taormina and Syracuse.

So for the best time-travelling, Sicily and the whole of the South offer the richest diversity, every invasion, every occupying power having left its mark: Arabo-Norman churches, like San Giovanni degli Eremiti in Palermo, castles, Norman (in Palermo), Swabian (Frederick II's famous Castel del Monte in Puglia), churches and palaces in typical Spanish baroque, and so forth.

Sometimes, though, minds are more interesting than places and things. Northern Italians are especially drawn to Naples, not so much for its architecture, nor even Vesuvius, but for the mentality, the philosophy of the Neapolitans. Northerners are both fascinated and repelled by them, and there is even a literary genre devoted to them, like Luciano de Crescenzo's popular "Così parlò Bellavista", which became a best-seller.

So it is that, driven by a passionate pride in the splendours of their country, and a deep curiosity to probe the mysteries of their fellow countrymen, Italians are forever on the move.

4.2 TAKE-A-BREAK

No. 1 LISTEN

Which dates have been booked for these holidays? Fill in the gaps.

A

1 ☐

B

2 ☐

C

3 ☐

D

4 ☐

No. 2

Weather forecast! Examine this weather map of Italy, and then circle each statement as either "vero" or "falso".

1. *Al nord la temperatura massima è di 21 gradi.* V F
2. *Il mar Ionio è mosso* .... V F
3. *Nelle regioni settentrionali (al nord) il cielo è coperto con piogge abbondanti* .... V F
4. *In Sicilia il cielo è nuvoloso* .... V F
5. *In Sicilia la temperatura massima è di 27 gradi.* V F

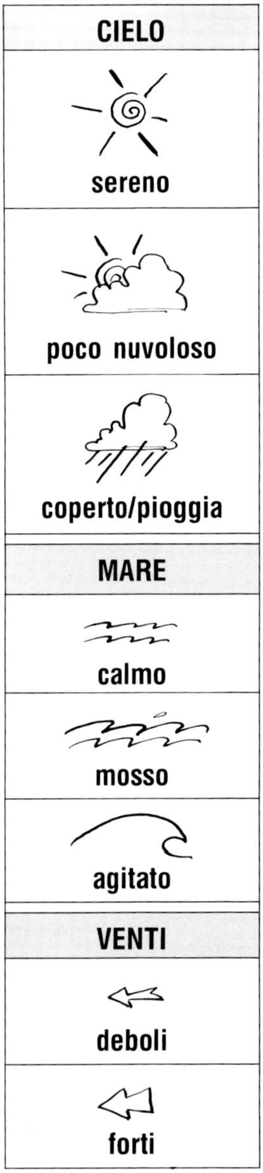

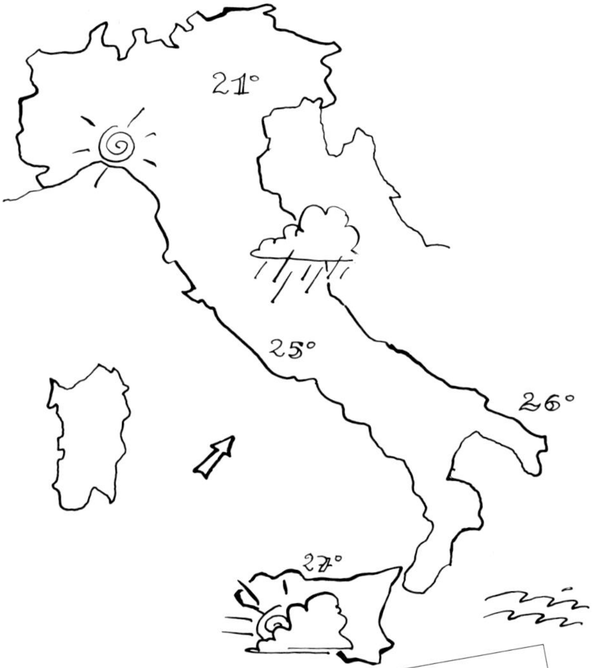

PROVERBIO

LISTEN

Rosso di sera bel tempo si spera
(lit., A red sunset indicates good weather)

Red sky at night, shepherd's delight

(Answers on page 29 of the booklet)

4.3 DIALOGUE

LISTEN

RACCONTARE UN'ESPERIENZA

When he gets home, Mr. Rizzi tells his wife what happened to him that afternoon.

Lei : *Come mai ritorni così tardi? Hai l'aria sconvolta! Che cosa è successo?*

Lui : *Non me ne parlare! Sai che oggi dovevo andare dall'avvocato. Ho preso l'autobus perché in centro è impossibile parcheggiare e mentre ero sull'autobus mi hanno rubato il portafoglio...*

Lei : *Oh, accidenti! C'erano molti soldi dentro?*

Lui : *No, per fortuna avevo solo 40,000 lire, ma c'erano tutti i documenti...*

Lei : *Ma come è successo?*

Lui : *Guarda, non te lo so dire: era l'ora di punta. Come al solito l'autobus era molto affollato. A un certo punto qualcuno mi ha dato una spinta mentre l'autobus frenava, ma io non ci ho fatto caso. Mi sono accorto che non avevo più il portafoglio solo dopo.*

Lei : *Dove lo avevi messo?*

Lui : *Nella tasca dei pantaloni, come sempre. Mi sono accorto che non c'era più solamente quando sono sceso. Sono andato a prendere un caffè con l'avvocato, e al momento di pagare...non ti dico il mio imbarazzo! Il portafoglio: sparito!*

Lei : *Ma non hai visto il ladro?*

Lui : *Ma no, se ti dico che non mi sono reso conto di niente! Con tutta la gente che c'era...e poi probabilmente il ladro è sceso subito.*

Lei : *Hai sporto denuncia, almeno?*

Lui : *Naturalmente, anche se penso che non serva a molto.*

Lei : *Speriamo che il ladro ti restituisca i documenti, a volte capita.*

Lui : *Ah! che rabbia!*

Lei : *Non ti arrabbiare, dai! Sono cose che capitano! In fondo non è grave.*

Lui : *Hai ragione, però è talmente sgradevole subire un furto, soprattutto in un modo così stupido!*

Lei : *Ma sei sicuro di non averlo dimenticato a casa? Ora che ci penso mi sembra di averlo visto sul mobile dell'ingresso...*

Lui : *Ma no! È impossibile...*

Lei : *E questo che cos'è?*

Lui : *Santo cielo! È proprio il mio portafoglio! Ero così sicuro di averlo preso...*

LISTEN AND REPEAT

You will find the translation on page 30 of the booklet.

1. The Gilli bar (Florence)
2. Giotto's famous Campanile
3. Rooftops
4. A bar in the Piazza della Signoria
5. A typical Florentine street
6. On the Ponte Vecchio

1

2

3

4

5

6

4.3 VOCABULARY

NOUNS

l'esperienza (f) — experience
l'aria (f) — air
il portafoglio — wallet
l'ora di punta (f) — rush hour
la tasca — pocket
i pantaloni (m.pl) — trousers
l'imbarazzo (m) — embarassment
il ladro — thief
la denuncia — report (to the police)
il furto — theft
il modo — way/manner
il mobile — piece of furniture
l'ingresso (m) — entrance

---

il borsellino — purse
la rapina — robbery
il rapinatore — robber
lo scippo — pickpocketing
la polizia — police
la questura — police station
il poliziotto — policeman

ADJECTIVES

sconvolto — distressed
affollato — crowded
grave — grave, serious
gradevole/sgradevole — pleasant/unpleasant
stupido/intelligente — stupid/intelligent

VERBS

raccontare — to tell
succedere — to happen
parcheggiare — to park
rubare — to rob/steal
dare una spinta — to give a shove/push
farci caso — to pay attention
accorgersi — to realise
sparire — to disappear
rendersi conto — to realise
sporgere denuncia — to report to the police
restituire — to give back
capitare — to happen
arrabbiarsi — to get angry
subire — to undergo
dimenticare — to forget

MISCELLANEOUS

così — so
mentre — while
accidenti! — damn!
per fortuna — luckily
che rabbia! — how maddening!
dai! — give over! ***(1)***
probabilmente — probably
almeno — at least
a volte — at times
in fondo — in the end
talmente — so
Santo cielo! — Heavens!
proprio — really

HOW TO SAY IT

1. ASKING WHAT HAPPENED

Che cosa è successo? (che cosa è capitato?) — What happened?
Che cosa ti è successo? (che cosa ti è capitato? — What happened to you?

2. SAYING WHAT HAPPENED

È successo questo — This is what happened.
Non è successo niente — Nothing happened.
Mi è capitato un fatto strano — Something strange happened to me.
Mi hanno rubato il portafoglio — They stole my wallet.
Ho subito un furto — I was victim of a theft.

3. LETTING OFF STEAM

Che rabbia! — It's infuriating!
Accidenti! — Blast!
Non me ne parlare! — Don't ask!
Che sfortuna! — What bad luck

4. CALMING SOMEONE DOWN

Non ti arrabbiare, dai! — Come on, don't be so angry!
In fondo non è grave! — All in all, it's not serious!
Sono cose che capitano! — These things happen.

5. PROMPTING SOMEONE .....

E poi? — And then?
E allora? — And so?
Ma come è successo? — However did it happen?
Quando è successo? — When did it happen?
Dove è successo? — Where did it happen?
Come è finita? — How did it all end?

6. EXPRESSING YOUR OPINION

Penso (credo) di sì — I think so
Penso (credo) di no — I don't think so.
Penso che non serva a molto — I think it's pointless. ***(2)***
Credo che sia vero — I believe it is true. ***(2)***

REMARKS REMARKS REMARKS REMARKS

(1) This is used only in informal speech. — (2) Verbs that express opinion/point of view take the subjunctive. See Grammar, L.11.

4.3 ORAL PRACTICE

1. SAYING WHAT HAPPENED

LISTEN

Rubare il portafoglio

- *Mi hanno rubato il portafoglio*

Continue saying what happened.

Rubare il portafoglio — Rubare la valigia — Accusare di furto — Seguire per strada — Ritirare la patente — Dare una spinta — Dire che non c'è posto — Dare l'orario sbagliato.

(See Grammar , L.)

2. BEING FORMAL

WITH DOUBLE PRONOUNS

LISTEN

Non te lo so dire

- *Non glielo so dire*

Change these sentences into formal speach.

Non te lo so dire — Non te lo so spiegare — Non te lo so precisare — Non te lo so descrivere — Non te lo so indicare — Non te lo so raccontare — Non te lo so dire.

(See Grammar, E.4.)

3. OFFERING HELP (FORMAL)

LISTEN

Chi mi da la valigia?

- *Gliela do io*

Chi mi indica l'albergo?

- *Glielo indico io*

Continue offering help as in the model.

Chi mi da la valigia? — Chi mi indica l'albergo? — Chi mi apre la porta? — Chi mi da il libro? — Chi mi compra i biglietti? — Chi mi prenota le camere? — Chi mi offre una sigaretta? — Chi mi indica la fermata dell'autobus?

(See Grammar, E.4.)

4. GIVING ORDERS

NEGATIVE FORMS (using 'tu')

LISTEN

Compra il giornale!

- *Non comprare il giornale!*

Spedisci la lettera!

- *Non spedire la lettera!*

Put these orders into the negative.

Compra il giornale! — Spedisci la lettera! — Leggi il libro! — Prendi il treno! — Bevi il caffè! — Attraversa la strada! — Fai le valigie! — Di la verità! — Va'a teatro!

(See Grammar L.10)

5. THE PRESENT SUBJUNCTIVE

ESSERE/AVERE

LISTEN

È vero?

- *Penso che sia vero*

Ha ragione?

- *Penso che abbia ragione*

Continue saying what you think, using "pensare" followed by the subjunctive.

È vero? — Ha ragione? — È italiano? — Ha 20 anni? — È interessante? — È giovane? — Ha l'aria condizionata? — È faticoso? — È sposato? — Ha la macchina? — È avvocato?

(See Grammar L.11)

6. EXPRESSING NEED

"BISOGNA" SUBJUNCTIVE

LISTEN

Mi dia un documento!

- *Bisogna che Lei mi dia un documento*

Mi ascolti!

- *Bisogna che Lei mi ascolti*

Change the sentences as in the model.

Mi dia un documento! — Mi ascolti! — Mi dica la verità — Mi faccia un favore! — Mi accompagni alla stazione! — Mi telefoni alle 9! — Mi compri il giornale! — Mi dia un consiglio! — Mi capisca!

(Se Grammar, L.11)

WHEN THE LIGHTS ARE FOREVER AMBER

It is a curious thing, that colours seem to change from country to country, an extension perhaps of the grass being greener. Italians call egg-yolks "red", but they also call the colour between red and green on their quaintly named semafori (traffic-lights) "yellow", rather than "orange" or "amber"... which probably has nothing to do with what, to foreign eyes at least, appears to be the complete pandemonium of their traffic system.

Why exactly do foreign visitors go on so about the traffic in Italy? Because it is a major problem in the cities: Italy may be larger than, for instance, the U.K., but its population is about the same, and much more concentrated in the urban areas. Italy is a country with wide open spaces, dotted with a multiplicity of seething towns.

The "macchina" is every Italian's sacred right. What started in the fifties and sixties as a status symbol has become part of life. Gone are the days when foreigners thought of Italy as the land of the small car, of the Fiat 500, and the endearingly named "Topolino". The variety of cars found in Italy today is as wide as anywhere in Europe, the only difference being the continuing popularity of two-wheeled vehicles, with the Vespa, as always, taking the lion's share.

FIAT (Fabbrica Italiana Automobili Torino) , belonging to one of Europe's great industrial dynasties, the Agnelli, has played a prominent part in the economic development of the country, not least in creating

jobs, and drawing its labour-force from every part of Italy. Fiat's empire has now spread throughout the European community, building lorries as well as cars.

At the other end of the scale, Italy is also synonymous with some of the most fast, stylish, luxurious ... in short, most prestigious cars ever made: legendary names like Alfa-Romeo, Lamborghini, Maserati and Ferrari.

From the race-track to the street is but an imaginative leap, although these days, the traffic barely moves at all, let alone with any degree of speed. This is because, like everywhere else, everyone in Italy wants to use their car at the same time. What is more, because of their eating habits, described in a previous chapter, there are not two daily rush-hours, but four! In cities like Rome, the volume of traffic, with its attendant pollution problems, (especially the corrosion it causes to buildings), is calamitous. They have been forced from time to time to introduce a system whereby cars are only allowed on the roads on certain days, according to their registration number: one day for even numbers, next day for odd numbers.

As far as the actual driving is concerned, beware! The way in which the Romans, Neapolitans and Palermians drive may be surprising, but the idea of the typical Italian as one who drives like a maniac, hooting incessantly, and jumping the lights, is just the sort of preconception best treated with caution. Interestingly enough, it is one of the pictures that Northern Italians have of the South.

And let's be fair: in major cities everywhere, drivers are un-disciplined, ill-tempered, agressive, and heavy-handed on the horn. In some of the cities of Northern Italy particularly, where there are excellent traffic directions, respected by the drivers in general, the foreign visitor may feel very much safer than on his home ground.

Nevertheless, there is still a sharp contrast between the driving found in the North and in the South. Once Rome is behind you, such things as "Stop" signs and traffic-lights are more or less ornamental and not intended to be obeyed, and the horn becomes a legitimate way of asserting your existence. Natural selection has ensured that the policemen accept this situation as normal, and would not dream that elsewhere such banalities could be worthy of comment.

Neapolitans, with their easy-going attitude to life, would argue that it is relationships between people which are the main thing, and that the lights are not there to order anyone about, but to remind them, gently, to be careful: you do not have to stop just because the lights are red, but it might be as well to remember that, on the other side, somebody else has not stopped just because they are green.

4.3 TAKE-A-BREAK

No. 1 LISTEN

Fill in Mr. Cammelli's statement, by ticking off the stolen goods.

DENUNCIA DI FURTO

COGNOME E NOME : . . . .

DATA DEL FURTO : . . . . 1999 . . . .

ORA (APPROSSIMATIVA) IN CUI È AVVENUTO

IL FURTO . . . .

OGGETTI RUBATI :

- Argenteria ☐
- Elettrodomestici ☐
- Mobili ☐
- Quadri ☐
- Tappeti ☐
- Pellicce ☐
- Gioielli ☐
- Impianto Stereo ☐
- Dischi ☐
- Televisore a colori ☐
- Televisore bianco e nero ☐
- Vestiti ☐
- Libri ☐
- Macchina fotografica ☐

Altri . . . .

No. 2

Anagram. By rearranging the letters of the following words you will get the name (first and second) of a famous international thief.
LUI, NIRO PENSA...

. . . .

No. 3

Dingbat.

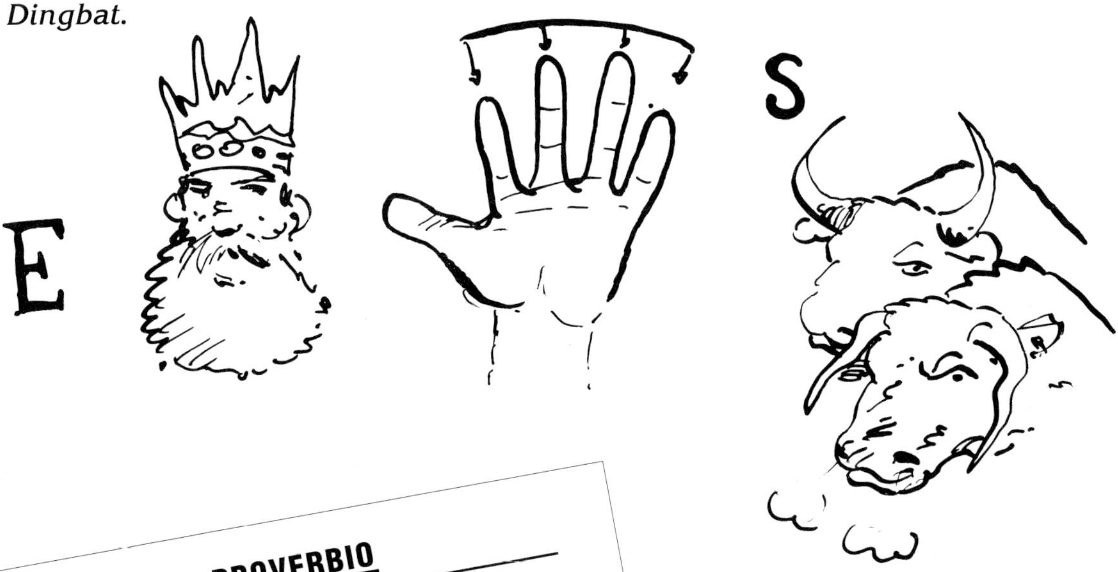

CA

PROVERBIO

LISTEN

La casa nasconde ma non ruba
(lit., A house may conceal, but never steal)

Things lost at home always come to light

(Answers on page 31 of the booklet)

4.4 DIALOGUE

LISTEN

LUOGHI COMUNI SUGLI ITALIANI

The Rizzi are at a cocktail party. It is an international gathering, and the conversation turns to the differences between various nationalities.

Signora Rizzi : *E così Lei è convinto che gli italiani siano pigri…è questa dunque la reputazione che abbiamo all'estero!*

L'inglese : *Non solo pigri! Nel mio paese si pensa che gli italiani siano tutti romantici, espansivi e un po' mafiosi… Naturalment si tratta solo di luoghi comuni, e immagino che in Italia ci siano altrettanti luoghi comuni sugli inglese…*

Signora Rizzi : *In effetti, prima di andare in Inghilterra credevo che tutti gli inglesi fossero freddi, seri e portassero la bombetta e l'ombrello in tutte le stagioni.*

L'inglese : *E adesso ha cambiato idea?*

Signora Rizzi : *Diciamo che ho imparato a non generalizzare, anche se penso che ci sia sempre un fondo di verità in tutti i luoghi comuni…*

Il tedesco : *E che cosa si dice dei tedeschi? Sono curioso di saperlo.*

Signora Rizzi : *Oh! I tedeschi hanno la fama di essere disciplinati, alti, biondi e con gli occhi azzurri, e appassionati di musica.*

Il tedesco : *Da noi si pensa che gli italiani, invece, siano tutti piccoli di statura, bruni, con gli occhi neri e la carnagione scura e mangino solo spaghetti…*

Il francese : *Scusate se mi intrometto nella vostra conversazione, ma l'argomento mi interessa: mia piacerebbe sapere che cosa si dice sui francesi…*

Signora Rizzi : *Sui francesi…non saprei dirLe. Chiediamolo a mio marito, che li conosce bene.*

Signor Rizzi : *Forse sono un po' meno espansivi di noi, però hanno la fama di essere simpatici, raffinati e buongustai. Io credo che in realtà siamo molto simili e se potessi vivrei volentieri in Francia.*

Signora Rizzi : *E che cosa faresti senza la tua mamma?*

Signor Rizzi : *Mia moglie mi prende in giro perché qui in Italia siamo tutti un po' mammoni, ma la Francia è un paese che mi attira molto…*

LISTEN AND REPEAT

You will find the translation on page 32 of the booklet.

1. Florence
2. Palazzo della Signoria
3. David and Perseus
4. A Florentine signorina
5. The Neptune Fountain, Piazza della Signoria

3

2

4

5

4.4 VOCABULARY

NOUNS

i luoghi comuni (m.pl) — commonplaces/clichés
la reputazione — reputation
l'estero (m) — abroad
la bombetta — bowler hat
l'ombrello (m) — umbrella
la stagione — season
la fama — reputation/fame
la statura — height ***(1)***
la carnagione — complexion
la conversazione — conversation
l'argomento (m) — topic
il buongustaio — gourmet
la mamma — mummy
il mammone — mummy's boy

---

il papà — daddy
l'ambiente (f) — setting/ambiance
il popolo — the people/population
la caratteristica — characteristic
le parti del corpo umano — parts of the human body
la mano — hand ***(2)***
il braccio — arm ***(3)***
la testa — head
la vita — waist
la pelle — skin
il peso — weight
(more words on p.145)

ADJECTIVES

pigro — lazy
romantico — romantic
espansivo — extrovert
serio — serious
disciplinato — disciplined
alto/basso — tall/short
grasso/magro — fat/lean, slim ***(4)***
biondo, bruno. rosso, castano — blond, dark, red, auburn (haired)
scuro/chiaro — dark/light
raffinato — refined
simile — similar

VERBS

trattarsi — to deal with
immaginare — to imagine/suppose
cambiare idea — to change one's mind
generalizzare — to generalise
imparare — to learn
insegnare — to teach
avere la fama (di) — to have the reputation (of)
intromettersi — to join in
prendere in giro (qualcuno) — to pull someone's leg/to tease
attirare — to attract

MISCELLANEOUS

altrettanto/a/i/e — as well, as many
in realtà — in reality

HOW TO SAY IT

1. SAYING WHAT PEOPLE LOOK LIKE

I tedeschi sono alti, biondi e con gli occhi azzurri — Germans are tall, blond with blue-eyes.
Gli italiani sono piccoli, bruni e con gli occhi neri — Italians are small, dark and dark-eyed.
I tedeschi hanno la carnagione chiara — Germans have fair skin.
Gli italiani hanno la carnagione scura — Italians have a dark complexion.

2. MORE DESCRIPTIONS OF PEOPLE

Quella ragazza è magra — That girl is slim.
È bionda, con i capelli lunghi — She is fair with long hair.
È un uomo abbastanza alto e robusto — He is a fairly tall, well-built man.
È un ragazzo con gli occhiali — He's a boy with glasses.
Ha dei bellissimi occhi verdi — He/She has very beautiful green eyes.

3. DESCRIBING CHARACTER

È una persona intelligente e dinamica — He/she is an intelligent, dynamic person.
È un ragazzo simpatico e espansivo — He is a pleasant, lively boy.
Non è una persona molto seria — He/she is not a very serious person.

4. ASKING ABOUT OTHER NATIONALITIES

Che cosa si dice dei tedeschi? — What do they say about Germans?
Che reputazione hanno i francesi in Italia? — What reputation do the French have in Italy.
Che fama hanno gli italiani all'estero? — What reputation do Italians have abroad?

5. CONDITIONAL, USING "se" PLUS SUBJUCTIVE

Se potessi, vivrei in Francia! — If I could, I'd live in France! ***(5)***
Se volessi, potrei partire domani — If I wanted to, I could leave tomorrow.
Se dovessi farlo, lo farei — If I had to do it, I could.

REMARKS *REMARKS* *REMARKS* *REMARKS*

(1) *"Altezza" can be used as well.* — ***(2)*** *This is the only feminine noun ending in -o (pl. "le mani")* — ***(3)*** *Plural = "le braccia" (f)* — ***(4)*** *These words, as in English, are also used as nouns, both masc.* — ***(5)*** *See Grammar L.12.*

4.4 ORAL PRACTICE

1. EXPRESSING YOUR POINT OF VIEW

LISTEN

Gli italiani sono comunicativi

- *Credo che gli italiani siano comunicativi*

I tedeschi amano la musica

- *Credo che i tedeschi amino la musica*

Continue expressing your point of view in this way.

Gli italiani sono comunicativi — I tedeschi amano la musica — Gli inglesi portano sempre l'ombrello — I francesi sono buongustai — I russi bevono tutti la vodka — I napoletani mangiano ogni giorno la pizza. (See Grammar, L. 11.)

2. THE IMPERFECT SUBJUNCTIVE (essere/avere)

LISTEN

Credo che lui sia inglese

- *Anch'io credevo che fosse inglese*

Credo che abbia la patente

- *Anch'io credevo che avesse la patente*

Continue changing the sentences as in the model.

Credo che lui sia inglese — Credo che abbia la patente — Credo che sia ricco — Credo che abbia la macchina — Credo che sia in Francia — Credo che abbia gli occhi azzurri — Credo che sia una persona seria — Credo che abbia due figli. (See Grammar L.12.)

3. IMPERFECT SUBJUNCTIVE (other verbs)

LISTEN

Pensavi che venisse?

- *Sì, pensavo proprio che venisse!*

Pensavi che lo facesse?

- *Sì, pensavo proprio che lo facesse*

Continue answering the questions as in the model.

Pensavi che venisse? — Pensavi che lo facesse? — Pensavi che tornasse? — Pensavi che capisse? — Pensavi che arrivasse subito? — Pensavi che dormisse ancora? — Pensavi che dicesse la verità!

(See Grammar L.12.)

4. CONDITIONAL USING "se" AND THE SUBJUNCTIVE

LISTEN

Usciresti volentieri?

- *Sì, se potessi uscirei*

Lo faresti volentieri?

- *Sì, se potessi lo farei*

Continue answering the questions as in the model.

Usciresti volentieri? — Lo faresti volentieri? — Partiresti volentieri? — Ritorneresti volentieri? — Dormiresti volentieri? — Resteresti volentieri? — Continueresti volentieri?

(See Grammar, L.12.)

5. DESCRIBING PEOPLE

LISTEN

Quel ragazzo pesa 100 chili

- *È grasso*

Quella ragazza misura 1,80 m.

- *È alta!*

Describe each person in this way.

Quel ragazzo pesa 100 chili — Quella ragazza misura 1,80 m — Lui non ha mai voglia di fare niente — Loro fanno molto sport — Voi siete vestiti molto bene — Loro mangiano solo cose buone — Tu segui sempre gli ordini — Lei pesa solo 45 chili.

6. COMPARING

LISTEN

Sono più espansivi gli italiani o gli inglesi?

- *Gli italiani sono più espansivi degli inglesi*

Continue making comparisons in this way.

Sono più espansivi gli italiani o gli inglesi? — Sono più disciplinati gli spagnoli o i tedeschi? — Sono più buongustai i francesi o i tedeschi? — Sono più romantici gli italiani o i francesi? — Sono più alti gli svedesi o i siciliani?

(See Grammar, H.1.)

WHO EXACTLY ARE THE ITALIANS?

Clichés about a particular nation never really do justice to reality: to attempt to reduce a whole people to a few stereotypes is absurd. This is never more the case than with the Italians, amongst whom, as we have already shown, there are innumerable contradictions and contrasts.

These are particularly spetacular in political and social matters. At least three are worth looking at closely. Politically, Italy is famous for its frequent changes of government. Voted in, voted out, it is hard to break the habit, and sometimes, no one seems to be in power. This may seem true at first glance, but in fact, since the war, Italy has enjoyed a period of remarkable political stability, thanks to the "combinazioni" between various political figures and parties. This ensures that the same people are always in power. Take a look at the successive governments, and you will constantly see the same names. They say that if only one Italian were left, it would be Andreotti (who embodies this characteristic obsession for always being on the spot).

Still on the political front, Italian democracy, notorious for its juicy scandals, grappling with particular problems, such as the Mafia, dogged during the seventies by savage terrorism, flourishes nonetheless. The proof: their freedom of information. At least scandals in Italy always come to light, which is more than might be said for other countries…

Socially, there is one astonishing fact to bear in mind: Italy, this country of deep Catholic tradition, with its prolific population, especially in the South, where foreigners picture families of six as the norm, has today, in fact, the lowest birth-rate in the world! which is particularly surprising for a country where children are worshipped. This cult of the child has been known to lead to excesses in their up-bringing, the spoilt child lording it over his besotted parents, who make no attempt to resist. But this has not stopped the trend in Italy of having fewer and fewer children.

One of reasons that Italy is so fascinating is precisely because of the surprises it keeps up its sleeve. It is a modern country, with a developed economy, and a society resolutely up to date in the way it regulates its life, including in the family. Artistically, too, Italy is in no way inhibited by the richness of its heritage; on the contrary, its artists are deliberately amongst the most audacious, their experiments playing an important role in the art-world, as is seen by the Tras-avant-garde movement, so popular in the States.

But this centre for the avant-garde has nonetheless retained a bed-rock of fearsome superstition, (even discounting popular traditional cults, like San Gennaro in Naples), which are not only held in each individual breast, but are enshrined in officialdom: in Italy, 13 and especially 17 are unlucky numbers. So you will find, in theatres and hotels, on Alitalia planes, in blocks of flats where the flats are numbered, that no seat , room or door ever bears the number 13 or 17.

Perhaps this is the real Italian miracle. An advanced, capitalist society, with luxury boutiques where you can still ask for "un po' di sconto", a country overrun with the most depressingly mediocre television, and which yet, despite everything that is said about the "crisis in the Italian cinema", still retains one of the liveliest film industries in Europe, a nation which, perhaps more than any other these days, values the human dimension more highly than anything else.

Oceans of ink could be wasted in trying to unravel the various contradictory threads of the Italian character, to no avail. They will never cease to amaze us.

4.4 TAKE-A-BREAK

No. 1

LISTEN

Who is the surgeon? Find the answer to the mystery!

No. 2

Find the answers to the clues and fit them into the grid.

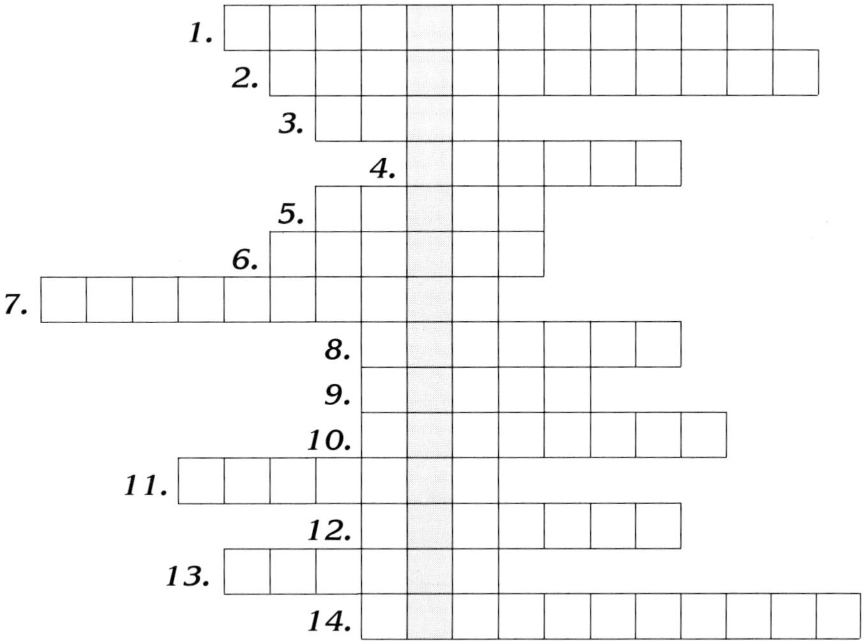

Orizzontali:

1. *Rispettano le regole.*
2. *Colore della pelle.*
3. *Contrario di bassi.*
4. *Fuori del proprio paese.*
5. *Persona che ride poco.*
6. *Capelli chiari.*
7. *Amano la buona cucina.*
8. *Lo sono spesso gli occhi chiari.*
9. *Amano il dolce far niente.*
10. *Tipico cappello portato dagli inglesi.*
11. *Non possono vivere senza la mamma.*
12. *Individuo compromesso con la mafia.*
13. *Quasi uguale.*
14. *Fama.*

Verticali:
Senza frontiere.

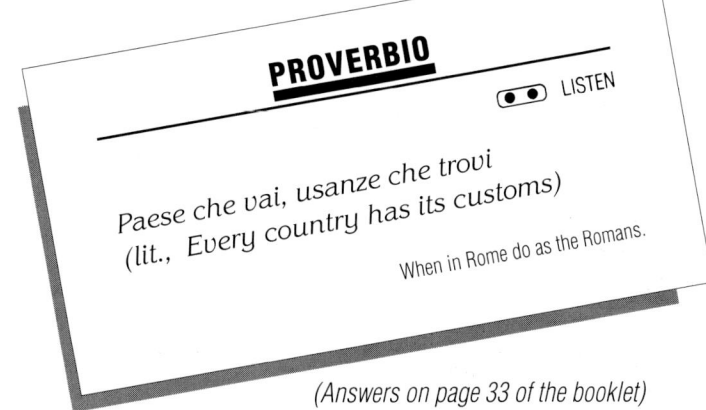

PROVERBIO

LISTEN

Paese che vai, usanze che trovi
(lit., Every country has its customs)

When in Rome do as the Romans.

(Answers on page 33 of the booklet)

4.5 DIALOGUE

LISTEN

UNA VISITA DI FIRENZE

The Rizzi are advising Mario (a visiting relative) on what to see in Florence.

Sig.ra Rizzi : *Per prima cosa, per quanto tempo ti fermi?*

Mario : *Mi trattengo per due o tre giorni al massimo.*

Sig.ra Rizzi : *In così poco tempo non potrai visitare tutto. Firenze è talmente rica di cose da vedere!*

Sig. Rizzi : *Secondo me innanzi tutto dovresti visitare Piazza della Signoria.*

Sig.ra Rizzi : *Sì, Piazza della Signoria con le sue statue e poi il Palazzo Vecchio, e naturalmente gli Uffizi.*

Sig. Rizzi : *Gli Uffizi vanno visitati con calma, e con delle scarpe comode...*

Mario : *E dov'è il famoso Ponte Vecchio?*

Sig. Rizzi : *Oh, guarda è proprio lì vicino, a pochi passi.*

Sig.ra Rizzi : *Vedrai è bellissimo! Pensa che dal '500 il ponte è sempre stato occupato dagli orefici e ancora oggi gode per questo di una vasta fama...*

Mario : *E la cattedrale?*

Sig. Rizzi : *Beh, la cattedrale va visitata assolutamente!*

Sig.ra Rizzi : *Vi si trovano marmi, ceramiche, affreschi e mosaici di diversi periodi e poi la cupola è del Brunelleschi.*

Mario : *Ah, sì, il celebre architetto del XV' secolo.*

Sig. Rizzi : *Ma tu che sei un appassionato di letteratura italiana dovresti andare a vedere la casa di Dante. È solo una curiosità, ma le stradine intorno alla casa sono molto caratteristiche.*

Mario : *Non c'è anche la sua tomba?*

Sig. Rizzi : *Eh no! La tomba di Dante non è a Firenze perché è morto in esilio a Ravenna.*

Sig.ra Rizzi : *Però nella chiesa di Santa Croce ci sono le tombe di alcuni dei più famosi scrittori, pittori e poeti italiani.*

Mario : *Ho capito! Due giorni non mi basteranno mai...!*

LISTEN AND REPEAT

You will find the translation on page 33 of the booklet.

1. Florence, the famous Duomo
2. The Bargello Museum
3. A Botticelli painting in the Uffizi Gallery
4. The Baptistry door, detail
5. Traditional, ceremonial dress

1

2

3

4

5

4.5 VOCABULARY

NOUNS

la piazza — square (in town or a village)
la statua — statue
il ponte — bridge
l'orefice (m) — goldsmith
la cattedrale — cathedral
il marmo — marble
la ceramica — ceramics
l'affresco (m) — fresco
il mosaico — mosaic
la cupola — dome
l'architetto (m) — architect
la stradina — narrow street/alley
la letteratura — literature
la curiosità — curiosity
la tomba — tomb
l'esilio (m) — exile
la chiesa — church
lo scrittore — writer
il pittore — painter
il poeta — poet

---

l'arte (f) — art
lo stile — style
il Medio Evo — Middle Ages
il Rinascimento — Renaissance

ADJECTIVES

comodo/scomodo — comfortable/uncomfortable
famoso (celebre) — famous
vasto — vast
caratteristico — characteristic/typical

VERBS

fermarsi (trattenersi) — stay ***(1)***
visitare — to visit
godere di — to enjoy
morire — to die
nascere — to be born
crescere — to grow
bastare — to be enough
capire — to understand
consigliare — to advise

MISCELLANEOUS

al massimo — maximum
al minimo — minimum
in così poco tempo — in such a short time
talmente — so
innanzi tutto — above all
con calma — calmly
a pochi passi — a few paces away
intorno a — around
alcuni — some
il secolo — century
il XV° secolo — 15th century
il '400 — the 1400s (15th century)

HOW TO SAY IT

1. DIFFERENT WAYS OF SAYING " SHOULD"

La cattedrale deve essere visitata
La cattedrale va visitata
La cattedrale è da visitare
La cattedrale, bisogna visitarla
} — The cathedral should be visited.

2. PERIODS OF HISTORY

Il Ponte Vecchio è del '200 (del XIII° secolo) — The Ponte Vecchio dates from the 13th century.
Dante è un poeta del '300 (del XIV° secolo) — Dante is a 14th century poet.

3. STYLES

È una chiesa romanica — It's a Romanesque church.
È una chiesa gotica — It's a Gothic church.
È un palazzo rinascimentale — It's a Renaissance palace.
È una statua barocca — It's a baroque statue.

4. IT WAS WRITTEN/PAINTED BY...

La Divina Commedia è stata scritta da Dante Alighieri — The Divine Comedy was written by Dante Alighieri.
La Gioconda è stata dipinta da Leonardo da Vinci — The Mona Lisa was painted by Leonardo da Vinci.

5. SAYING WHAT IT'S MADE OF

Questa statua è di marmo bianco — This statue is made of white marble.
La parete è di ceramica — The wall is ceramic.
Il Ponte Vecchio era di legno — The Ponte Vecchio was made of wood.

REMARKS REMARKS REMARKS REMARKS

(1) *This verb means literally "to stop oneself".*

4.5 ORAL PRACTICE

1. EXPRESSING NEED

LISTEN

La cattedrale deve essere visitata

● *Va visitata assolutamente!*

Le lettere devono essere scritte a macchina

● *Vanno scritte a macchina assolutamente!*

Change the sentences by using* "andare" *followed by the past participle of the verb, as in the model.

La cattedrale deve essere visitata — Le lettere devono essere scritte a macchina — I documenti devono essere spediti domani — L'esercizio deve essere fatto — L'appuntamento deve essere preso per domani — Le cassette devono essere ascoltate.

(See Grammar L.15)

2. EXPRESSING NEED

LISTEN

Il libro è da comprare

● *Bisogna comprarlo*

Le cassette sono da ascoltare

● *Bisogna ascoltarle*

***Change the sentences by using* "bisogna" *and replacing the noun with the appropriate pronoun,* (lo, la, li, le).**

Il libro è da comprare — Le cassette sono da ascoltare — La lettera è da spedire subito — Il film è da vedere — La città è da visitare a piedi — Gli esercizi sono da finire — La cena è da preparare.

(See Grammar L.15)

3. CENTURIES

LISTEN

Dante è un poeta del XIV° secolo

● *Dante è un poeta del '300*

Continue as in the model

Dante è un poeta del XIV° secolo — Caravaggio è un pittore del XVI° secolo — Alberto Moravia è uno scrittore del XX° secolo — Brunelleschi è un architetto del XV° secolo— Alessandro Manzoni è uno scrittore del XIX° secolo — Antonio Vivaldi è un compositore del XVIII° secolo — Michelangelo è uno scultore, pittore e architetto del XVI° secolo.

(See Grammar K.3)

4. VERBS IN THE PASSIVE

LISTEN

Dante ha scrito "La Divina Commedia"

● *"La Divina Commedia" è stata scritta da Dante*

Vivaldi ha composto "Le Quattro Stagioni"

● *"Le Quattro Stagioni" sono state composte da Vivaldi*

Put the following sentences into the passive.

Dante ha scritto "La Divina Commedia" — Vivaldi ha composto "Le Quattro Stagioni" — Leonardo da Vinci ha dipinto "La Gioconda" — Brunelleschi ha progettato la cupola della cattedrale di Firenze — Umberto Eco ha scritto "Il Nome della Rosa" — Marcello Mastroianni ha interpretato molti film di Fellini.

(See Grammar L.14)

5. SUPERLATIVES

LISTEN

"La Gioconda" è un famoso quadro di Leonardo da Vinci

● *"La Gioconda" è il quadro più famoso di Leonardo da Vinci.*

Il Ponte Vecchio è un ponte antico di Firenze

● *Il Ponte Vecchio è il ponte più antico di Firenze.*

Continue as in the model.

"La Gioconda" è un famoso quadro di Leonardo da Vinci — Il Ponte Vecchio è un ponte antico di Firenze — "La Divina Commedia" è una grande opera della letteratura italiana — Milano è una grande città del nord dell'Italia. — Il calcio è uno sport diffuso e amato in Italia.

(See Grammar H.2)

FLORENCE - MOTHER OF CITIES

Not content with giving Italy its literary language, Florence remains at the forefront in every sphere of Italian thought, and proves the fact, by being the cradle of the new, typically Italian rock music, complete with Italian vocals.

The Florentines, on the whole the nicest people in the world, do have a fairly high opinion of themselves. They are right. Between 1865 and1871, before Rome, Florence was the capital of the united Italy; its newspaper, one of Italy's most prominent daily papers, is still called "La Nazione". Is this symbolic? Florence is equidistant from Rome, the political capital, and Milan, the financial capital. Yet it is not an especially large town, nor does it seem to have any particular ambition. But it has always played an influential part in cultural affairs, throughout Europe.

Take art first. Think of Florence, and you think of the Renaissance, of the Duomo, and of the Baptistry, of the countless marvels created by Botticelli, Donatello, Cellini, Michelangelo, Uccello, (there is a huge, wonderful, battle scene by him in London's National Gallery), of the Piazza Signoria, of the Uffizi Gallery. Florentine artists launched a new style, and worked in every country in Europe, even Russia.

It is also true of politics. One of Florence's sons was the redoubted Macchiavelli, the political theorist who, in his book "The Prince", laid the basis of current political thought. The Medici family ruled Renaissance Florence, of course, but members of that family were also in power in France, so their influence over European history at the crucial time of the Reformation was enormous. Catherine de Medici was, among other things, Mary, Queen of Scots' first mother-in-law!

There are other ways in which Florence has been ahead of its time. In the XVIIIth century their ruler, Grand-Duke Leopold II of Tuscany, had the revolutionary idea of abolishing the death penalty. He was certainly the first in Europe, and perhaps in the world, to have thought of it.

Florence has also played a formative role in cooking. Florentines proudly boast that they taught every European court the best way to cook meat. Right up to to-day, it can be sampled, as the famous "bistecca alla fiorentina". This influence extended to vegetables, which is why dishes using spinach are known as "florentine". For the sweet-toothed, there is also a delectable biscuit, of nuts and glacé fruit on a chocolate base, named after the city.

In point of fact, despite the queues at the museum doors, the hoards of tourists swarming over the Ponte Vecchio, through the Duomo, across the Piazza Signoria, Florence does not live entirely for, nor off, its visitors, only 2% of the population does. Simply take a stroll outside the - amazing - tourist centres, and look at the shop windows. Florence offers you the biggest bookshop in Italy, as well as some of the country's finest shops for clothes, shoes and leather-goods.

There is a definite Florentine style, consisting of elegance, grace (a long tradition, you might say), civility, the picture people have of the city, with its monuments, parks, like the superb Giardino dei Boboli, behind the Pitti Palace. This style, like Chianti, is the fruit of both labour and experience. In fact, Florence is a very industrious city, it is one of the places in Italy where people work hardest. So do not be taken in! The Arno, still as it looks, can wreak havoc, and the Florentines are warm-hearted, despite their reserve. Florence, a city in aspic? quite the contrary! Florence is living, breathing, buzzing.

4.5 TAKE-A-BREAK

LISTEN

Nel blu, dipinto di blu (Volare)
(D Modugno - F. Migliacci)
Sung by Domenico Modugno
© Edizioni Curci

Penso che un sogno così non ritorni mai più,
Mi dipingevo le mani e la faccia di blu
Poi d'improvviso venivo dal vento rapito

E incominciavo a volare nel cielo infinito...

Volare...oh, oh...cantare...oh, oh, oh, oh!
Nel blu, dipinto di blu, felice di stare lassù

E volavo, volavo felice più in alto del sole ed ancora più su
Mentre il mondo pian piano spariva lontano laggiù
Una musica dolce suonava soltanto per me...
Volare...oh, oh...cantare...oh, oh, oh, oh!
Nel blu, dipinto di blu, felice di stare lassù

Ma tutti i sogni nell'alba svaniscono perché
quando tramonta, la luna li porta con sè

Ma io continuo a sognare negli occhi tuoi belli
Che sono blu come un cielo trapunto di stelli

Volare ...oh, oh...cantare...oh, oh, oh, oh!
nel blu degli occhi tuoi blu
felice di stare quaggiù
E continuo a volare felice più in alto del sole ed ancora di più su
mentre il mondo pian piano scompare negli occhi tuoi blu,
la tua voce è una musica dolce che suona per me..
Volare...oh, oh...cantare...oh, oh, oh, oh!
nel blu degli occhi tuoi blu
felice di stare quaggiù
Con te!

In the Blue, Painted Blue (Flying)

I think such a dream will never return
I was painting my hands and face blue
Then all of a sudden I was taken away by a gust of wind

And I started to fly in the infinite sky...

Flying...oh, oh...singing...oh, oh, oh, oh
Happy to be up there in the blue, painted blue,

Happy flying higher than the sun and even higher
While the world slowly slowly disappeared far below
Sweet music playing just for me
Flying...oh, oh...singing...oh, oh, oh, oh!
Happy to be up there in the blue, painted blue.

But all dreams disappear at sunrise
because the disappearing moon takes them with her.

But I continue to dream of your beautiful eyes,
which are as blue as a starlit sky

Flying...oh, oh...singing...oh, oh, oh, oh!
in the blue of your blue eyes!
happy to be down here
And I go on flying happily over the sun and still higher
while the world slowly disappears in your blue eyes.
Your voice is sweet music which is playing for me.
Flying...oh, oh...singing...oh, oh, oh, oh!
in the blue of your blue eyes
Happy to be down here
With you!

AVERE IL DENTE AVVELENATO

(lit. to have a poisoned tooth)

to have a poisonous tongue

ATTACCARE BOTTONE

(lit. to sew on a button)

to buttonhole (somebody)

PRENDERE QUALCUNO PER IL NASO

(lit. to take someone by the nose)

to lead someone by the nose

ANDARE CON I PIEDI DI PIOMBO

(lit. to go with lead feet)

to tread cautiously

4. WRITTEN PRACTICE

4.1

FILL IN THE BLANKS WITH THE POSSESSIVE WITH AN ARTICLE IF REQUIRED: *Signor Verdi, Le presento ....moglie. — Carlo ha una sorella:..............sorella si chiama Giulia. — Marco e Claudio hanno un negozio di abbigliamento: ....negozio è in centro. —Io ho molti amici: ....amici vivono in Italia. — Laura ha due fratelli: ....fratelli sono ancora piccoli.*

TRANSLATE: *Le signore stanno prendendo il tè. — Come al solito andranno in campagna per il fine settimana. — Mi piacerebbe fare un viaggio all'estero.*

He plays the guitar very well. — My children play tennis. — We don't know how to swim. — It's a difficult choice.

4.2

ANSWER EACH QUESTION USING me, lo, la, li, le AS REQUIRED: *Mi presti la piantina? — Mi racconti il tuo viaggio? — Mi scrivi una cartolina dalla Sicilia? — Mi racconti le tue vacanze? — Mi prendi un dépliant all'agenzia? — Mi dai il tuo indirizzo?*

TRANSLATE: *Nell'albergo c'è l'aria condizionata. — La formula comprende la pensione completa. — Qual è l'orario di chiusura dei musei?*

We'd like to go away for the Christmas holidays. — Are there any package tours to Sicily? — It's a very beautiful place. — He would like to spend a few days at the seaside.

4.3

ANSWER EACH QUESTION IN THE AFFIRMATIVE, USING THE FORM te, lo, la, le OR glielo/la/li/la, AS NECESSARY WITH "tu" OR "Lei": *Mario, mi racconti la storia del furto? — Signor Verdi, mi racconta la storia del furto? — Antonio mi ripeti il nome di quella persona? — Signor Neri, mi ripete il nome di quella persona? — Sandro, mi porti i documenti? — Signor Santi, mi porta i documenti? — Giacomo, mi dai le riviste nuove? — Signor Rossi, mi da le riviste nuove?*

TRANSLATE: *Non ti preoccupare! — Può succedere... — Sull'autobus c'era molta gente.*

What happened? — I wasn't aware of anything. — I reported it to the police. — What bad luck!

4.4

PUT THE VERBS IN BRACKETS INTO THE CORRECT PART OF THE PRESENT SUBJUNCTIVE: *Credo che Marco (essere) ...... a Londra. — Penso che la mamma (arrivare) ...... domani. — Penso che Giulio (avere) ...... l'appuntamento alle 8. — Credo che loro (prendere) ...... l'aereo. — Penso che tu (essere) ...... soddisfatto. — Credo che voi (capire) ...... un po' l'italiano.*

TRANSLATE: *Pensavano che gli italiani fossero tutti romantici. — Credevo che tu fossi a Roma in vacanza. — Se potessi, lo farei volentieri.*

Nordic people have light eyes and blond hair. — Italians have the reputation of being short with dark hair. — These are only common myths.

4.5

FILL IN THE BLANKS WITH "va" OR "bisogna", AS REQUIRED: *La cattedrale ....visitata assolutamente. — Il museo .... visitarlo di mattina. — La grammatica .... studiata. — I biglietti dell'autobus .... comprarli dal tabaccaio. — La città .... girata a piedi. — I mosaici .... vederli assolutamente.*

TRANSLATE: *Nella basilica si trovano meravigliosi affreschi. — Firenze è una delle città italiane più visitate dai turisti.*

It is a book written by a famous author. — It is a beautiful marble statue. — It's the oldest church in Rome. — It's a Renaissance palace.

(Answers on page 37 of the booklet)

MORE VOCABULARY

WEATHER

acquazzone (m) — downpour
afa (f) — mugginess
brina (f) — frost
cielo (m) — sky
clima (m) — climate
fulmine (m) — thunder
ghiaccio (m) — ice
grandine (f) — hail
inondazione (f) — flood
lampo (m) — lightening
luna (f) — moon
nebbia (f) — fog
neve (f) — snow
nuvola (f) — cloud
pioggia (f) — rain
siccità (f) — drought
sole (m) — sun
stella (f) — star
temporale (m) — storm
terremoto (m) — earthquake
tuono (m) — clap of thunder
umidità (f) — humidity
vento (m) — wind

A BIT OF GEOGRAPHY

mare (m) — sea
lago (m) — lake
fiume (m) — river
affluente (m) — tributary
torrente (m) — torrent
monte (m) — hill
montagna (f) — mountain
collina (f) — small hill
valico (m) — mountain pass
pianura (f) — plain
altopiano (m) — plateau
golfo (m) — gulf
foce (f) — mouth of a river
delta (m)— delta
estuario (m) — estuary
le Alpi (f/pl) — Alps
gli Appennini (m) — Apennines
le Dolomiti (f/pl) — Dolomites
il traforo del Monte Bianco — the Mont Blanc tunnel
la pianura padana (f) — Po valley
la frontiera — frontier
il confine — border
il Mar Mediterraneo — Mediterranean Sea
il Mar Tirreno, Ionio, Adriatico — Tyrrhenian, Ionian, Adriatic Sea
l'oceano Atlantico, Pacifico, Indiano — Atlantic, Pacific, Indian ocean

GAMES

giochi di società (m/pl) — board-games
giocare a carte — to play cards
picche — spades
fiori — clubs
quadri — diamonds
cuori — hearts
fare un solitario — to play patience
giocare a dama — to play draughts
giocare a scacchi — to play chess
giocare a dadi — to play dice

FAMILY MEMBERS

padre (m) — father
madre (f) — mother
genitori (m/pl) — parents
parenti (m/pl) — relatives
nonno/a — grandfather/mother
bisnonno/a — great grandfather/mother
figlio/a — son/daughter
fratello (m) — brother
sorella (f) — sister
zio/a — uncle/aunt
cugino/a — cousin
nipote (m/f) — nephew /niece, grandson/daughter
cognato/a — brother/sister-in-law
suocero/a — father/mother-in- law
genero (m) — son-in-law
nuora (f) — daughter-in-law
fratellastro (m) — half-brother
sorellastra (f) — half-sister
patrigno (m) — stepfather
matrigna (f) — stepmother

THE ITALIAN SCHOOL SYSTEM

asilo nido (m) — kindergarten
scuola materna (f) — nursery school
scuola elementare (f) — primary school
scuola media inferiore (f) — lower secondary school
scuola media superiore (f) — upper secondary school
liceo classico (m) — further education college/high school
liceo scientifico (m) — technical college
liceo linguistico (m) — language school
liceo artistico (m) — art school
istituto tecnico (m) — technical school
scuola magistrate (f) — teacher training college
università (f) — university

AT THE UNIVERSITY

facoltà (f) — faculty
di ingegneria — of engineering
di medicina — of medicine
di economia e commercio — of business and commerce
di legge — of law
di scienze politiche — of political science
di lettere — of arts
di lingue straniere — of foreign languages
di chimica — of chemistry
di fisica — of physics
di biologia — of biology
di farmacia — of pharmacy
di agraria — of agriculture
di architettura — of architecture

DIPLOMAS/CERTIFICATES

licenza elementare(f) — junior school certificate
licenza media — secondary-school certificate
maturità liceale — high school diploma, university entrance
laurea — university degree
diploma di instituto tecnico — technical school diploma

4. TEST YOURSELF

1. COMPLETE WITH DOUBLE PRONOUNS ACCORDING TO THE MEANING

Maria vuole il mio libro e io...presto.
Se vuoi un caffè, io .... offro volentieri.
Signora, non ho capito il Suo nome!...............................può ripetere, per cortesia?
Ho visto una commedia divertente e ....racconto, Mario.
Il signor Verdi ha bisogno dei documenti e io...do.

2. CHANGE THE FOLLOWING INTO THE PAST CONDITIONAL

imperfect subjunctive + conditional
Se posso, vengo con voi...
Se fa bello, vado al mare ....
Se vado a Roma, visito la fontana di Trevi ....
Se ho tempo, gioco a tennis ....
Se ci sono 4 giorni di vacanza, parto ....

3. MAKE THE FOLLOWING SENTENCES PASSIVE

Tutti gli italiani seguono il calcio...
Umberto Eco ha scritto Il Nome della Rosa ....
Il direttore ha chiamato la segretaria ....
Cristoforo Colombo ha scoperto l'America ....
Gli americani hanno inventato la pop-art ....

4. WHAT WOULD YOU SAY IF YOU WANTED TO ...

ask someone if he/she does a lot of sport ....
ask someone what he/she is doing at the weekend ....
ask for a map of the town at the tourist office...
ask someone what happened ....

say that someone stole your wallet ....
ask what they think of the English in Italy ....
say that this palace dates from the 1400s...

5. ONLY ONE SENTENCE IN EACH SET IS CORRECT. CAN YOU FIND IT?

A. *Mi piacerei andare in Sicilia*.. ☐
B. *Piacerebbemi andare in Sicilia*.. ☐
C. *Mi piacerebbe andare in Sicilia*... ☐

A. *Vuole una cartina? Sì, mi dia una*.. ☐
B. *Vuole una cartina? Sì, me ne dia una*... ☐
C. *Vuole una cartina? Sì, mi ne dia una* .... ☐

A. *Bisogna che voi andiate all'agenzia*.. ☐
B. *Bisogna che voi andate all'agenzia*.. ☐
C. *Bisogna che voi andaste all'agenzia*.. ☐

A. *È il quadro il più famoso di Leonardo*.. ☐
B. *È il quadro più famoso di Leonardo*... ☐
C. *È il quadro più famosissimo di Leonardo*.. ☐

6. MATCH EACH QUESTION TO ITS ANSWER

A. *Non abbiamo ancora un programma preciso.*
B. *Grazie, volentieri!*
C. *Nella tasca dei pantaloni.*
D. *Per fortuna avevo solo 40.000 lire.*
E. *Mi trattengo per due o tre giorni.*

1. *C'erano molti soldi nel portafoglio?*
2. *Dove avevi messo il portafoglio?*
3. *Gradisce ancora una tazza di tè, signora?*
4. *Per quanto tempo ti fermi a Firenze?*
5. *Che cosa fate per le vacanze?*

(Check your answers on page 38 of the booklet)

IN BOCCA AL LUPO

Throughout the day, there had been no relief from the unremitting grey of the sky, with hardly enough light to see in the streets. From dawn to dusk, the lights had all been on in the office, and as Ambrogio stepped out into the gloom of the street, his eyes were streaming. He felt wearier than usual, and did not really want to go home. He had been all the readier to accept Lucia's invitation.

The dull light reminded him of Milan. He was downcast; an old story came back to him, he was not sure why, perhaps the gloom of the moment lent itself to such thoughts. Leaning back in his armchair in Lucia's flat, he recounted it to her:

"You know, when I lived in Milan, I often used to have breakfast in a bar on the corner of via Pioppette and corso di Porta Ticinese. It was a funny sort of place, at that time. In the evening, the yuppies would rub shoulders with drug pushers and God knows what. But in the morning, it was back to a normal, run of the mill, local bar. Anyhow, every morning, at the same time, I would run into the same couple. They were completely ordinary people, still young.The man looked a bit haggard, gaunt....as if he had some hidden disease gnawing away at him, or was recovering from a long illness. They always sat at the same table, at the back, beside the door to the lavatories, and talked uninterruptedly, in low, muted voices, barely above a whisper. They spoke in English, which was what first attracted my attention. Apart from their way of huddling together, never paying the least attention to their surroundings, they had nothing remarkable about them. Except, perhaps, that they looked so casual, so relaxed. They would arrive at exactly quarter past eight, but without seeming hurried: at an hour when everyone else would tear in, down their coffee at a gulp before rushing off for the tram, which stopped just opposite. Then one day, they had gone. I didn't see them again, for a month or more."

"È allora?"

"And then, one fine morning, they were back again, at the same table, as if nothing had happened. The man looked paler, iller, than before, but their behaviour had not changed in any way. Only, when he got up, to go and pay at the cash-desk, I realised that he no longer had his right hand. Just a stump."

"Ma è straordinario," *exclaimed Lucia.* "È proprio la stessa storia che ho letta nel libro che interessava la Piper-Sharp!"

Ambrogio went white: once again, the ground fell away from beneath his feet. He clutched the arms of his chair.

"No. Non è possibile."

"Ma , sì, te lo giuro. Una storia così morbosa, non potevo fare a meno di notarla. Aspetta che vado a cercare una copia del libro."

When she returned, triumphantly brandishing a copy of "In bocca al lupo", *the telephone jangled. She handed him the book, said:* "Scusi un attimo", *and lifted the receiver. Ambrogio glanced at the page she had opened for him; it was again the chapter* "Gelsi in via Pioppette". *Before he could read further, Lucia was already calling him:*

"C'è un tizio che ti vuole parlare. Non ha detto il nome. Te lo passo?"

Ambrogio seized the receiver. His hand was sweating. He could guess whose voice he was about to hear.

"Pronto, Ambrogio? Hai letto il libro che ti ha gentilmente consigliato Mrs. Piper-Sharp? Avresti tante cose da dimenticare. Purtroppo, temo che sia ormai un po' tardi. Mi spiace."

The line went dead. Ambrogio rushed to the window. The street was white with snow. A couple were walking arm in arm on the pavement opposite. A car roared at high speed into view, and disappeared at the cross-roads.

Ambrogio turned round. Lucia looked at his face in dismay.

"Cosa ti succede? Guarda che sei pallidissimo. Cosa ti ha detto quest'uomo?"

She took his hand, he pulled it away, he stammered, hesitatingly:

"Forse...forse mi conviene lasciarti. Sarebbe anche meglio per te. Credo proprio di essere nei guai."

"Non dire stupidaggini. Vedrai che passerà."

He was not listening to her. He picked the book up again, and continued reading from where he had left off that very morning. The story of the one-armed man was indeed there, just as he had told it to Lucia, but while the couple were not named, another witness was, dubbed "A" by M.S. :

"Era proprio lo stesso A che aveva visto della finestra del suo appartamento in via Pioppette l'assassinio del banchiere Gelsi. Questo non mi avrebbe per nulla disturbato se i miei clienti non avessero richiesto un lavoro pulitissimo. Quindi non potevo lasciare in vita un testimone. Dovetti rintracciarlo perché, nel frattempo, si era trasferito all'estero."

Ambrogio's knees turned to water. He skimmed rapidly over the next few lines:

"...certi delitti rimangono impuniti perché sono inspiegabili. Mi era facile eliminarlo nella città dove viveva: mai nessuno avrebbe scoperto un qualsiasi collegamento tra la fine del banchiere Gelsi e la morte di questo giovanotto perbene. Nel mio mestiere, l'improbabile è l'unica cosa sicura. Dovevo giocare questa carta anche con A. Non era uno del giro dei affari della finanza; non aveva niente da nascondere, tranne le solite cose: tresche di cui tutti sanno sempre tutto, piccoli vizi che fanno piuttosto tenerezza. Quasi una vita da impiegato."

Ambrogio went on frenziedly thumbing the book. At a glance, he just had time to take in:

"...mi rincresce una cosa: è morta anche la ragazza con cui stava. Peccato non aver potuto più tempo a disposizione, ma c'era un aereo che partiva da Heathrow un'ora dopo; non potevo rimanere di più a Londra."

And he crumpled to the floor beside Lucia.. — The silent impact of the two bullets had shattered the glass.

THE END.

PRACTICAL INFORMATION

To travel hopefully you need to feel well-informed.
The following brief guide will help you discover
Italy, from A to Z

Trentino-Alto Adige
Trento
Friuli-Venezia Giulia
Valle d'Aosta
Aosta
Milano
Veneto
Lombardia
Torino
Venezia
Trieste
Piemonte
Emilia-Romagna
Liguria
Genova
Bologna
Firenze
Ancona
Toscana
Perugia
Marche
Umbria
L'Aquila
Roma
Abruzzo
Lazio
Campobasso
Molise
Sardegna
Napoli
Bari
Campania
Puglia
Potenza
Basilicata
Cagliari
Catanzaro
Calabria
Palermo
Sicilia

APERITIFS

Italians generally prefer to go out for a drink with friends, rather than stay in their own homes. When you order a drink in a bar, you are usually served olives, crisps, pickled onions, cocktail biscuits, peanuts and sometimes even a small portion of pasta. The Italians often have a glass of dry or sparkling white wine, such as a Pinot Grigio. But Italy is the home of vermouth, the famous Martini among others, so cocktails are also popular. A piece of advice: try a "Negroni": it is a mixture of sweet vermouth, gin and Campari. You won't be disappointed! And, as the Italians say, "Cincin!"

ART

Italy is a kind of immense museum in itself, as well as being the repository of an extraordinarily rich artistic heritage. Everybody, (except lovers of highly specialised exotic art!) can find the form of art that particularly interests them: the proto-historic ruins of Sardinia's nuraghi, examples of Etruscan art, Greek (especially in Sicily), Roman, early Christian (St. Apollinare Nuovo and St. Vitale in Ravenna), Romanesque (the Cattedrale di Torcello in the Venetian lagoon, or Cefalù in Sicily), Norman-Arabic in Sicily (the cathedral of Amalfi or Saint John of the Hermits in Palermo), and Gothic (from Castel del Monte, the palace of Frederick II in Puglia to the Piazza del Campo in Siena, and from the Doges' Palace in Venice, to the Duomo in Milan), and so on. And then there is the beauty and classicism of the Renaissance (Palladio's villas, such as the Villa Rotunda) and the Baroque period (Bernini's wild stone baldacchino in St. Peter's, or the Trevi fountain, also in Rome, or the extraordinarily Hispanic-American architecture of Lecce). There is neoclassic art (with Canova's Pauline Bonaparte), plus romanticism, realism, symbolism, cubism, modernism, futurism, anything you care to name!

BOLOGNA

The Italians have nicknamed this city "Red", both for its brick monuments (such as the Church of Saint Petronius) and its politics! Bologna is a friendly city, known for the straightforward good nature of its citizens. It has other claims to fame: the famous tomato and meat sauce, called "ragù" (which has become the archetypal Italian dish in the Anglo-Saxon mind) and the arcades - over 27 miles of them - to keep off both sun and rain. Among the principal sights are the two leaning towers of Asinelli and Garisenda, and the magnificent cluster of early Christian and Romanesque churches of Santo Stefano.

BREAD

Bread is one of Italy's staple foods. In the country particularly, it is easy to find fat, round loaves called "micche" or "pagnotte". But what is really fascinating is the enormous variety of "panini" (rolls), each with a different name and shape, changing as you go from from region to region. The taste also varies, from bread without salt to bread with oil. The "panifici" (bakers) have other things on offer, such as "grissini", the breadsticks found on restaurant tables, to be nibbled while you wait for your meal. Or "focaccia" from Liguria, which is a kind of soft pancake (watch out: it can be very greasy!), usually garnished with basil, anchovies, olives, or onions; still in Liguria, you can find "farinata", an ancient recipe made with chick-pea flour.

CAFES

Some of Italy's famous cafés are an integral part of its culture. Among the best known are: the Florian and the Quadri, both in Venice's St. Mark's Square, with the magnificent décor of their salons inside, and their Viennese orchestras playing outside; the Greco, in Rome, on the Via Condotti, one of the most fashionable places in the city, frequented over the years by many of Europe's intellectuals; Padua's Caffe Pedrocci, just off the Piazza Cavour, like a neoclassical, Greek-Egyptian monument, founded in 1831, (the French writer, Stendhal, thought it was Italy's finest café); the Doney and the Rivoire, both high-spots for Florence's rich and famous; the Florio on the Via Po in Turin, the best place to buy ice-cream in the city; the Calfish, well-known in Naples, and the

Sant'Ambroseus, on the Corso Matteotti in Milan, particularly celebrated for its chocolates.

FLORENCE

Florence is the capital of Tuscany, cradle of the Renaissance, and considered by many to be the most beautiful city in Italy. Beware of the affliction, so well portrayed in "Room with a View", where the visitor becomes dazed and helpless, glutted by the city's beauty. There are too many things to see in Florence to mention them all here, so be sure to arm yourself with a good guidebook, and it is worth reading up on it before you go.

Tourist offices: at the central station, open every day from 9.00 am to 9.00 pm., and on the Via Manzoni.

FOLK FESTIVALS

There are numerous festivals, fairs, and celebrations each year. Here are a few:

- *January 6: Festival of the Befana (Epiphany) in Rome.*
- *January 17: In Sardinia, the procession at Maimoiada, with Mamutone masks, a tradition whose origins are lost in the mists of time.*
- *February: Many pre-Lenten carnivals take place, apart from the world-famous one in Venice, including one in the Piedmont town of Ivrea (famous for its battle of the oranges), and one in Viareggio, near Lucca in Tuscany, with floats and political satire.*
- *March 1st: In Oristano, Sardinia, the Sartiglia - a horse race and tournament in XVIth century costume.*
- *March/April: At Piana degli Albanesi in Sicily, an Easter celebration according to the rites of the Albanese Orthodox Church.*
- *May 15: At Gubbio, in Umbria, the Feast of the Candles.*
- *May 31: Also at Gubbio, a crossbow tournament.*
- *The first Thursday in May: At Cocullo (in the province of Aquila) in Abruzzi, a procession with live snakes, in honour of the village's patron saint, San Domenico.*
- *During May: In Camogli, Liguria, the "Sagra del Pesce", the Fish Fair.*
- *End of May/beginning June: In Genzano, Latium, the feast of the Infiorata. The procession of Corpus Domini takes place through streets carpeted with pictures made from flowers.*
- *July 2: The first run of Siena's "Palio", in mediaeval dress, a horse race which pits riders from the 17 ancient districts of the city against one another.*
- *Third Saturday and Sunday in July: The Feast of the Redeemer in Venice - a great celebration marking the end of a devastating plague in 1576.*
- *August 16: The second run of the Palio in Siena.*
- *First Sunday in September: In Venice, the "Regate Storiche", (historical regattas) on the Grand Canal.*
- *Beginning of September: At Marostica (Vicenza) the town square is turned into a giant chess-board with living chess-pieces.*
- *End of October: in the Val d'Aoste, the finale of the "Battaglia di Regine" (battle of queens, with fighting cows.)*
- *End of November: At Gorgonzola (Lombardy) the gigantic Polentata, during which polenta with Gorgonzola cheese is prepared and eaten. Scrumptious!*

FOOD

Pasta is being dealt with separately, but it would be unthinkable not to mention some of the other specialities of Italy's delectable cuisine. First, two or three typical dishes. Polenta originated in the poor parts of the Veneto. It is a simple mixture of cornmeal, salt and water and it forms the staple food of certain regions. Despite its humble origins, it is sufficiently popular to be available in many modern supermarkets. Risotto, with its thousand and one flavourings, from saffron to seafood, is typical of the region of the Po Valley, where rice has been grown since the time of Napoleon. Finally, pizza, the famous and immensely popular open crust, covered with whatever comes to hand, including left-overs, is a purely Neapolitan creation - it was originally lunch for the dock workers of Naples.

These are the basics, but let's consider some of the specialities you might encounter on restaurant menus. "Saltimbocca alla Romana" is a sautéed veal escalope, wrapped in ham and flavoured with Marsala. Other Roman recipes include tripe in a mint sauce and "abbachio", roasted spring lamb. "Pasta al pesto" is any type of pasta mixed with a delicious sauce of basil, (hence the bright green colour), garlic , olive oil, and pine nuts: wonderful! In Venice, besides fish and seafood dishes, you should taste the "fegato alla veneziana" (thin slithers of pigs' liver gently fried with onions), "risi e bisi" (rice and baby peas cooked in beef stock), and "pasta e fagioli" (a hearty soup of pasta and kidney-beans). In Liguria, a region between the mountains and the sea and, therefore, with no tradition of meat-eating, there are superb vegetable dishes: stuffed or frittered vegetables (verdure fritte), and different vegetable flans. Bread-crumbed and deep-fried foods appear in all parts of Italy, from the famous Milanese escalope (similar to what English-speakers call "Wiener Schnitzel"), fried in butter, to the equally famous "scampi fritti", plump prawns fried in oil. To round off, there is "carpaccio", very fine slices of raw meat served with a wedge of lemon, or "melanzane alla parmigiana" (aubergines with parmesan), or "stracciatella", a soup made with parmesan cheese and beaten egg. But, there are still so many more local dishes it is impossible to name them all!

GENOA

Genoa, like many frontier posts, is often overlooked by tourists, who are heading for the more "Italian" parts of Italy. But in fact it is full of charm, and worth a stop. The sumptuous mansions along the Via Garibaldi are a reminder of Genoa's glorious past. For many years the city was neglected, but 1992 Genoa cleaned itself up to celebrate the 500th anniversary of the discovery of America by its native son, Christopher Columbus. Among the structures chosen for restoration was the house where Columbus was supposedly born (authenticity doubtful!). Genoa has two notable landmarks: the Lanterna (the lighthouse) which is the city's symbol, and the cemetery of Staglieno, one of the most fascinating in Europe.

MILAN

Milan is a busy city, famous for having more public clocks than any other city in Italy, (time, after all, is money). Girded by its "tangenziali", (ring-roads), and trapped in the centre of a web of motor-ways, Milan is particularly easy to get to! It has become Italy's most fashionable city in every sphere, its dress-designers famous throughout the world, and there are treasures there not to be missed, starting with its celebrated cathedral, and equally exalted opera house, La Scala.

- *Tourist Office: Palazzo del Turismo, Piazza Duomo; or at Milano Centrale station.*

MONEY

Be warned! Not all bank notes are exchanged at the same rate. For example, a 100,000 lire note, which for years has not been allowed to leave the country, is, along with the 50,000 lire note, exchanged at a lower rate in banks outside Italy. It is better, therefore, to leave Italy with notes of no greater value than 10,000 lire, since the exchange is more advantageous. Also, be aware that banks are generally closed in the afternoon. Cheques and credit cards are not used as widely in Italy as in many other countries. On the other hand, automated cash dispensers are plentiful, and accept all the major credit cards.

MOTORING

Petrol costs more in Italy than in many other countries and the Italian government has devised a voucher system. Foreigners, or expatriot Italians who own a car registered abroad, can buy coupons for discounted petrol, and toll-tokens for the motorways. These can be acquired at Italian tourist offices or border crossings, or outside the country. There are different discounts according to your destination: (the whole of Italy, the South, or the South plus islands). These coupons must be purchased with foreign currency and include automatic membership of the ACI (Automobile Club of Italy). Italy's 3,780 mile (6,086 km) motorway-network is one of the best in Europe but remember that motorways are toll roads, except for one or two, such as in Calabria or Sicily, which are free.

- *To get these coupons, ask at a travel agent's before you leave.*

MUSEUMS

There are several museums in Italy that must not be missed:

- *The Pinacoteca di Brera in Milan, 28 via Brera: Open daily from 9.00 am to 7.00 pm; closed: Mondays, (closed on Tuesdays if the preceding Monday is a public-holiday). Open on Sundays from 9.00am to 5.00 pm.*

- *The Egyptian Museum of Turin, 6 via Accademia delle Scienze. One of the richest in Europe. It's open from 9.00 am to 2.00 pm; closed: Mondays, public holidays, and any Tuesday following a public-holiday Monday.*
- *The Galleria dell'Accademia in Venice, on the Campo della Carità. One of the largest museums in Italy. Open daily from 9.00 am to 2.00 pm. Sundays from 9.00 am to 1.00 pm; closed: Mondays.*
- *The Peggy Guggenheim Collection, Palazzo Venier dei Leoni, Calle San Cristoforo in Venice. A magnificent collection of modern art. Open every day, April to October, from 12.00 noon to 6.00 pm, Saturdays from 2.00 pm to 9.00 pm. Closed: Tuesdays.*
- *The Uffizi Gallery, 6 Loggiato degli Uffizi, Florence. Open from 9.00 am to 2.00 pm daily, Sundays from 9.00 am to 1.00 pm, closed: Mondays.*
- *The National Archaeological Museum, 35 Piazza Museo, Naples. One of the best in Europe. Open daily from 9.00 am to 2.00 pm. Sundays until 1.00 pm, closed: Mondays.*
- *The Capodimonte National Gallery and Museum, Parco di Capodimonte, also in Naples. Open daily from 9.00 am to 2.00 pm, Sundays until 1.00 pm., closed: Mondays.*

As for Rome, truly the museum city par excellence, there are too many to mention.

NAPLES

Naples is a city of generosity and excess, a city at once mythical yet a bit absurd, a city that completely defies logic. Naples attracts and repels at the same time. To discover it, leave any photographic equipment and luggage at the hotel and stroll through the alley-ways of Spaccanapoli, old Naples. How can you resist the inimitable charm - playful and tragic - of the Neapolitan people?

Apart from its unique atmosphere and breath-taking position, with the incredible view of Mount Vesuvius across the bay, Naples, quintessential baroque city, offers a number of monuments and museums well worth a visit.

Its surrounding area has for over two hundred years been a centre of attraction for those interested in the ancient world: (Pompeii, Herculaneum).

- *Tourist Office: Piazza Gesù Nuovo, or Central Station.*

OPENING TIMES

Taking into consideration local differences, the most usual opening and closing times are as follows:-

- *Banks: 8.30 am - 1.30 pm (and 3.00 pm - 4.00 pm in major towns). Closed: Saturday, Sunday, and public holidays.*
- *Post Offices: 8.30 am - 2.00 pm. Closed from mid-day on Saturdays and the last day of each month. Central post offices in major towns are open in the afternoon until 7.00 pm. Post Offices at airports and central post office services like telegrammes and registered mail are available 24 hours a day.*
- *Chemists: Usual hours 8.30 am - 1.00 pm, 4.30 pm - 8.00 pm, night-time opening: 8.00pm-8.30 am. At all chemists you will find the rota ("di turno") of emergency chemists for night-times and Sundays.*
- *Shops: Shops that stay open all day are rare. In the north of Italy, the hours are generally 9.00 am - 1.00 pm and 4.00 pm - 7.30 pm, in the south they are usually 5.00 pm - 8.30 pm. All shops are closed on Sunday and half a day during the week.*
- *Petrol stations: Usually closed from 11.30 am - 4.00 pm and after 7.00 pm.*

PASTA

Pasta is basic to Italian civilization and there is a huge variety available, with evocative names and interesting shapes.

These are just a few of the most common:

- *long and cylindrical: spaghetti, spaghettini (thinner), bucatini, ziti.*
- *short: maccheroni, penne (bevelled), rigatoni (tubes), fusili (twists), farfalle (bows) conchiglie (shells).*
- *Flat: fettucine (also called tagliatelle) and lasagna. When pasta is stuffed, it is called ravioli (or agnolotti), cannelloni, or tortellini (ring-shaped).*

Finally, there are pastas used mainly in soups, such as capellini (angel hair) or occhi di pernice (partridge eyes), .

The full catalogue of pasta would run into volumes.......

PLACES OF INTEREST

An arbitrary choice from the huge number of beautiful places in Italy. In Venice, Torcello, the farthest island, is the ancient queen of the lagoon. All that remains are a few churches amongst the reeds; it is a strange place, that lends itself to meditation. To get there, take a boat at the Fondamenta Nuove (about three quarters of an hour).

Since Venice is our point of departure. it would be tragic not to take a boat along the Canale de la Brenta, linking Venice and Padua. This beautiful waterway is lined with magnificent villas - former country houses of the Venetian aristocracy - among them, several designed by Palladio, such as the Malcontenta (Villa Foscari).

In the area round Milan, Lake Maggiore is particularly ravishing, not least thanks to the Borromean Islands in the middle. These islands can be reached from Stresa. Of the three islands - Isola Bella, Isola dei Pescatori, (which, as its name suggests, harbours a fishermen's village), and Isola Madre, it is the first, often called the "pearl" of lake Maggiore, that is the most fascinating: there is a beautiful palace, surrounded by trees....like a fairy-tale.

On the Italian Riviera there are several enchanting spots, such as Portofino or Cinque Terre. Portofino, where the European jet-set moors its yachts, is incomparable, with its sheltered port, its promontory, its cemetery by the sea, and the delightful monastery of San Fruttuoso. You can get there by boat, from either Santa Margherita Ligure or Genoa. Cinque Terre - or Five Lands - is the name given to five villages breathtakingly clinging to the cliffs: Monterosso, Vernazza, Corniglia, Manarola and Riomaggiore, all between Levanto and La Spezzia. The path that links them is known as "via dell'amore" (lovers' lane). Astonishingly enough, these villages also have a train service and can be reached by car, following a strange route that uses the rail tunnels. The pleasantest way to arrive, however, is by boat.

In Tuscany, who could resist San Gimignano, the city of towers. In this entrancing town, the visitor can picture life as it was in Tuscany in the Middle Ages. Scarcely 60 miles from Rome, between Viterbo and Orte, lies Bomarzo, and its famous "parco dei mostri" (park of monsters). The "Bosco Sacro" (sacred wood) was created by Prince Pierfrancesco Orsini in the middle of the sixteenth century and Bomarzo Park - where the natural rock was used to form grotesque figures - is a fascinating excursion into the world of ancient mythology. In the middle of the park stands a terrifying fantastic dragon, its gaping mouth a challenge to all who come "in search of knowledge". One of the most magical places!

When visiting Naples, it would be unthinkable not to see Herculaneum (Ercolano) or Pompeii, the two famous Roman towns destroyed by an eruption of Mount Vesuvius in AD 79. The visit is an emotional one, as the volcano's human victims can still be seen, their contorted bodies preserved by lava, but these two towns also give us a uniquely clear picture of life in ancient Rome. There is a private rail link, the Circumvesiana, which leaves from Naples central station.

There are too many extraordinary places in Italy to mention them all, but here are just a few more: Alberobello, in the ancient province of Apulia (now called Puglia), with its unbelievable "trulli", cone-shaped stone huts that are more reminiscent of Turkey than of Italy. There is a marvellous nature reserve on the island of Alcudi (15 inhabitants, one of the Lipari, the Aeolian islands off the north-east coast of Sicily), or the countryside of Sardinia, whose natural beauty has remained untouched; on the north side of the island, you can wonder at the rocks of Capo d'Orso, worn by erosion into fantastic forms, or at the "nuraghi", megalithic ruins of fortified villages dotted all over the island.

PUBLIC TRANSPORT

Each city has its own transport system and tickets can generally be bought at newstands.

In Rome there are two underground lines and numerous bus routes. A ticket is valid for one hour, but you can also buy books of tickets and a tourist pass called the Roma Pass. Milan also has two underground lines but there are buses, trams and trolley-buses as well. A ticket is valid for 75 minutes. In Naples there is one underground line, plus buses and several funiculars that link the low-lying parts of the city with the higher area. In Turin , you can go by tram or bus. In Genoa the long-awaited underground is still on the drawing-board. As yet, you have to make do with the buses, lifts and funiculars. A ticket is valid for an hour and a quarter.

For all these cities, one ticket allows you to use all the various parts of the transport system, changing

from bus to tram to funicular, for the specified amount of time.
Finally, a word about the very special form of transport available in Venice. The famous "vaporetti", (water-buses), are splendid for visiting the city and islands, like a sort of delightful mini-cruise. There are both express and local routes. You can buy tickets singly, but you can also get a ticket for the whole day on all lines (the "biglietto giornaliero"). For crossing the Grand Canal there are also the "traghetti", which are ferry boats like big, public, gondolas. You pay when you get on and stand during the crossing. Gondolas, which are not really a form of public transport, are much more expensive: 50,000 lire for 50 minutes, for no more than five people.
There are taxis in all cities, even in Venice where they are actually motor-boats. Fares vary greatly from place to place.

RAILWAY STATIONS

There are tourist information offices in all major stations where you can, for example, find somewhere to stay, be given a map, and get all sorts of information. There will also be a "cambio" (bureau de change), staying open much later than banks (usually until 7.00 pm). There are left-luggage facilities, of course, and the "albergo diurno" - or daytime hotel - where you can have a wash, or shower, shave and even take a nap.

ROME

It's hard to define Rome, capital not only of Italy but also of the Catholic Church, living museum, centre for films, a city at once ancient, Renaissance, baroque, and modern, where all the styles are inextricably mixed. It is impossible to list all the attractions - remember simply the Coliseum (Rome's symbol), the Via Vittoria Veneto (Rome's premier shopping-street), Trastevere (the part of town "across the Tiber", the "arty" district), the Spanish Steps of the Trinita dei Monti, (where the locals collect to chat up the girls), the Castel Sant'Angelo, the pyramid of Caius Cestius, the Piazza Navona, with Bernini's glorious Fountain of the Four Rivers. And then there is the E.U.R., a whole, monumental neighbourhood built under Mussolini , which houses government buildings, and halls for exhibitions, meetings and concerts, all in an immense park.

- *Tourist office: 5 Via Parigi or at the Termini station.*

SAN MARINO

The Italian Peninsula is divided into three states: the Italian Republic with 116,316 square miles (301,260 km²), the Republic of San Marino with 23.4 square miles (60.57 km²), and Vatican City with only .17 square miles (.44 km²). The oldest of the three is the Republic of San Marino, established in the fourth century. The capital, San Marino, perched on a rock, is a haven for drinkers (there is no tax on alcohol) and philatelists (manufacturing postage-stamps is the Republic's largest industry).

SHOPPING

Impossible to list all the shops in Italy! so here are just a few of the high-spots: in Rome, the Piazza Barberini (at the end of the Via Vittorio Veneto), Via del Corso, which links the Piazza Venezia to the Piazza del Popolo, and the streets between the Via del Corso and the Piazza di Spagna (the Spanish Steps), like the Via Condotti or Via Frattina. One of Italy's best known department stores is Rinascente and there are two branches in Rome - Piazza Fiume and Piazza Colonna.
The chic shopping in Milan is done in the Brera area, where connoisseurs of fashion and design will be in their element. Shops are located around the central axis of the Via Monte Napoleone, particularly in the Via Bigli, Via Sant'Andrea, Via della Spiga or the Corso Matteotti.
In Naples, you must head for the Via dei Mille, Via Filangieri or Via Carlo Poerio, in the residential area behind the Cellamare Palace.
In Florence, avid shoppers will want to visit the part just southwest of the Duomo around the Piazza della Repubblica. This forms a kind of square that corresponds to an ancient Roman city. At the western boundary is the Via de' Tornabuoni, to the north, Via de' Cerretani, to the east Via de' Calzaioli where, as the name implies, shoes have always been sold.
No one goes to Venice just to shop, but there are lovely boutiques. The best are to be found between the Piazza San Marco and the Teatro la Fenice, in the Calle Larga XXII Marzo, the Salizada San Moise, the Calle Vallaresso, the Frezzeria San Marco, or the

Ramo Fuserie. Remember, too, that there are two specialities made on Venice's islands: glass from the island of Murano and lace from Burano. Watch out, though, for the tourist traps.

SPAS

The popularity of spas dates back to ancient Rome, but this is not about the Roman baths at Caracalla, in Rome, nor other such monuments. This is about the Italian spas still in use today, and offering all the traditional amenities that have made these watering-places so popular over the years, such as orchestras, gardens and colonnades. In some of these spas, there is also that certain "je-ne-sais-quoi" that comes from taking the same waters as the Romans or Etruscans.

The best known are Albano Terme in Venetia (province of Padua); Ischia, an island off Naples; Salsomaggiore in Emilia-Romagna (the province of Parma); Montecatini (province of Pistoia); and Chianciano (near Siena in Tuscany), patronised by Etruscans with liver problems; and Giuggi (province of Frosinone in Latium). If you celebrate Christmas and New Year in Italy, these names might well come in handy.

TELEPHONES

There are telephone booths in the streets, railway stations, etc., and a lot of bars and restaurants have a public phone, indicated by a sign. You can use the phone or consult the directories without having a drink. These telephones take money or tokens, called "gettoni". Gettoni have the interesting feature of also being used as ordinary coins, whose value actually increases with inflation. Use of the phone-card is becoming more widespread.

THEATRE

Certain Italian theatres are renowned throughout the world, the most famous being La Scala, Milan's opera house (Teatro Lirico della Scala, Piazza della Scala). Milan is also the setting for one of the brightest jewels of modern European theatre, the Piccolo Teatro de Giorgio Strehler (2 Via Rovanello). Venice is home to another great lyric theatre, the Teatro La Fenice (Campo San Fantin), the only opera house that has canals on two sides...and then there is the famous Theatre of San Carlo in Naples, which is even older than La Scala and La Fenice.

In the summer, at the end of the theatre season, there are festivals throughout Italy: the summer season of opera and ballet held each year in the arena at Verona, lasts all through July and August (Arena di Verona, Piazza Bra 28, Verona 37121); open-air theatres also hold festivals, one in Rome at the Baths of Caracalla and two in Sicily in the Greek theatres of Syracuse and Taormina. And let's not forget the Rossini Festival in Pesaro (in August and September, in the Marches), nor the famous Festival of Two Worlds in Spoleto, Umbria, (from April to July), nor Stresa's Musical Weeks beside Lake Maggiore, (in the province of Novara).

Speaking of Festivals, three very famous and popular ones must be mentioned: The Venice International Film Festival which begins at the end of August and lasts into September, the International Festival of Italian Music in San Remo (province of Imperia), held in February, and in September, Naples' Festival of Neapolitan Songs.

TURIN

On the banks of the River Po, Turin, largest city in the Piedmont , may be Italy's industrial heartland, (home of FIAT), but it nonetheless has a certain charm. Its royal past, from the time when it was the capital of Savoy, has left it a certain gracious solemnity, with its strict , rectilinear streets, squares and colonnades. The heart of Turin consists of a group of majestic buildings: the Royal Palace, the Madamma Palace, the Carignano Palace, the Piazza San Carlo, with its twin churches, and the Mole Antonelliana, whose high slender tower is a symbol of the city. Its palaces and numerous bronze statues give Turin the air of a great European capital of the past.

- *Tourist office: 226 via Roma or the Porta Nuova Station.*

VATICAN

In the heart of Rome, Vatican City is an independent state. With only .17 square miles (.44 km^2). it may be the smallest state in the world, *but it is one of the richest, and attracts Catholics and art lovers from all over the world. St. Peter's, the largest basilica in the world, is an extraordinary feat, both artistically and architecturally. As for the Vatican's museums, they are so full of works of art that a day's visit is not enough. Anyone pressed for time should concentrate on the works of Raphael and Michelangelo's stunning Sistine Chapel .*

- *St. Peter's Basilica: Open from 7.00 am to 7.00 pm.*
- *The Vatican Museum: Open from 9.00 am to 4.00 pm except Sundays and public holidays.*
- *Papal audiences: Every Wednesday from 11.00 am in the Hall of Paul IV, near the south side of St. Peter's. Those who wish an audience should write in advance to the Prefetto della Casa Pontificia.*

VENICE

Everything in Venice is wonderful: the buildings, the museums, the location. Byron summed this up: "Venice sat in state, throned on her hundred isles", and it is precisely the canals and the lagoon that give Venice her unique beauty. To get the feel of Venice, start with the Gran Canale, the most extraordinary "street" in the world, but then simply wander, explore as the fancy takes you, lose yourself beside narrow canals, and in tiny piazzas. On foot and by boat. No matter where you go - and Venice is not large - you will eventually come across signs to direct you, and if not, the Venetians will always be happy to help. With its canals, bridges and views which change with every hour and every season, Venice never fails to thrill. Especially if you leave the main areas, which are full of tourists, and stroll towards the Fondamente Nuove or the Arsenal and the part called San Pietro, or to the Giudecca. There is a dreamlike unreality about Venice, which is perhaps the reason that everyone finds there what he seeks.

- *Tourist office: Piazza San Marco (Calle dell'Ascenzione); Santa Lucia Station;*
- *Piazzale Roma (for those who arrive by car).*

WINES

Italy boasts nearly 1,500 different wines, among which 200 or so have been awarded the DOC (Denominazione di Origine Controllata), a mark of their high quality. Among these fine wines, there are, (for reds): Chianti from Tuscany (the best have a black cockrel on the neck of the bottle); Barolo, Nebiolo, Barbera, Dolcetto, all from the Piedmont; Valpolicella from the Verona area. Among the white wines are: Bianco dei Castelli Romani from the Rome area, Soave from near Verona, Lacrima Christi from Vesuvius, Cortesi di Gavi from the Piedmont, Vernaccia de San Gimignano from Tuscany. There are also special wines such as Lambrusco, a light sparkling wine from Romagna, (very popular abroad as a white wine, but generally the red is more popular in Italy); the famous Asti Spumante, a champagne-type wine from the Piedmont, and Marsala, a strong, heady, fortified wine, sometimes thickened with a beaten egg yolk.
Connoisseurs of wine would be interested in visiting the Enoteca Italica Permanente, in Siena. This is a government-run collection of all the different wines Italy can offer, where they can be studied, and even sampled!

COMMON ITALIAN ABBREVIATIONS

ACI	*Automobile Club d'Italia* (Automobile Club of Italy)
ANSA	*Agenzia nazionale stampa associata* (National Press Association)
BI	*Banca d'Italia* (Bank of Italy)
BR	*Brigate rosse* (Red Brigade)
CAP	*Codice di avviamento postale* (Post Code)
CGIL	*Confederazione generale italiana del lavoro* (General Confederation of Italian Workers)
CISAL	*Confederazione italiana sindacati autonomi dei lavoratori* (Italian Confederation of Independent Trade Unions)
CISL	*Confederazione italiana sindacati lavoratori* (Italian Confederation of Trade Union Workers)
CIT	*Compagnia italiana turismo* (Italian Tourist Office)
CP	*Casella postale* (Post Box)
DC	*Democrazia cristiana* (Christian Democratic Party)
DP	*Democrazia proletaria* (Democratic Proletarian Party)
ENAL	*Ente nazionale assistenza lavoratori* (National Worker's Assistance Office)
ENEL	*Ente nazionale per l'Energia elettrica* (National Organisation for Electric Power)
ENIT	*Ente nazionale italiano per il turismo* (Italian National Tourist Board)
EPT	*Ente provinciale per il turismo* (Regional Tourist Board)
FI	*Frequenza intermedia* (Frequency Modulation (FM))
FIA	*Frequenza intermedia audio* (Audio Amplitude Modulation (AM radio))
FIV	*Frequenza intermedia video* (Video Amplitude Modulation (AM video))
FS, FF.SS	*Ferrovie dello stato* (National railway system)
G.C.	*Gesù Cristo* (Jesus Christ)
GR	*Giornale radio* (Radio news)
G.U.	*Gazzetta ufficiale* (Official news)
IACP	*Instituto autonomo per le case popolari* (Independent Institute for Low-Income Housing)
INPS	*Instituto nazionale per la previdenza sociale* (National Institute for Social Services)
INT	*Instituto nazionale trasporti* (National Transport Office)
IVA	*Imposta sul valore aggiunto* (Value-added Tax (VAT))
MEC	*Mercato comune europeo* (European Common Market)
MSI	*Movimento sociale italiano* (Italian Social Movement, a neo-fascist party)
PA	*Posta aerea* (Air Mail)
PLI	*Partito liberale italiano* (Italian Liberal Party)
PREI	*Partito repubblicano italiano* (Italian Republican Party)
PSDI	*Partito socialista democratico italiano* (Italian Social-Democratic Party)
PSI	*Partito socialista italiano* (Italian Socialist Party)
POLSTRADA	*Polizia stradale* (Traffic Police)
PS	*Polizia di stato* (State Police)
PT	*Posta e telegrafi* (Post Office and Telegraph)
PTP	*Posto telefonico pubblico* (Public telephone box)
PU	*Polizia urbana* (City police)
RAI	*Radio televisione italiana* (Italian Radio and Television)
RR	*Ricevuta di ritorno* (Acknowledgement of receipt)
SP	*Strada statale* (National highway)
TG	*Telegiornale* (Television news)
TUT	*Tariffa urbana a tempo* (Urban unit fare)
TVC	*Televisione a colori* (Colour television)
US	*1. Ufficio stampa* (Press office)
	2. Uscita di sicurezza (Emergency exit)
VU	*Vigile urbano* (Police officer)

VOCABULARY

About 1,500 words and expressions are listed alphabetically in this Italian-English glossary. Where a word has several meanings, only those which appear in this book are given. Adjectives are in the masculine singular, and verbs in the infinitive. Irregular forms can be found in the grammar section of the booklet. Place-names where the Italian and English are identical have been omitted.

VOCABULARY

A

abbastanza — quite/enough
abbigliamento — clothing
abbondante — abundant
abitare — to live (somewhere)
accappatoio — dressing-gown
accettare — to accept
accidenti! — damn!
acciuga — anchovy
accomodarsi — 1:to come in; 2: to sit down; 3: to proceed to . . .
accompagnare — to accompany
accorciare — to shorten
accorgersi — to realise
aceto — vinegar
acqua (minerale) — (mineral) water
acquavite — brandy
acquazzone — downpour
acquisto — purchase
adesso — now
adottivo — adopted
aereo — aeroplane
aeroporto — airport
afa — mugginess
affettuoso — affectionate
affittare — to rent
affitto — rent
affluente — tributary
affollato — crowded
affresco — fresco
agente (immobiliare) — (estate) agent
agenzia — agency
aggiungere — to add (on)
agiato — comfortably off
aglio — garlic
agosto — August
agraria — agriculture
alba — dawn
albergo — hotel
albicocca — apricot
alcoolici — alcoholic drinks
alcuni — some (pl)
allegro — happy
allevamento — rearing
alloggiare — to lodge
allora — then
allungare — to lengthen
almeno — at least
Alpi — Alps
altitudine — altitude
alto — 1: tall; 2: high
altoparlante — loudspeaker
altopiano — plateau
altrettanto — as well, as many
altrimenti — otherwise
altro — other
amare — to love
amaro — bitters
ambiente — setting/ambiance
americano — American
ammalarsi — to fall ill
ammirare — to admire
amore — love
analcoolici — non-alcoholic drinks
ananas — pineapple
anatra — duck
anche — also, too
anche di più — even more
ancora — again/yet
andare — to go
andata — oneway ticket
anguilla — eel
anguria — watermelon
animale — animal
anno — year
annoiarsi — to be bored
Antartide — Antarctica
antibiotico — antibiotic
Antille — Antilles
antipatico — unpleasant (esp. of people)
anzianità — seniority
aperitivo — drink before a meal
apparenza — appearance
appartamento — apartment/flat
appassionato — enthusiast/lover of (dance etc.)
appena — hardly
Appennini — Apennines
appetito — appetite
approvare — to approve
appuntamento — appointment
aprile — April
aprire — to open
Arabia Saudita — Saudi Arabia
aragosta — lobster
architetto — architect
architettura — architecture
argenteria — silverware
argento — silver
argomento — topic
aria — air
aria condizionata — air conditioning
armadio — wardrobe
arrabbiarsi — to get angry
arrivare — to arrive
arrivo — arrival
arrosto — roast
arte — art
artista — artist
ascoltare — listen
asilo nido — kindergarten
aspettare — to wait for
aspirina — aspirin
assegno — cheque
assistente — assistant
assistente sociale — social worker
attendere — to wait
attenzione — attention
attimo — instant
attirare — to attract
attore/attrice — actor/actress
attraversare — to cross
autista — driver
autobus — bus
automobile — car
autopullman (il pullman) — coach
autunno — autumn
avere — to have
aver intenzione di... — to intend to..
aver mal di gola — to have a sore throat
aver mal di testa — to have a headache
avere fretta — to be in a hurry
avere la fama (di) — to have the reputation (of)
avere un certo appetito — to be quite hungry
avere una fame da lupi — to be as hungry as a hunter
avere voglia — to feel like/want
avvertire — to warn
avvocato — lawyer
azienda — business/company
azzurro — pale blue

B

bagagli (pl) — luggage
bagno — bath
balcone — balcony
ballare — to dance
ballerina — dancer
bambino/a — child
banana — banana
banca — bank
bandiera — flag
bar — bar
barbiere — barber
barella — stretcher
basilico — basil
basso — 1: short; 2: low
bastare — to be enough
battere — to beat
Belgio — Belgium
bello — beautiful
bene — well
benissimo — very well
bere — to drink

berretto — cap
bevande — drinks
bianco — white
bicchiere — drinking glass
bicicletta — bicycle
biglietteria — ticket office
biglietto — ticket
binario — platform (lit. rail)
biologo (m) — biologist
biondo — fair-haired
birra — beer
birreria — beer house
bisnonno — great-grandfather
bisogna — it is necessary
bistecca — steak
blu — dark blue
bocca — mouth
bollito — boiled
bombetta — bowler hat
Bosnia-Erzegovina — Bosnia
borsellino — purse
bottiglia — bottle
bottoncino — small button
bottone — button
box — garage/parking place
braccio (m)/bracchia (f.pl.) — arm (s)
Brasile — Brazil
bravo — talented/good
brillante — brilliant
brina — frost
bruno — dark-haired
brutto — ugly
bue (m.plur.:buoi) — ox, oxen
buio — dark
buono — good
buonasera — good evening
buongiorno — goodmorning
buongustaio — gourmet
bustapaga — pay-packet

C

cabina — booth/fitting-room
cabina telefonica — phone box
cacciagione — game (meat)
caffè — coffee
calamaro — squid
calcio — football
caldo — heat/hot
calma — calm
calze — socks
calze di nylon — tights
calzolaio — shoemaker
calzoleria — shoe shop
cambiare — to change/exchange
cambiare idea — to change one's mind
cambio — change/exchange
camera — room
camera da letto — bedroom
camera doppia — double room
camera matrimoniale — room with double bed
camera singola — single room
cameriere — waiter
camicetta — blouse
camicia — shirt
camicia da notte — nightdress
campaggio — campsite
canarino — canary
canottiera — vest
cantare — to sing
cantina — basement storage/cellar
canzone — song
capelli — hair
capire — to understand
capitare — to happen
capo — head/chief
capolinea — terminus
cappello — hat
cappotto — coat
capra — goat
capriolo — venison
capufficio — office manager
caratteristica — characteristic (n.)
caratteristico — characteristic/typical
carciofo — artichoke
carnagione — complexion
carne — meat
carnevale — carnival
caro — dear/expensive
carota — carrot
carpa — carp
carrozza — coach (train)
carta d'identità — identity card
carta di credito — credit card
cartina geografica — map
casa — house
casa editrice — publishing house
casalinga — housewife
caso — case
cassa — cash desk
cassetta — cassette
cassetto — drawer
castagno — brown-haired
categoria — category
cattedrale — cathedral
cattivo — wicked
causa — cause
cauzione — downpayment/ deposit
cavallo — horse
cavolo — cabbage
cece — chick pea
ceco — Czech
cena — dinner
cenare — to dine/have dinner
centrale — central
centralinista — telephone operator
centro — centre
ceramica — ceramics
cercare — to search/look for
certamente — certainly, of course
certo — certainly (indeed)
che rabbia! — how maddening!
chi — who
chiacchierare — to chat
chiamare — to call
chiamarsi — to be called
chiaro — clear, light
chiave — key
chiesa — church
chilo — kilo
chimico — chemist
chiostro — cloister
chirurgo — surgeon
chitarra — guitar
chiudere — to close
Ciad — Chad
cibo — food
ciclismo — cycling
cielo — sky
Cile — Chile
ciliegia — cherry
Cina — China
cinema — the pictures/cinema
cinghiale — wild boar
cintura — belt
cioè — that is
cipolla — onion
circuito — circuit/tour
citofono — intercom
città — city, town
classe — class
classico — classic
clima — climate
coda — tail, end
cognac — cognac
cognato — brother-in-law
cognome — surname
coincidenza — (train) connection
colazione — breakfast
collega — colleague/associate
colletto — collar
collina — small hill
collo — neck
colore — colour
coltello — knife
comico — comical
cominciare — to begin

commedia — comedy
commercialista — businessperson
commerciante — dealer, trader
commesso — assistant
commissario — police inspector
comodo — comfortable
compilare — to fill in
completo — complete/full
complimento — compliment
comprare — to buy
compressa — tablet
compromesso — compromise
comunque — however
con — with
con calma — calmly
concerto — concert
condimento — seasoning
condizione — condition
confine — border
coniglio — rabbit
conoscere/conoscersi — to know (someone)/to know each other
consegna dei bagagli — left-luggage counter
considerare — to consider
consigliare — to advise
contare — to count
continuare — to go on
conto — bill
conto corrente — current account
contorno — side dish of vegetables
contrario — contrary
contrattempo — hitch/mishap
contratto d'affitto — lease
controllare — to check
conversazione — conversation
convincere — to convince
coperto — covered
coppa — brawn
Corea — Korea
correre il rischio di — to run the risk of
corridoio — corridor
corsista — participant on a course
corso — course
corto — brief
cosa — thing
coscia — thigh
così — so
costa — coast
costare — to cost
costume da bagno — swimsuit
cotone — cotton
cottura — cooking, as in "cooking time"
cratere — crater
credere — to believe
crema di bellezza — beauty cream
crescere — to grow
Croazia — Croatia
crudo — raw
cuccetta — berth/couchette
cucchiaino — small spoon
cucchiaio — spoon
cucina — kitchen
cugino/a — cousin
cuore— heart
cuori — hearts (cards)
cupola — dome
cura — treatment/care
curare — to look after/to cure
curiosità — curiosity
curioso — curious

D

dai! — give over!
Danimarca — Denmark
danza (classica, moderna) — dance (ballet, modern)
dare — to give
dare (darsi) del Lei — to call each other "Lei" (formal "you")
dare (darsi) del tu — to call each other "tu" (familiar "you")
dare una spinta — to give a shove/push
darsi delle arie — to give oneself airs
datore di lavoro — employer
davanti (a) — in front (of)
davvero? — really?
debole — weak
debolezza — weakness
decentrato — out of town/in the suburbs
decidere — to decide
decimo — tenth
delta (m)— delta
denaro — money
dente — tooth
dentista — dentist
dentro — inside
denuncia — report (to the police)
dépliant — brochure
depresso — depressed
desiderare — to want, require
destinazione — destination
destino — fate
destra — right (hand)
dettagliato — detailed
dicembre — December
dietro — behind
difficile — difficult
digestivo — "digestif" (usu. spirits after a meal)
dimenticare — to forget
dimostrare — to show/demonstrate
dimostrare l'età — to show one's age
dinamico — dynamic
dio — god
dipendente — salaried worker
dipendere (da) — to depend on
dire — to say/tell
diretto — through train
direttore — director/manager
direttore amministrativo — administrative/executive director
dirigente — manager
disciplinato — disciplined
disco — record
discoteca — discotheque
disegnatore industriale — industrial designer
disoccupato — unemployed
disoccupazione — unemployment
disonesto — dishonest
disponibile — available
disporre — to have available
distratto — distracted/absent-minded
disturbare — to disturb
dito (m) dita (f.pl.) — finger (s)
ditta — company
divano/sofà — sofa
diventare — to become
diverso — different/several
divertente — amusing
divertirsi — to enjoy oneself
divorziare — to divorce
divorzio — divorce
documento — document
dogana — customs
dolce — dessert, pudding
dollaro USA — American dollar
Dolomiti — Dolomites
domanda — question
domandare — to ask
domani — tomorrow
domenica — Sunday
donna — woman
dopo — after
doppi servizi — kitchen, bathroom etc.
doppia — double
dormire — to sleep
dottore — doctor
dove — where
dovere — to have to
dramma — drama
drammatico — dramatic
dritto — straight ahead
drogheria — grocer's shop
droghiere — grocer
dunque — therefore/thus

E

ecco — here you are
eccolo — here it is
economico — cheap
effettivamente — really
Egitto — Egypt
elegante — smart
elenco telefonico — phone book
elettricista — electrician
elettrodomestico — electrical household goods
elevato — elevated
entrare — to enter
eppure — and yet...
equitazione — horse riding
eredità — heritage
esclamarsi — to exclaim
esatto! — exactly!
escursione — excursion
esilio — exile
esistere — to exist
esitare — to hesitate
espansivo — extrovert
esperienza — experience
esposizione — aspect
espresso — express train
essere — to be
essere indeciso — to be undecided
essere matto — to be crazy
essere pronto — to be ready
essere stonato — to sing off-key
est — east
estate — summer
estero — abroad
estuario — estuary
età — age
etto — a hundred grammes/hectogramme
Europa (f) — Europe

F

fabbro — locksmith
faccia — face
facile — easy
facoltà — faculty
fagiano — pheasant
fagiolino — green bean
fagiolo — bean
falegname — carpenter
falso — false
fama — reputation/fame
fame — hunger
famiglia — family
famoso (celebre) — famous
fantascienza — science-fiction
fare — to do/make
farci caso — to pay attention
fare colazione — to have breakfast
fare il biglietto — to take a ticket
fare in tempo — to have enough time
fare sport — to do sport
fare un solitario — to play patience
fare une telefonata — to telephone
farfallino — bow-tie
farmacia — chemist shop
farmacista — chemist
farsi un'idea — to get an idea
fascino — appeal/fascination
fatica — fatigue
fattorino — errand boy, delivery man
febbraio — February
febbre — fever/temperature
felice — happy
ferie — paid holidays
fermarsi (trattenersi) — stay
fermata (dell'autobus) — (bus) stop
fiammiferi — matches
fico — fig
fidanzato — fiancé
fidarsi (di) — to trust
fiero — proud
figlio/a — son/daughter
figlio maggiore — oldest son
figlio minore — youngest son
fila — line
filetto — filet
fine — end
fine-settimana — weekend
finestra — window
finire — to finish
fino a — until
finocchio — fennel
fiore — flower
fiori — clubs (cards)
firma — signature
fisico — physicist
fiume — river
foce — mouth of a river
foglio — leaf
foglio-paga — pay-slip
fondo — end
fontana — fountain
forchetta — fork
formaggio — cheese
formazione — training
formula — formula/type
forno — oven
forse — perhaps
forte — strong
fortunato — lucky
fotografo — photographer
fra — in (time), amongst (place)
fragola — strawberry
francese — French
Francia — France
franco — franc
frase — sentence
fratellastro — half-brother
fratello — brother
freddo — cold
fritto — fried
fronte — forehead
frontiera — frontier
frutta — fruit
frutta e verdura — green-grocer's shop
frutti di mare — seafood
fruttivendolo — green-grocer
fulmine — thunder
fumare — to smoke
fungo — mushroom
fuori — outside
furto — theft

G

gabinetto — lavatory
galleria — gallery, arcade
gallina — hen
gamba — leg
gamberetto — shrimp
gambero — crayfish
gazzosa — fizzy drink
gatto — cat
gelateria — icecream parlour
generalizzare — to generalise
genero — son-in-law
genitori — parents
gennaio — January
geologo — geologist
Germania — Germany
gessato — striped
gestione — management
gettone — token
ghiaccio — ice
già — already
giacca — jacket
giallo — 1.yellow,2.thriller
Giappone — Japan
ginecologo — gynaecologist
ginnastica — gymnastics
ginocchio — knee
giocare (un gioco) — to play (a game)
giocare a carte — to play cards
giocare a dadi — to play dice
giocare a dama — to play draughts
giocare a scacchi — to play chess
giochi di società — board-games
gioco — game

gioielleria — jewellery shop
gioielliere — jeweller
Giordania — Jordan
giornalaio — newsagent
giornale — newspaper
giornalista — journalist
giorno — day
giovane — young
giovedì — Thursday
girare — to turn
giro della città — tour of the city
girocollo — polo-necked
giubbotto — blouson/bomber-jacket
giugno — June
goccia — drop
godere di — to enjoy
gola — throat
golf — sleeveless pullover
golfo — gulf
gomito — elbow
gonna — skirt
gradevole — pleasant
grammo — gramme
granchio — crab
grande — big/large
grande magazzino — department-store
grandine — hail
grappa — Italian brandy
grasso — fat
grave — grave, serious
grazie — thanks
Grecia — Greece
grigio — grey
guanti — gloves
guardare — to watch/look at
guarire — to get better
guida — guide

I

idea — idea
idraulico — plumber
ieri — yesterday
illuminato — well-lit (floodlit)
imbarazzo — embarassment
immaginare — to imagine/suppose
imparare — to learn
impegno — obligation/thing to do
impermeabile — raincoat
impianto stereo — hifi-system
impiegato/a — clerk/employee
importante — important
impossibile — impossible
impressionante — impressive
in effetti — actually, in effect
in fondo a — at the end of
in genere — in general
incidente — accident
incominciare — to commence
incontrarsi — to meet/run into
incredibile — incredible
indeciso — undecided
indennità — indemnity
individuo — individual
indovinello — riddle
industriale — industrialist
influenza — flu
informarsi — to get information
informatica — computing
ingegnere — engineer
ingegneria — engineering
Inghilterra — England
inglese — English
ingresso — entrance
inizio — start/beginning
innamorato — in love
innanzi tutto — above all
inondazione — flood
inquilino — tenant
insalata — salad
insegnante — teacher
insieme — together
insomma — in short
insonnia — insomnia
insupportabile — intolerable
intelligente — intelligent
intenzione — intention
interessare — to interest
internazionale — international
interprete — interpreter
intorno a — around
intraprendente — enterprising
intromettersi — to join in
invece — instead, rather
inverno — winter
Irlanda — Ireland
iscrivere (si) — to enrol/register
isola — island
Israele — Israel
istituto tecnico — technical school
Italia — Italy
italiano — Italian
itinerario — route/itinerary
Iugoslavia — Yugoslavia

K

Kenia — Kenya

L

labbra — lips
ladro — thief
lago — lake
lampo — lightening
lampone — raspberry
lana — wool
lardo — bacon-fat
largo — loose/wide
lasciare — to leave
lasciar detto qualcosa — to leave a message
lato — side
lattaio — milkman
latte — milk
latteria — dairy
laurea — university degree
lavorare — to work
lavoro — job/work
legge — law
leggero — light (weight)
Lei — you (formal)
lei — she/it
lenticchia — lentil
lepre — hare
lettera — letter
letteratura — literature
letto — bed
lì — over there
Libano — Lebanon
libero professionista — freelance professional
Libia — Libya
libretto degli assegni — cheque-book
libro — book
licenza elementare — junior school certificate
licenza media — secondary school certificate
licenziamento — sacking (job)
liceo classico (m) — further-education college/high school
linea — line
lingua — language
lingue straniere — foreign languages
liquore — liqueur
lira italiana — Italian lira
litro — litre
lontano (da) — far (from)
luccio — pike
luglio — July
luminoso — well-lit
luna — moon
lunedì — Monday
lunghezza — length
lungo — 1.long; 2. (of coffee) weak
luogo — place
luoghi comuni — common-places, clichés

lupo — wolf (in bocca al lupo = and the best of luck!)
Lussemburgo — Luxembourg
lusso — luxury

M

ma — but
ma dai! — come on!
macchina — car
macchina fotografica — camera
macellaio — butcher
macelleria — butcher's shop
madre — mother
maestro — school teacher
maggio — May
maglietta — T-shirt
magnifico — magnificent
magro — lean
mai — ever (never)
maiale — pig
male — badly/harm
maleducato — impolite
malinconia — melancholy
mamma — mummy
mammone — mummy's boy
mancare — to lack
mancia — tip (money)
mandarino — mandarine
manica — sleeve
mano — hand
mare — sea
Mar Mediterraneo — Mediterranean Sea
Mar Tirreno, Ionio, Adriatico — Tyrrhenian, Ionian, Adriatic Seas
marco tedesco — German mark
marito — husband
marmo — marble
marrone — brown-haired
martedì — Tuesday
marzo — March
massimo — maximum
matrigna — stepmother
matrimonio — marriage
mattina — morning
maturità liceale — high school diploma, university entrance
meccanico — mechanic
medicina — medicine
medico — doctor
Medio Evo — Middle Ages
meglio — better
mela — apple
melanzana — aubergine
melone — melon
meno — less
mensa aziendale — works canteen
menta — mint
mento — chin
mentre — while
menù — menu
meraviglioso — wonderful
mercoledì — Wednesday
merluzzo — cod
meso — month
messaggio — message
Messico — Mexico
meteorologico — weather-forecast
metro — metre
mettere — to put
mettere piede — to set foot
mezza pensione — half board
mezzo — half
mezzo etto — fifty grammes
mezzogiorno — mid-day
Mezzogiorno — Southern Italy
mi dispiace! — I'm sorry!
milanese — Milanese
minestra — soup
minimo — minimum
minuto — minute
mirtillo — bilberry
misura — size
mobile — piece of furniture
modello — model/style
modo — way/manner
modulo — form
moglie — wife
molluschi — mulluscs
molto — very/much/a lot
momento — moment
montagna — mountain
monte — hill
monumento — monument
mora — blackberry
morire — to die
morte — death
mosaico — mosaic
moscato — muscatel
Mozambico (m) — Mozambique
mucca — cow
muscolo — mussel
museo — museum
musica — music
mutandine — pants

N

napoletano — Neapolitan
nascere — to be born
nascondere — to hide
nasello — hake
naso — nose
Natale — Christmas
naturalmente — naturally
nave — boat, ship
nazionalità — nationality
nebbia — fog
necessario — necessary
negozio — shop
nero — black
nessuno — no one
neve — snow
niente — nothing
nipote — nephew/niece/grandchild
noioso — boring
nome — name
non — not
non vedere l'ora (di) — to be unable to wait (can't wait to)
nonno/a — grandfather/mother
nono — ninth
nord — north
normale — normal
Norvegia — Norway
notte — night
novembre — November
nulla — nothing
numero di telefono — phone number
nuora — daughter-in-law
nuoto — swimming
Nuova Zelanda — New Zealand
nuovo — new
nuvola — cloud
nuvolosa — cloudy

O

oca — goose
occasione — opportunity
occhio — eye
oceano — ocean
odiare — to hate
oggetto — object
oggi — today
olio — oil
oltrepassare — to exceed
ombrello — umbrella
onesto — honest
operaio — worker
operare — to operate
ora — 1. now, 2. hour
ora di punta — rush hour
ordinare — to order
orecchio — ear
orefice — goldsmith
organizzare — to organise
organizzazione — organisation
ormai — from now on

oro — gold
orologiaio — watchmaker
orologio — watch/clock
ostrica — oyster
ottavo — eighth
ottobre — October
ovest — west
ozio — idleness

P

pacchetto — package
padre — father
padrino — godfather
padrone di casa — owner of the building
paese — country
Paesi Bassi — Netherlands
pagare — to pay
paio — pair
palazzo — block of flats
pallacanestro — basket-ball
pancetta affumicata — smoked bacon
pancetta — bacon
panetteria — bakery/breadshop
panettiere — baker
paninoteca — sandwich bar
panna — cream
pantaloncini — shorts
pantaloni — trousers
pantofole — slippers
papà — daddy
parcheggiare — to park
parecchi — several
parenti — relatives
parlare — to speak/talk
parola — word
parrucchiere — hairdresser
partenza — departure
partire — to leave, depart
Pasqua — Easter
passaporto — passport
passante — passerby
passare — to pass by/pass
passeggero — passenger
passegiata — walk
pasticcere — pastry-cook
pasticceria — cake-shop
pasto — meal
patate — potatoes
patatine fritte — chips
patente — driving-licence
patrigno (m) — stepfather
pattinaggio — skating
paura — fear
pausa — pause
pavimento — floor
pazzia — madness
pecora — sheep
pelle — skin
pelliccia — fur coat
penisola — peninsular
pensare — to think
pensionato/a — pensioner
pensione — pension
pensione completa — full board
pepe — pepper (spice)
peperone — pepper (vegetable)
per — for/by
per caso — by chance
per cortesia — please
per esempio — for example
per fortuna — fortunately (Thank goodness!)
pera — pear
perbacco! — Wow!
perché — why/because
perfetto — perfect
periodo — period
pernice — partridge
pernottamento — a night's stay
però — but, however
persona — person
Perù — Peru
pesante — heavy/warm (clothes)
pesca — peach
pesce — fish
pescespada — swordfish
pescheria — fish shop
pescivendolo — fishmonger
peseta spagnola — Spanish peseta
peso — weight
pettegolezzo — gossip
petto — chest
piacere — to please
piacevole — agreeable
piano — floor/storey
piantina della città — town plan
pianura — plain
pianura padana — Po valley
piatto — plate
piazza — square (in town or a village)
picche — spades (cards)
piccolo — small/little
piede — foot
piega — pleat
Piemonte — Piedmont
pieno — full
pigiama (sing.) — pyjamas
pigro — lazy
pioggia — rain
piscina — swimming-pool
piselli — peas
pista — path
pittore — painter
più (di) — more (than)
piumino — anorak
piuttosto — rather
pizzeria — pizza house
poco — a bit/few
poeta — poet
poi — then, after
polizia — police
poliziesco — detective (story)
poliziotto — policeman
pollo — chicken
Polonia — Poland
polpaccio — calf
polpo — octopus
polso — wrist
poltrona — armchair
pomeriggio — afternoon
pomodoro — tomato
ponte — bridge
popolo — a people/population
porro — leek
porta — door
portafoglio — wallet
portare — to bring/wear
portinaio — caretaker
portineria — porter's lodge
porto — port
Portogallo — Portugal
portoghese — Portuguese
posate — cutlery
possibile — possible
possibilmente — possibly
posto — 1.place,2.space
posto da sedere — seat
potere — to be able to
povero — poor
pranzare — to have lunch
pranzo — lunch
preferibilmente — preferably
preferire — to prefer
prefisso — code
prego — please, of course
prendere — to take
prendere in giro (qualcuno) — to tease/pull someone's leg
prenotare — to reserve
prenotazione — reservation
prenotazione obbligatoria — compulsory reservation
prepararsi — to get ready
prescrivere — to prescribe
presentarsi — to introduce oneself
pressione — blood pressure
presto — quickly
prezzemolo — parsley

prima — before
primavera — spring
primo — 1. first; 2. first course
principale — boss
probabilmente — probably
problema — problem
professione — profession
professore — lecturer
profumo — perfume
programma — programme
pronto! — Hello! (telephone)
pronto soccorso — first-aid post
proporre — to propose/ suggest
proprio — really
prosciutto — ham
proseguimento — the continuation (of the tour)
prossimo — next
protagonista — main actor/character
provare — to try (on)
proverbio — proverb
prugna — plum
psichiatra — psychiatrist
psicologico — psychological
psicologo/a — psychologist
pullman — coach
punti cardinali — cardinal points
purtroppo — unfortunately

Q

quadretto — square
quadri — diamonds (cards)
quadro — picture
quaglia — quail
qualche — some/a few
qualcosa — something
qualcuno — someone
qualità — quality
quando — when
quanto — how much
quarto — fourth
quasi — nearly
quello — that
questione — matter
questo — this
questura — police station
qui — here
quindi — therefore/thus
quintale — 100 kilos
quinto — fifth
quotazione — exchange-rate

R

racchetta — racket
raccomandarsi — to implore
raccontare — to tell
raffinato — refined
raffreddore — a cold
ragazza — girl
ragazzino/a — little boy/little girl
ragazzo — boy
raggiungere — to reach
ragione — reason
ragioniere — accountant
rapido — fast train
rapina — robbery
rapinatore — robber
rappresentante — representative
realtà — reality
recentemente — recently
recitare (un ruolo) — to play (a role)
recuperare — to recover
refurtiva — stolen goods
reggiseno — bra
regione — region
regista — film director
Regno Unito — United Kingdom
regola — rule
rendersi conto — to realise
reparto — department
Repubblica Ceca — Czech Republic
Repubblica Sudafricana — South Africa
reputazione — reputation
residenza — residence
responsabile — director, manager, head
restare — to remain
restituire — to give back/return
resto — change (money)
riattaccare — to hang up
ribes — redcurrant
ricco — rich
ricetta — prescription
ricevere — to receive
ricevuta — receipt
richiamare — to call back
ricordarsi — to remember
ridere — to laugh
ridicolo — ridiculous
riflettere — to think over/reflect
riga — stripe
rimanere — to stay/remain
rimettere a nuovo — to do up/renovate
rimpianto — regret
Rinascimento — Renaissance
rinfrescare — to renew/redecorate
ringraziare — to thank
ripetere — to repeat
ripetere lettera per lettera — to spell out
riposarsi — to rest
ripostiglio — storeroom
riscaldamento — heating
rischiare — to risk
riservato — reserved
rispettare — to respect
rispondere al telefono — to answer the phone
risposarsi — to remarry
risposta — answer
ristorante — restaurant
ristretto — strong (coffee)
ritardo — late (ness)
ritorno — return
riunione — reunion
riuscire — to succeed
rivedere — to see/meet again
rivista — magazine
romantico — romantic
romanzo — novel
rosa — pink
rossetto — lipstick
rosso — red
rosticcere — rotisserie owner
rosticceria — rotisserie (cooked meat dishes)
rubare — to rob/steal

S

sabato — Saturday
sala — room/hall
sala d'attesa — waiting room
salario — salary
sale — salt
salire — to go up/to get on (a bus, etc)
salmone — salmon
salone (salotto) — sitting room
salumeria — prepared pork (salami, ham etc) shop
salumiere — pork butcher
salutare — to greet
sandali — sandals
sangue — blood
sapere — to know
Sardegna — Sardinia
sardina — sardine
sbagliare — to make a mistake
sbrigarsi — to hurry
scaffale — shelf/bookcase
scaloppina — veal cutlet
scampo — giant prawn
scarpe — shoes
scegliere — to choose
scellino austriano — Austrian schilling
scelta — choice
scena — scene

scendere — to go down/to get off
scherma — fencing (sport)
scherzare — to joke
schiena — back
sci — skiing
sciare — to ski
scialle — shawl
sciarpa — scarf
scioglilingua — tongue-twister
sciopero — strike
scippo — pick-pocketing
sciroppo — syrup
scomodo — uncoomfortable
scomparire — to disappear
scontrino — ticket-stub
sconvolto — distressed
scorso — last
scrittore — writer
scudo portoghese — Portuguese escudo
scuola elementare — primary school
scuola magistrate — teacher training college
scuola materna — nursery school
scuola media inferiore — lower secondary school
scuola media superiore — upper secondary school
scuro — dark
scusare/scusarsi — to excuse / apologise
se — if
secolo — century
secondo — 1.second, 2.main course
secondo — according to
sedia /seggiola — chair
segretario/a — secretary
seguire — to follow
sembrare — to seem
sempre — always
senape — mustard
seno — breast
sentimentale — sentimental
sentire — to listen/hear
sentirsi — to feel
senza — without
seppia — cuttlefish
sera — evening
serata — evening (as a length of time)
serie — series
serio — serious
servire — to serve
sesto — sixth
seta — silk
sete — thirst
settembre — September
settimo — seventh
sgradevole — unpleasant
si — 1. yes; 2. oneself
si figuri! — not at all
siccità — drought
Sicilia — Sicily
sicuramente — surely
signora — 1. lady, 2. Mrs.
signore — 1. gentleman, 2. sir
signorina — 1. young lady, 2. Miss
silenzio — silence
simile — similar
simpatico — nice/friendly
sindacato — trade-union
sinistra — left
singola — single
Siria — Syria
sistemazione — arrangement
sito — site
Slovacchia — Slovakia
socio — member/partner
soffitto — ceiling
soffrire — to suffer
soggiornare — to stay
soggiorno, salotto — living-room
sogliola — sole
sognare — to dream
sogno — dream
solamente — only
soldi (pl) — money
sole — sun
solo, solamente, soltanto — only
somma — total amount
sorella — sister
sorellastra — half-sister
sottile — fine
Spagna — Spain
spagnolo — Spanish
spalla — shoulder
sparire — to disappear
spaventarsi — to take fright
spazioso — spacious
spendere — to spend (money)
sperare — to hope
spese di amministrazione — administrative charges
spesso — often
spettacolo — show
spiaggia — beach
spinaci (pl) — spinach
splendido — splendid
sporgere denuncia — to report to the police
sport — sport
sportello — bank counter
sportivo — casual
sposarsi — to get married
spostamento — transfer
spremuta d'arancia — fresh orange juice
spremuta di limone — fresh lemon juice
spumante — sparkling wine
squadra — team
stage — training course
stagione — season
stanza — room
stare a casa — to stay at home
stare bene/male — to feel well/ill
stasera — tonight
Stati Uniti — the United States
statua — statue
statura — height
stazione — station
stella — star
sterlina inglese — Sterling
stesso — same
stile — style
stimare — to esteem
stipendio — wage
stivali — boots
strada — road
stradina — narrow street/alley
strano — strange
stretto — narrow
stringere — to clasp
studente — student
studio — consulting-room/chambers etc.
stupido — stupid
stupire — to surprise
stupirsi — to be surprised
subire — to undergo
subito — suddenly
succedere — to happen
succo di frutta — fruit juice
succo di pomodoro — tomato juice
sud — south
sugo — sauce
suocera — mother-in-law
suocero — father-in-law
suonare (uno strumento) — to play (an instrument)
suora — nun
superficie — floor area
supposta — suppository
sveglia — early morning call
svegliarsi — to wake up
Svezia — Sweden
Svizzera — Switzerland
svizzero — Swiss

T

tabaccaio — tobacconist's
tacco — heel
taglia — size/fit
Tailandia — Thailand
talmente — so
tappeto — rug
tardi — late
tasca — pocket
tassista — taxi-driver
tavola calda — snack bar
tavola — table
tavolo — board
té — tea
teatro — theatre
tedesco — German
telefonare — to phone
telefonata — phone call
telefono — telephone
televisore — television set
temperatura — temperature
tempo — time
temporale — storm
tennis — tennis
termosifone — radiator
terrazza — terrace
terremoto — earthquake
terzo — third
testa — head
tinca — tench
tinta unita — plain, self-coloured
tintoria — cleaner's
tipico — typical
tomba — tomb
tonnellata — tonne
tonno — tuna
tornare — to return, come back
toro — bull
torrente — torrent
Toscana — Tuscany
tosse — cough
tovaglia — tablecloth
tovagliolo — napkin
tra — between
traduttore/trice — translator
traffico — traffic
traforo del Monte Bianco — Mont Blanc Tunnel
tragedia — tragedy
tram — tram
tranquillo — quiet
trasferimento — transfer
traslocare — to move
trasloco — moving house
trattarsi (di) — to deal with
trattoria — small restaurant
traversa — road junction
tredicesima — holiday pay
treno — train
Trentino-Alto-Adige — Italian Tyrol
triste — sad
troppo — too, too much
trota — trout
trovare — to find
truccarsi — to put on make-up
truccato — wearing make-up
trucco — make-up
tuono — clap of thunder
Turchia — Turkey
turismo — tourism
tutti — everyone
tutto — everything

U

uccidere — to kill
Ucraine — Ukraine
ufficio — office
uguale — the same
ultimamente — lately
ultimo — last
umidità — humidity
undicesimo — eleventh
Ungheria — Hungary
Unione Sovietica — Soviet Union
unità — unit
università — university
uomo (pl.: gli uomini) — man
uovo — egg
urgenza — emergency
usanza — custom
uscire — to go out
uva (sing.) — grapes

V

va bene — certainly/O.K.
vacanza — holiday
vagone — carriage
vagone letto — sleeper
valere — to be worth
valico — mountain pass
valigia — suitcase
valore — value
vano — room
vario — various
vasto — vast
vecchio — old
vedere — to see
vedersi — to see each other/meet
vela — sailing
venerdì — Friday
venire — to come
ventesimo — twentieth
vento — wind
veramente — really
verde — green
verdura (sing.) — vegetables
vero — true
versare — to put down (a deposit)
verso — towards
vestaglia — dressing-gown
vestirsi — to dress oneself
vestito — dress/suit
vetrina — shop-window
viaggiatore — traveller
viaggio organizzato — package holiday
vicino — near
vino (rosso, bianco, rosato) — wine (red, white, rosé)
viola — purple
violento — violent
violino — violin
visita — visit
visitare — to visit
viso — face
vita — 1.life, 2.waist
vitello — veal
vivace — lively
vivere — to live
vizio — vice
voce — voice
vodka — vodka
volare — to fly
volere — to want to
volo — flight
volta — a time
vongola — clam
vulcano — volcano

Z

zero — zero
zio/a — uncle/aunt
zona archeologica — archaeological site
zucchero — sugar
zucchino — courgette

PHOTO CREDITS

P. 6-7 : GRAZIA NERI, Cavicchioni ; p. 9 : COSMOS, Carmichael ; p. 17 hg : EXPLORER, Pelletier ; p. 17 hd : EXPLORER, DPA : p. 17 mg : OVERSEAS, Villarosa ; p. 17 md : GRAZIA NERI, Walker ; p. 17 bg : OVERSEAS, Villarosa ; p. 17 bd : OVERSEAS, Villarosa ; p. 25 h : MAGNUM, Scianna ; p. 25 mg : MAGNUM, Scianna ; p. 25 bg : GRAZIA NERI ; p. 25 bd : MAGNUM, Scianna ; p. 33 hg : GRAZIA NERI ; p. 33 hd : GRAZIA NERI, Bonomo ; p. 33 md : GRAZIA NERI, Walker ; p. 33 bd : GRAZIA NERI, Walker ; p. 33 bg : GRAZIA NERI, Bonomo ; p. 41 hg : OVERSEAS ; p. 41 hd : MAGNUM, Scianna ; p. 41 md : MAGNUM, Scianna ; p. 41 bg : MAGNUM, Scianna ; p. 41 bd : MAGNUM, Scianna ; p. 54-55 : MAGNUM, Erwitt ; p. 57 h : EXPLORER, Wolf ; p. 57 b : ZEFA, Kerth ; p. 65 hg : MAGNUM, Scianna ; p. 65 hd : GRAZIA NERI, Lanzelloto ; p. 65 mg : MAGNUM, Kalvar ; p. 65 md : OVERSEAS, De Angelis ; p. 65 bg : MAGNUM, Scianna ; p. 65 bd : GRAZIA NERI, Lanzelloto ; p. 73 h : COSMOS, Budnick ; p. 73 b : EXPLORER, Wolf ; p. 81 hg : MAGNUM, Scianna ; p. 81 bg : EXPLORER, Paul ; p. 81 hd : GRAZIA NERI ; p. 81 md : GRAZIA NERI, Marcarini ; p. 81 bd : OVERSEAS ; p. 89 h : ZEFA, Keycolor ; p. 89 bg : ZEFA, Pittins ; p. 89 bd : MAGNUM, Kalvar ; p. 102-103 : MAGNUM, Zachmann ; p. 105 h : ZEFA, Eugen ; p. 105 b : GRAZIA NERI, Sparavigne ; p. 113 hg : EXPLORER, Roy ; p. 113 hd : MAGNUM, Henri Cartier-Bresson ; p. 113 bg : OVERSEAS, Piromallo ; p. 113 bd : GRAZIA NERI, Sparavigna ; p. 121 h : GRAZIA NERI, Sparavigna ; p. 121 bg : EXPLORER, Wolf ; p. 121 bd : MAGNUM, Glinn ; p. 129 hg : GRAZIA NERI, Sparavigna ; p. 129 hd : EXPLORER, Wolf ; p. 129 mg : MAGNUM, Glinn ; p. 129 md : MAGNUM, Riboud ; p. 129 bg : EXPLORER, Wolf ; p. 129 bd : GRAZIA NERI, Bini ; p. 137 hg : OVERSEAS, Semacapriola ; p. 137 hd : MAGNUM, Silverstone ; p. 137 mg : GRAZIA NERI, Sparavigna ; p. 137 md : GRAZIA NERI, Sparavigna ; p. 137 bg : COSMOS, Budnick ; p. 137 bd : COSMOS, Budnick ; p. 150-151 : MAGNUM, Barbey ; p. 153 : GRAZIA NERI, Bettini ; p. 161 hg : MAGNUM, Scianna ; p. 161 hd : MAGNUM, Depardon ; p. 161 m : MAGNUM, Freed ; p. 161 b : MAGNUM, Stock ; p. 169 hg : MAGNUM, Barbey ; p. 169 hd : GRAZIA NERI, Bettini ; p. 169 mg : EXPLORER, Veiller ; p. 169 md : MAGNUM, Scianna ; p. 169 bg : MAGNUM, Barbey ; p. 169 bd : GRAZIA NERI, Bettini ; p. 177 hg : MAGNUM, Scianna ; p. 177 hd : GRAZIA NERI, Guaita ; p. 177 bg : MAGNUM, Scianna ; p. 177 md : COSMOS, Ferorelli ; p. 177 bd : MAGNUM, Barbey ; p. 185 h : MAGNUM, Gruyaert ; p. 185 mg : MAGNUM, Barbey ; p. 185 md : MAGNUM, Barbey ; p. 185 bg : GRAZIA NERI, Guaita ; p. 185 bd : GRAZIA NERI, Bettini.